PANIC ATTACK

PANIC ATTACK

YOUNG RADICALS IN THE AGE OF TRUMP

ROBBY SOAVE

ALL
POINTS
BOOKS

www.allpointsbooks.com

Library of Congress Cataloging-in-Publication Data

Names: Soave, Robby, author.
Title: Panic attack : young radicals in the age of Trump / Robby Soave.
Description: First edition. | New York : All Points Books, 2019. |
    Includes bibliographical references and index.
Identifiers: LCCN 2019001951| ISBN 9781250169884 (hardcover) |
    ISBN 9781250169907 (ebook)
Subjects: LCSH: College students—Political activity—United States. |
    Protest movements—United States. | College environment—United States. |
    Freedom of speech—United States. | Academic freedom—United States. |
    United States—Politics and government—2017-
Classification: LCC LA229 .S57 2019 | DDC 378.1/980973—dc23
LC record available at https://lccn.loc.gov/2019001951

Our books may be purchased in bulk for promotional, educational, or business use. Please contact your local bookseller or the Macmillan Corporate and Premium Sales Department at 1-800-221-7945, extension 5442, or by email at MacmillanSpecialMarkets@macmillan.com.

First Edition: June 2019

10 9 8 7 6 5 4 3 2 1

For my grandmothers,
Dolores and Martha

CONTENTS

PANIC ATTACK

ARRESTED DEVELOPMENT

This is a roundup
This is a low-flying panic attack
—Radiohead, "Burn the Witch"

On November 4, 2008, I was a college junior working as an assistant editor in the offices of the *Michigan Daily,* the University of Michigan's primary student newspaper, when Barack Obama was elected president of the United States. As a libertarian who opposed big government and the Iraq War with equal fervor, I hadn't felt positively about Obama or his rival, John McCain, and was thus disinterested in the outcome.

But at UM, I was almost completely alone on that front: Obama's landslide victory provoked campus-wide celebration. An impromptu band formed on the Diag, the campus's main public square, and played the national anthem. Hundreds cheered "Yes we did!" and "Go-bama!" Students flooded the streets of Ann Arbor—including many of my colleagues at the left-leaning newspaper.

One student, a young woman, summed up the general sentiments of a campus that felt like its own political activism—rallies, voter registration drives, campaign grunt work—played at least a small role in Obama's victory. She told a *Daily* reporter, "I feel this is the greatest moment of our lives."[1]

Eight years later, America elected Donald Trump to be its next president. No one danced or sang at Michigan, though many shed tears.

The night of the election, as Trump's victory became evident, the energy drained from the *Daily*'s typically convivial newsroom. The mood changed "from tipsy to holy shit," according to Emma Kinsey, a senior news editor and later editor in chief of the *Michigan Daily*. Literally and metaphorically sobered by the results, the editors dispatched reporters to cover the student reaction on campus. But the only thing to write about was everyone's overwhelming sadness.

"Everyone was just upset," Kinsey told me. "My roommates were crying. Some classes the next day were canceled. Then campus Republicans were pissed that classes were canceled, which is valid. It was a weird time.

"That night there was some sort of mourning," Kinsey continued. "Then there were a bunch of protests the next day. After that, there were many protests across campus—constantly, it felt like."

A similar thing took place at other campuses. A day after Trump won the presidency, left-leaning professors at such lofty institutions as Columbia and Yale postponed midterms, or made them optional, in order to give students time to heal.[2] (Yale, notably, did not even cancel classes on September 11, 2001.)[3] The *Cornell Daily Sun*—the student publication of Cornell University—invited members of the community to attend a public "cry-in." The University of Michigan provided its students with coloring books, Play-Doh, and Legos, while the University of Pennsylvania made small animals available for cuddling.

"There were actual cats and a puppy there," Penn student Daniel Tancredi told the *College Fix*. "The event as a whole seemed to be an escape from the reality of the election results."[4]

The weekend after the election, Alex, a student at Reed College who identifies as bipolar, black, and queer, posted a message on Facebook asking students to email the administration and demand Monday off because "students of color and other marginalized students need a day to rest . . . classes should be cancelled tomorrow and also there should be no work due tomorrow."

Trump's victory came as a shock to many Americans on the left, on the right, and in the middle of the political spectrum—including the author of this book, whose own politics don't fit neatly in any one spot. But for young progressive activists, the election wasn't just a surprise or a disappointment: it was a declaration of war, an act of outright violence, a hate crime.

"It really is their 9/11," said Laila, a twenty-six-year-old Muslim woman and political activist, recalling the emotional impact of the election on Generation Z—an age cohort whose members were for the most part born after the events of September 11, 2001. "Not that I'm attempting in any way to equate the loss of so many precious lives to an individual that was elected to office," she added.

Still, the comparison is illustrative. According to leftist activist members of the millennial generation (birth dates 1980–2000) and Gen Z (birth dates post–2000), the election of Trump was psychologically scarring on an order of magnitude resembling the deadliest terrorist attack in American history. In fact, in the immediate aftermath of Trump's victory, countless students at some of the most elite college campuses in the country complained that they were suffering from a kind of self-diagnosed post-traumatic stress disorder.

"It was traumatizing," Juniper, a nineteen-year-old who transitioned from male to female and attends the University of California, Berkeley, told me. "Every time I realized that someone I knew voted for Trump, it was sort of a personal attack, or at least it felt that way."

Yet it would be a mistake to think young progressives did nothing but sit around and cry about Trump. Far from it. Leftist activism, on college campuses and elsewhere, is now enjoying a considerable resurgence. This resurgence began at least some years before Trump captured the White House, and it can trace its roots to the 2011 Occupy Wall Street movement, which started as a popular demonstration against economic inequality before degenerating into a series of smaller, zanier protests. (Echoes of the Bush-era Iraq War protest movement are present as well, though Trump's confused, occasionally constrained foreign policy may have prevented the anti-war movement—which prematurely dissolved around the time Obama won a Nobel Peace Prize—from properly reconstituting itself.)

For a variety of reasons, including the growing power of social media, revised federal guidelines from the Education Department that reward squeaky wheels, and sheer administrative capitulation, activists enjoy considerably more power on college campuses in the 2010s than they did in the 2000s. College is where their influence is concentrated, but they would like to control the conversation everywhere else as well. In this regard, the election of Trump was merely an intensifier: voters in Pennsylvania and Michigan may have kicked the hornet's nest, but the hive was already in motion.

In the political realm, the most energized contingent of the Democratic Party is the Democratic Socialists of America (DSA), which is pushing the party to move toward Bernie Sanders—and beyond—on a variety of issues: Medicare for all, free college tuition, and a federal jobs guarantee, among others. Today's young people grew up well after the Soviet Union ceased to exist, and thus they never came to view socialism as an existential threat. Socialism is all the good stuff they would like the government to provide: universal health care, a high minimum wage, and so on. For Democratic Socialists, getting rid of Trump isn't going nearly far enough, since Trump is just a symptom of the disease that's ailing America—capitalism.

"If Trump got impeached tomorrow, people's lives would improve, but we'd still have to work, we'd still have capitalism, we'd still have imperialism," Alex Pellitteri, an eighteen-year-old college freshman and cochair of New York City's Young Democratic Socialists, told me in an interview.

Sympathetic readers likely see the activism of millennials and

Gen Z—hereafter referred to as "Zillennials" when discussed collectively—as merely a continuation of the lofty, noble activism of previous generations. Radical activists in the 1960s, 1970s, and 1980s fought for racial equality, an end to the morally unconscionable Vietnam War, economic protections for the most vulnerable citizens, the rights of women, and the dignity of LGBT people. If Trump is as noxious as he seems—an obstacle to the kind of society that moderate and progressive people want to build—isn't he worth fighting with the same fervor, the same youthful passion?

Unfortunately for everyone who would like to see Trump humbled on some front, the Zillennial left suffers from several serious defects that make it fundamentally unlike the fondly remembered activist movements of decades past. In fact, these defects frequently lead Zillennial activists to embrace tactics that are at best counterproductive and often completely at odds with the successful strategies employed by their radical forebears. Some of these defects were apparent before Trump's election, but over the past two years, they have only become more glaring.

The purpose of this book is to explore these defects and chronicle the various ways in which they serve to undermine the progressive cause. I will explain how and why the various contingents of the new radical left are at odds with older activists, with moderate and liberal Americans who might otherwise support them, and even with themselves. I will delve into their tactics and goals, outline the structures of their organizations, and provide insight into where their leaders come from and what they think. Consider this a psychological profile of the Zillennial activist, an origin story for the selfie generation's social change agents: antifa, Black Lives Matter, #MeToo feminists, the Parkland kids, and many others.

In order to construct such a profile, I've interviewed, read, listened to, and engaged with hundreds of politically engaged millennials and Gen Zers from around the country over the last few years. I've visited campuses all over the country, attended protests, and even snuck into meetings. Whenever possible, I've asked the activists to explain themselves, and have used their own words to describe their views.

Assisting me in this effort is the fact that I was twenty-nine years old at the time this book was written. My 1988 birth date places me smack-dab in the middle of the millennial cohort. I speak the language ("person of color" instead of "African American"), know the culture (those *BuzzFeed* "You Might Be a Millennial if You Loved This TV Show/Band/Movie" quizzes were pretty much modeled after my exact tastes), and look the part (I wear sandals, skinny jeans, and a T-shirt to the office on most days).

My own libertarian views put me in the unlikely but usefully neutral position of being neither entirely hostile nor entirely friendly toward the activist movements I researched. We libertarians are for economic and social freedom, which makes me sympathetic to many of the left's goals with respect to the latter: civil rights, tolerance, peace. Indeed, one of the reasons I am so concerned about their tactics backfiring is that I would occasionally like them to succeed.

Frustratingly, my conversations with young activists left me concerned that they will struggle to translate their feelings into any sort of cohesive movement that wins undecided Americans to its cause. That's because they frequently seem almost hysterically opposed to building bridges with potential allies, preferring to settle scores with people who are for the most part already on their side. The college-aged activist of modern times is radically exclusionary and often views the principles of open debate with skepticism, if not outright hostility. Indeed, many of the young people interviewed for this book thought speech that offends them should be illegal, or was *already* illegal.

Reflexive opposition to speech is perhaps the most noticeable quirk of the new left, misunderstood though it is. While it's true that small numbers of campus radicals have always desired to shut down speakers with whom they disagree, student activists have grown more militantly opposed to free speech, and more successful at no-platforming (British slang for censoring) their critics—whether these critics are outside speakers, or even their own professors. The activists' rejection of broad First Amendment norms—norms that are central to the American experiment in participatory democracy—generally takes one of two forms.

Some activists simply reject the notion that people who do not share their views should be given rights at all; these activists are following in the intellectual tradition of a certain strain of Marxism, best articulated by the sociologist Herbert Marcuse in his 1965 essay "Repressive Tolerance," which held that it might be necessary to censor bad ideas so that the easily confused masses would be more likely to embrace good ideas (*good ideas like Marxism!* the Marxists would say).

That's the first argument against free speech; the second, which seems more common among the activists I spoke with, is a kind of repressive *safety*. Many young people think that speech is not speech at all if it inflicts emotional pain. Emotional pain, they say, is not fundamentally different from physical pain, and since violence is rightly restricted, speech should be as well. Thus the students who shouted down—and then attacked—the conservative writer Charles Murray at Middlebury College, no-platformed his colleague Christina Hoff Sommers at Lewis and Clark College, barred would-be attendees from hearing pro-police pundit Heather Mac Donald speak at Claremont McKenna College, chased left-leaning critic Bret Weinstein out of Evergreen State College, and tried to stop the feminist author Alice Dreger from delivering remarks deemed offensive by transgender activists on any number of occasions don't think they were corrupting free speech. Instead, they think they were merely practicing self-defense on behalf of the oppressed people within their community who would feel upset by the speech in question.

One of the most exhaustively reported of these kinds of incidents occurred at Yale University in the fall of 2015, when several dozen students surrounded Nicholas Christakis, a dean of one of Yale's colleges, and proceeded to berate him for daring to assert that the administration had no business policing offensive Halloween costumes. These students disagreed; Christakis was their father figure on campus, and the role of every father figure is to protect his children from pain.

"It is your job to create a place of comfort and home for the students," said one of the activists.

"It is not about creating an intellectual space!" insisted another. "It is not! Do you understand that? It's about creating a home here! You are not doing that. You're going against that."

"You have created space for violence," said yet another student.

Christakis, besieged on all sides, attempted to refute these claims but was simply told: "You can't."

Christakis eventually resigned his position. When I spoke with him, he told me something had changed among the students over the years.

"I've been an academic for thirty years," he said. "I don't recall these types of things before. And most of my colleagues can't either."

Many of Christakis's colleagues probably came of age following the Free Speech Movement of the 1960s, in which activist students were committed to making the college campus a welcome place for all viewpoints, no matter how offensive or controversial. Twenty-first-century college activism frequently appears alien to them. (Leftist activism relating to free speech is more fully explored in Chapter Two.)

Hostility to free speech divides leftists from ordinary liberals. Ironically, it's something the hard left has in common with an increasingly popular strain of far-right white nationalist conservatism known as the alt-right. Much has been written about this group over the last several years, since they are closely identified with Trump, a figure who they believe fits in with their worldview much more comfortably than do traditional Republican leaders such as Mitt Romney or Paul Ryan. Despite holding political views that are 180 degrees opposite from the left, the young and almost exclusively male members of the alt-right occasionally seem like insidious doppelgangers—a reaction against, and an extension of, the illiberal currents of the left. They are also hostile to free speech norms, distrustful of the media, and avowed enemies of societal elites, for instance. Their anti-Semitism occasionally overlaps with the far left's condemnation of capitalism, given the caricature of Jewish people as uniquely influential in the financial sector. The alt-right also shares the far left's appreciation for identitarianism—the idea that one's worth and meaning are derived from one's membership in an identity group based on an immutable characteristic such as race. The alt-right practices "white identity politics," having co-opted the term from the left's "identity politics." And the intellectual leader of the movement, the white nationalist Richard Spencer, has expressed admiration for the tribalism of the left. While it's still a marginal group, the alt-right is well worth parsing, and it is the subject of the final chapter of this book.

Discomfort with free speech norms is just one thing that makes young activists stand out from previous generations. These and other differences raise larger questions: How did Zillennials come to be this way? At what point did their tactics diverge?

One answer, frequently invoked by conservative media, is that Zillennials are too coddled. Most readers will be familiar with the "delicate snowflake" smear, which is often deployed against young people. "You are not special. You are not a beautiful or unique snowflake. You are the same decaying organic matter as everything else"—that is a quote from the 1999 film *Fight Club,* a mostly faithful adaptation of the 1996 Chuck Palahniuk novel of the same name, which explores themes of male dissatisfaction with consumerism and modernity. (These are chief concerns of the alt-right, for which *Fight Club* is something of an unintentional bible.) The line became a favorite of the movie's fans, and "snowflake" appeared in the cultural lexicon as a term of derision evoking fragility and sensitivity, mostly reserved for people on the left. In modern parlance, snowflakes are easily triggered. Snowflakes think offensive speech is violence. Snowflakes want safe spaces.

Of course, it's easy to make too much of this explanation. For one thing, the snowflake insult is often deployed hypocritically. Older Americans say that young people who demand censorship of controversial speakers are too easily offended, but many of these same Americans wanted the National Football League to punish players for engaging in what they saw as an offensive protest during the playing of the national anthem. If snowflake-ism exists, it's not exactly confined to the young left.

For another thing, Zillennials' hypersensitivity is hardly their own fault. Rather, it reflects their upbringing, which coincided with a number of inauspicious cultural phenomena—the rise of helicopter parenting, zero-tolerance school disciplinary measures, and safety paranoia in general—that might have made kids more frightened and less resilient. If Zillennials want to carve out safe spaces for themselves, it's probably because we made the world seem more dangerous than it actually is.

Let me briefly explain. In her brilliant book *Free Range-Kids,* journalist Lenore Skenazy, a colleague of mine at *Reason* magazine, pinpoints 1981—the birth year of the earliest millennials—as the beginning of a media frenzy over kidnappings. That was the year of the abduction and murder of six-year-old Adam Walsh, whose tragic death became the subject of a two-part miniseries. When it aired on NBC in 1983, it was watched by thirty-eight million people. Adam's real-life father, John Walsh, eventually created and hosted *America's Most Wanted.* It became more and more difficult to watch television without getting the feeling that kids were being abducted, murdered, or sold into slavery at record rates. The practice of printing pictures of missing youngsters on milk cartons, which originated in the late 1970s and reached its apotheosis in the 1980s, probably didn't help.

Child abductions are horrible. They are also blessedly rare. Most missing children either ran away from home or were taken by a family member during a custody dispute. In modern times, abductions of children by strangers account for 0.1 percent of the total.[5] (If you actually *wanted* your children to be kidnapped and held overnight, Skenazy observed, you would have to leave them outside by themselves for *750,000 years,* statistically speaking.)

This shouldn't be so surprising: the Zillennial generation has come of age during a time of unprecedented safety. Since the early 1990s, rates of murder and violent crime have fallen by half. The teen homicide rate decreased from 12 per 100,000 to 5.1 per 100,000 between 1993 and 2008. Most Americans are completely oblivious to these positive developments; a 2013 Pew Research Center poll found that a majority of respondents mistakenly thought crime had increased in the past two decades, and a 2016 *Vox* poll found the same thing.[6] We should thank the media, and television in particular, for this confusion: fear sells, and if it bleeds, it leads.

But while Zillennials enjoy lives that are less violence-prone than did members of previous generations, they enjoy fewer freedoms. Parenting trends have moved in the opposite direction of reality: being a kid keeps getting safer, parents keep getting more paranoid about safety. This gave rise to the pernicious helicopter parenting phenomenon, which saw parents become ceaselessly involved in their children's lives, supervising every step of their development. Explicit governmental policy encouraged families to move in this direction—in many jurisdictions, it is against the law to leave kids alone for any length of time, let them walk to school on their own, or even allow them to play in their own backyards without an adult present. Skenazy has documented thousands of cases of parents who were arrested for daring to give their children a fraction of the autonomy they themselves received when they were young. (Schools have implemented similarly counterproductive policies as a result of safety panic; these are covered more extensively in Chapter Seven.)

The end result, I suspect, is that some of the Zillennials who grew up in this environment have internalized society's push for safety at all costs. When today's youthful radicals assert a right to be protected from harms both real and imagined—like offensive

Halloween costumes—they are really just asking to be treated in the manner to which they have grown accustomed.

This explanation, however, does not by itself fully explain the current state of Zillennial activism. Another critical development—the theme to which the rest of this book will frequently return—is intellectual in nature, rather than cultural. It's a theory, concept, outlook, and analytical tool that has grown to dominate the academy, particularly the humanities and social sciences. This theory does not compromise, it makes little room for healthy disagreement, and it has nothing but scorn for the not yet converted.

Its name is intersectionality, and it most closely resembles an ouroboros devouring its own tail. As will become clear, it both haunts and actively sabotages the anti-Trump resistance movement.

ONE

INTERSECTIONAL A.F.

The Women's March came to Washington, D.C., on January 21, 2017, the day after Trump's inauguration. Its purpose was to call attention to the incoming president's history of appalling behavior toward women—behavior to which Trump had all but admitted during the infamous hot-mic moment that became known as the *Access Hollywood* tape. "When you're a star, they let you do it," Trump had said. "You can do anything. Grab 'em by the pussy."

This was a statement that rightly offended millions of Americans of all political stripes—indeed, Trump's electoral fortunes were never lower than they were immediately after the tape's release—and thus the march held the promise of uniting people around a universal, positive message: it's not okay to abuse women.

More than half a million people descended on D.C. for the march, making it the largest protest in the United States since the Vietnam War era. It was a fairly awe-inspiring spectacle. I live in D.C. and only had to walk a few blocks from my apartment before I happened across streets jam-packed with activists. A sea of pink hats greeted me. Many of the protesters had chosen to reclaim

Trump's own vulgar language, and I saw dozens of signs bearing some variant of the slogan "This pussy grabs back." Others were less intense; a young woman with pink streaks in her light brown hair held a sign that said, "To love, we must survive; to survive, we must fight; to fight, we must love." Her friend stood next to her, waving a sign that featured a hand-drawn Donald Trump with the universally recognized emoji for excrement atop his head and the words "Dump Trump."

All in all, the Women's March was a success for the nascent anti-Trump movement informally known as the Resistance. More people showed up to protest than to attend the inauguration—something that seemed to infuriate the president, forcing several Trump staffers to make misleading statements about the relative sizes of the crowds. (This was the genesis of presidential counselor Kellyanne Conway's line about "alternative facts.")

Still, the Women's March suffered from some noteworthy behind-the-scenes conflicts that occasionally spilled out into the open and hampered the protest's overall effectiveness and staying power.

Organizers claimed to have geared the event toward "inclusion," according to its website.[1] Inclusion would have been a good strategy, since many women of differing political beliefs had reason to be suspicious of Trump and cause to send him a message about disrespecting them. Inclusion can be difficult, however.

Right off the bat, the planned event ran into trouble.[2] It was organized primarily on Facebook, showcasing the incredible power of social media, and also its considerable disadvantages. The Facebook page was constantly besieged by infighting. A lot of people were upset that white women were running the event, given that they aren't as threatened by Trump's policies as black and Hispanic women are. (A much larger percentage of white women voted for Trump than did black and Hispanic women, which has led to continuing resentment—a sense that some significant mass of white women betrayed their sisters of color.) The protest was initially called the Million Women March, but critics said that was too much of a rip-off; a 1997 event of a similar name had intended to call attention to civil rights for women of color.

Then there was the issue of prostitution, a topic that often divides the left. For reasons that will be more fully explored in Chapter Four, modern feminism is largely split on the subject of whether sex workers are independent women boldly reclaiming their agency and their bodies from a system of male domination or victims of economic and sexual exploitation.

At first the Women's March stood firmly in column A, and its Unity Principles included a pledge to "stand in solidarity with sex workers' rights movements."[3] This was eventually replaced with a very different line about protecting "all those exploited for sex and labor," a column B position. Finally, the group compromised and included both positions: "We stand in solidarity with the sex workers' rights movement. We recognize that exploitation for sex and labor in all forms is a violation of human rights."

The abortion issue was even more contentious. Most people on the left are pro-choice, of course, and it's not surprising that the Women's March would broadly support abortion rights. But at least one pro-life group, the New Wave Feminists, signed on as an official partner of the march. At the time, many pro-life women were un-doubtedly feeling just as uncertain about Trump as their opponents; while Trump has governed as a fairly staunch social conservative during his first term, there was once ample reason to doubt whether the twice-divorced former Democrat and lifelong practitioner of what Senator Ted Cruz dubbed "New York values" would actually support the pro-life cause.

Organizers of the pro-life New Wave Feminists group told the *Atlantic* that they were "not just pro-lifers who are also feminists . . . we're feminists first and foremost," and "[we're] so grateful to have this opportunity to walk together with [our] sisters and brothers."[4]

Unfortunately for them, inclusion did not and could not extend to pro-lifers, and heaps of denunciation ensued.

"You cannot be anti-choice and feminist," wrote Amanda Marcotte, a leftist feminist writer, on Twitter.

"Inclusivity is not about bolstering those who harm us," wrote Jessica Valenti, a feminist columnist for the *Guardian*, on Twitter.

The backlash succeeded, and Women's March leadership de-certified the New Wave Feminists as an official partner. Inclusion only goes so far.

And yet despite the myriad ways in which the Women's March failed to live up to its stated goal of inclusivity, many of the young leftists I interviewed for this book told me they thought the protest turned out to be *too* inclusive.

"That's actually fucking right," Laila, the twenty-six-year-old Muslim woman and political activist mentioned in the introduction, agreed.

I asked Laila, who lives in Washington, D.C., whether she attended the march. She did not. In fact, she skipped town that weekend. "I'm tired of being a poster child for someone else's attempt at inclusivity," she said.

In her view, by including so many different perspectives, organizers had watered down the message and ended up marginalizing the people who should have been the focus. They took "an approach that co-opted the narratives of many who have already been fighting in this space, specifically, black women."

Laila is hardly the only young activist who felt that way about the Women's March. Juniper, the nineteen-year-old trans woman, castigated the march as "super white, super cisgender-centric." ("Cisgender," the opposite of "transgender," describes people who identify as the gender to which they were born.) She was skeptical of it at best, she said. And others were even harsher.

"I just felt like it wasn't very sincere," said Yanet, a woman of color and student at the University of Maryland. Yanet made a conscious decision not to participate. "It just felt like a moment for people who aren't as involved or didn't care as often or before to feel like, 'Oh, I did something.'"

"I hated it," Ma'at, a student of color at American University, told me. "It was super cis-centric. It was exclusive of trans identities.

It was whitewashed. It just in general was very co-opting and in-effective."

"Insincere" and "ineffective" will strike many readers as surprising ways for leftist activists to describe the most well-attended mass march in four decades. But it makes perfect sense when one considers the priorities of the new activist culture, which prefers quality—intellectual purity—over quantity. A protest is successful only if it highlights the correct issues, includes the *right* people—people who humbly check all the appropriate boxes—and is organized by a ruling coalition of the most oppressed.

This, of course, is what intersectionality dictates. Though the words "intersectionality" and "inclusion" sound like synonyms, they are actually in conflict with each other—a conflict perfectly encapsulated by the Women's March and the activists' dissatisfaction with it. In case there was any confusion, Roxane Gay, a celebrated feminist author and voice of the left, said this in response to the idea of inclusion: "Intersectional feminism does not include a pro-life agenda. That's not how it works!"

This chapter will define intersectionality, explain how it provides an ideological framework for safety-conditioned Zillennials, and describe the main problems with an intersectional approach to activism.

Intersectional Theory 101

Intersectionality is the operating system for the modern left. Understanding what it means and where it comes from is essential for comprehending the current state of activism on college campuses, at protests in major cities, and elsewhere.

Put simply, intersectionality means that various kinds of oppression—racism, sexism, homophobia, transphobia, economic inequality, and others—are simultaneously distinct from each other and inherently linked. They are distinct in the sense that they stack: a black woman suffers from two kinds of oppression (racism and sexism), whereas a white woman suffers from just one (sexism). But they are also interrelated, in that they are all forms of oppression that should be opposed with equal fervor. For instance, a feminist who isn't sufficiently worked up about the rights of the gay and transgender communities is at odds with the tenets of intersectionality. She is a feminist, but she is not an *intersectional* feminist.

Holly, a twenty-three-year-old Berkeley student whom I met at the April 2017 People's Climate March in Washington, D.C., told me that for her, intersectionality means all issues are "connected and tie in with each other, like indigenous rights, Black Lives Matter, and climate change."

Kimberlé Williams Crenshaw, a professor at UCLA Law School and Columbia University School of Law, coined the term *intersectionality* in her 1989 paper "Demarginalizing the Intersection of Race and Sex." She needed a word to describe the lives of black women who were discriminated against because of both their race and their sex. Their experiences were fundamentally different from those of black men, who were privileged to the extent that they were men, and from those of white women, who were privileged to the extent that they were white.

"Discrimination, like traffic through an intersection, may flow in one direction, and it may flow in another," wrote Crenshaw in the paper. "If an accident happens in an intersection, it can be caused by cars traveling from any number of directions and, sometimes, from all of them. Similarly, if a Black woman is harmed because she is in the intersection, her injury could result from sex discrimination or race discrimination."[5]

Crenshaw got the idea from a 1976 federal district court case, *DeGraffenreid v. General Motors,* in which five black women had sued GM. They argued that GM's policy of laying off the most recently hired employees violated Title VII of the 1964 Civil Rights Act, which prohibits both racial and gender-based discrimination. Since it had been only a little more than a decade since the law had required GM to hire black and female employees, the most recently hired employees tended to be black women, the plaintiffs argued.

But the court determined that black women enjoyed no special protection under the law—the employees were protected from racial discrimination and gender-based discrimination, but not from the combined effects of these two categories. "The plaintiffs are clearly entitled to a remedy if they have been discriminated against," wrote the court. "However, they should not be allowed to combine statutory remedies to create a new 'super-remedy' which would give them relief beyond what the drafters of the relevant statutes intended."[6]

Since GM policy allowed women to work in management positions, where there were several white women, it could not be said that the company engaged in sexism, and the court told the plaintiffs they should drop this aspect of their case and instead proceed with a purely race-based lawsuit. But the women had no interest in doing so—they felt they had been discriminated against not because they were black but because they were black women.

DeGraffenreid v. General Motors was Crenshaw's lightbulb moment. Black women lived in the midst of two kinds of discrimination—racism and sexism—and thus languished under an oppressive force greater than the sum of its parts.

"What Kimberlé is saying with intersectionality is that, in order to understand how power operates, you have to understand how people live their lives," Alicia Garza, an activist and cofounder of the Black Lives Matter movement, told me. "Intersectionality is the very basic notion that we live multiple experiences at once. It's not just, oh, I'm black and I'm a woman, and I'm a black woman. It's to say that I'm uniquely discriminated against. I uniquely experience oppression based on standing at the intersection of race and gender."

Though Crenshaw came up with the term, the concept itself predates her. As far back as 1892, the black feminist Anna Julia Cooper had criticized leading anti-racists for failing to advance the cause of black women. "Only the black woman can say when and where I enter, in the quiet undisputed dignity of my womanhood . . . then and there the whole race enters with me," she said.[7] (Cooper, who was born a slave in 1858, eventually became the first formerly enslaved woman to earn a Ph.D. She lived to be 105. Her sprawling Washington, D.C., residence still stands—in fact, I rented a room there for six months in 2012.)

For the Boston-based black feminist lesbian organization known as the Combahee River Collective, which existed in the 1970s, "simultaneity" was the word they used to describe the cumulative impact of the various oppressions they experienced. Their manifesto called not just for the abolition of racism and sexism but for "the destruction of the political-economic systems of capitalism and imperialism as well."[8] Avowed enmity toward all the various isms: this is the strategy required by the intellectual framework that became known as intersectionality.

Patricia Hill Collins, a professor of sociology at the University of Maryland, expanded upon Crenshaw's work, publishing *Black Feminist Thought: Knowledge, Consciousness, and the Politics of Empowerment* in 1990. Taking a cue from Crenshaw, she used the term "intersectionality" to refer to the interlocking matrixes of oppression that serve to marginalize people. Initially focused on race and gender, Collins gave additional consideration to class as a matrix in her 1992 book *Race, Class and Gender: An Anthology.* A decade later, *Black Sexual Politics* added sexual orientation to the mix. "Intersectional paradigms view race, class, gender, sexuality, ethnicity, and age, among others, as mutually constructing systems of power," she wrote in *Black Sexual Politics.* "Because these systems permeate all social relations, untangling their effects in any given situation or for any given population remains difficult."[9]

That's quite the understatement, since every new addition to the list of interrelated oppressions makes the task even more cumbersome. There are more of these categories than most people might imagine, and every year, intellectual peers of Crenshaw and Collins propose new ones. Meanwhile, intersectionality has become a ubiquitous force on college campuses, where young people are taught to perceive all social issues through the lens of interrelated oppression, and to find smaller and smaller grievances to add to the pile. Young people who grasp the truth of intersectionality are said to be "woke," Zillennial slang that describes someone who has awakened to the reality of their own privilege and adopted a progressive worldview.

The spread of intersectionality poses some problems for the left, since the theory divides people as often as it unites them. In the wake of Trump's election, Hulu's *The Handmaid's Tale*, a prestige drama based on feminist author Margaret Atwood's beloved novel, became mandatory #Resistance viewing for its depiction of an oppressive society where women have been enslaved by theocratic authoritarians—a future toward which Trump's America is hurtling, according to many on the left. But season two of *The Handmaid's Tale*, which debuted in 2018, drew criticism; the show was accused of a "failure of intersectionality" because it never grappled with racism, only sexism. "This is a show all about gender—it is built entirely around that concept—but until *The Handmaid's Tale* learns to make its feminism intersectional, it's going to keep letting its audience down," commented *BuzzFeed* TV writer Louis Peitzman.[10]

Spreading the Gospel

In the years since Crenshaw introduced the term, intersectionality has broadened in both scope (that is, more kinds of oppression have been identified) and reach (more people are aware of the concept and what it implies).

The academy loves intersectionality, and the theory's popularity has soared in sociology, psychology, English, philosophy, history, and other social science and humanities departments. Indeed, more and more universities have created entire academic wings dedicated to studying specific kinds of oppression and explaining how they relate to others. Thus the rise of women's studies, African American studies, Hispanic studies, Asian studies, queer studies, and others.

Indeed, what began at the intersection of race and sex now

includes economic class, gender identity (the gender category to which a person feels attachment—it may be different from the person's biological sex), gender expression (the way a person looks and behaves), sexual orientation, immigration status, age, disability status, religious belief (though certain believers—among them Muslims—are perceived as more oppressed than others), and size (whether you are overweight or not).

Take that last example. I'm betting you might not believe that intersectionality requires its adherents to denounce "sizeism" as a form of oppression against differently bodied people.

Well, consider that in recent years Tufts University, Dickinson College, Oregon State University, and Portland State University all added courses aimed at studying and reducing sizeism.[11] Portland State's course is called Every Body Matters: Embracing Size Diversity.[12] According to its online description, the course "focuses on fatness as a social and cultural construction, examining the relationship between discrimination caused by body size and gender, race, and social class." Students in the class "will use social justice and healthcare perspectives to question weight bias and explore ways in which the fat community and its supporters resist sizeism." Readers might quibble with the blanket assertion that obesity is a social construct. They might also ask whether students in the course are being taught—or trained.

At Colorado College, a young activist named Jade penned a manifesto against the institution's outdoorsy culture and conventionally attractive, physically fit student body.[13] Jade lacked "body privilege," which caused her "emotional injury." Not to worry, Jade: sizeism and all the other isms have been informally banned on college campuses across the country. The New Republic estimated that at least a hundred institutions of higher education employ what are known as "bias response teams," or BRTs, which investigate complaints.[14] BRTs consist of students, academics, and administrators, though campus police often have a seat at the table as well. BRTs will investigate the complaint based on the information given. Some maintain hotlines that ask complainants to provide the accused party's contact info and identifying details. The BRT will then intervene: administrators have a conversation with the accused about the alleged offensive behavior, or refer the case to a campus authority with more explicitly punitive powers, such as a diversity czar or conduct enforcer.

Complaints are often filed anonymously, by members of the student body who feel they have been victims of bias, unintentional or otherwise. The relevant categories typically include all the familiar matrixes of oppression: race, gender, sex, orientation, class, disability status, age, size, and so forth. The kinds of harms we're talking about here are very minor in effect but broad in scope, and go by the name of "microaggressions."

That term was first coined by Harvard University professor Chester Pierce in 1970 but gained little attention until Derald Wing Sue, a professor of psychology at Columbia University, helped to popularize the concept decades later. His definitive book on the subject, *Microaggressions and Marginality: Manifestation, Dynamics, and Impact,* was not published until 2010.

Sue defined microaggressions as "brief and commonplace daily verbal, behavioral, or environmental indignities, whether intentional or unintentional, that communicate hostile, derogatory, or negative racial slights and insults toward people of color." His 2007 paper in *American Psychologist,* "Racial Microaggressions in Everyday Life," provided numerous examples of things that counted as microaggressions.[15] It included:

- Asking "Where are you from?" The question presupposes the person being addressed is from somewhere other than the United States, and therefore "others" the person.
- Saying "I believe the most qualified person should get the job." This statement promotes the "myth of meritocracy" and suggests that perhaps certain people are getting an unfair advantage because of their race via affirmative action.
- Claiming "There is only one race, the human race," which denies a person's "racial/cultural being."

. Telling an Asian person to "speak up more" in class could also
be a microaggression, though the assertion that it *is* a microaggression relies on the lazy stereotype that Asian people are
less assertive than white people.

Some examples are more obvious than others, like a cabdriver
deliberately ignoring a potential customer who is black, or a white
woman clutching her purse when a man of color walks past her.
For Sue, it was self-apparent that "almost all interracial encounters
are prone to microaggressions."

The idea here is that these small, often unintentional acts of
hostility toward people for reasons of race, sex, orientation, et cetera
aren't just problematic but represent a form of aggression—a tiny
dose of violence. It's little wonder that a generation of young people
for whom everything is dangerous and safety is the most important factor—including safety from verbal and emotional harm—
sees the elimination of microaggressions as an important task for
the authorities.

When asked by the *Chronicle of Higher Education* in 2016 about
the tremendous growth in appreciation for his work, Sue struck
a cautious note. "People who engage in microaggressions are of-
tentimes well-intentioned, decent individuals who aren't aware
that they are engaging in an offensive way toward someone else,"
he said.[16] Christina Capodilupo, an adjunct professor at Teachers
College and a coauthor with Sue of "Racial Microaggressions in
Everyday Life," said that the point had been to open people's minds,
not cause them to shut their mouths.

At some universities, the antics of the BRTs are kept private. At
others, the curtain is occasionally pulled back. In 2016, I obtained
the University of Oregon's annual report on its BRT. The report was
later removed from the university's website, and thus from public
view. Having read example after example of the kind of things its
BRT thought were worth investigating, I can see why. In one case,
a staff member reported that a poster featured a triggering image.
The type of bias listed was "body size." The report notes that the

administration offered "support" to the offended party. Another report concerned a "culturally appropriative themed party" and involved the BRT sitting down with students who dared to host it.

A student reported a professor for writing a negative comment on the student's blog—thus impugning the student's religion. A student reported the campus newspaper for failing to give adequate space in its pages to the opinions of transgender students. A student filed a report to complain that a sign encouraging cleaning up after oneself was sexist. In this last example, I gather that the sign, which was probably posted by a cafeteria worker or janitor, said something to the effect of "Clean Up After Yourself—We're Not Your Mother." This message, which made gendered assumptions about the kind of work mothers do in the household, was so offensive to a student that a campus agency had to investigate *and* intervene. One wonders if the intersectional feminist who called out the sign ended up getting the janitor or cafeteria worker fired.

Perhaps the strongest indictment of microaggression theory was made by Scott Lilienfeld, a clinical psychologist at Emory University. Lilienfeld evaluated the core claims of the theory and found them lacking. For one thing, there isn't a widely agreed-upon list of things that *definitely* count as microaggressions, and a significant segment of the minority population consistently fails to take offense at various proposed examples. For another, the evidence that microaggressions cause mental health problems just isn't there. In fact, Lilienfeld expressed concern that educating people about microaggressions could itself exacerbate mental health issues.

I asked Lilienfeld what his recommendation to university administrators would be, given these findings.

"My negative recommendation—what not to do—is to stop distributing microaggression lists on campuses and to cease training faculty and students to identify microaggressions, at least until the concept is far better defined," he told me. "Undoubtedly, there's some truth to the idea that many or most of us at times inadvertently offend others. But at present, the microaggression concept is so vaguely defined and open-ended that it can encompass almost any statement or behavior that offends other people."

In 2017, the Cato Institute surveyed people of color and asked whether they were offended by various examples taken from a list of possible microaggressions. Sure enough, in nearly all cases, a majority of the respondents who ought to have felt victimized said that they were not.

The point isn't that microaggressions are completely harmless, or that offended people need to just get over it, or something similarly insensitive. What's remarkable, though, is the radical transformation that has taken place on campuses over the last twenty years. Pursuing truth is still the purpose of higher education, but education can be uncomfortable, and *discomfort* is now considered oppressive.

Only a small percentage of students move through the academic disciplines where intersectionality has taken hold most strongly. But it would be a mistake to think that microaggression training and awareness are primarily in-class experiences. Bias response teams don't just intervene inside the classroom: they're an omnipresent facet of campus life—inside the residence halls and cafeterias, on the quad, and elsewhere. At Oberlin College, the school's Multicultural Resource Center teaches activist students about microaggressions—and it also pays them $8.15 an hour to run training modules designed to teach other students.[17]

Part of the story here is administrative bloat: over the past quarter century, universities have hired an army of bureaucrats to micromanage the lives of students outside the classroom. Between 1993 and 2009, universities more than doubled the number of administrators they employed.[18] These employees are often handsomely paid. According to the American Enterprise Institute's Mark Perry, the University of Michigan, for instance, currently employs a hundred different administrators whose sole job is to advance diversity on campus—and more than a quarter of them make more than $100,000 per year.[19] (Meanwhile, faculty salaries have barely budged the entire time I've been alive.)

More presidents of diversity, vice presidents of diversity, and diversity coordinators mean more bias response teams, more attention to microaggressions, and more attempts to make campus as diverse, sustainable, equitable, and emotionally calming as possible. In addition to their primary functions, these bureaucrats act as the enforcement arms of intersectionality. The administration trains young people to identify the various flavors of oppression, hunt for new ones, and expect protection from them.

It's not pleasant being oppressed by a wide range of connected isms. Thus the overhyped (albeit accurate in some small way) "snowflake" phenomenon itself intersects with intersectionality. Young people have learned that the world is scary and violent, and that there are overlapping matrixes of oppression rooted in distinct but interrelated forms of exploitation. The campus—and perhaps one day the rest of society—should be structured as a safe haven from intersectional oppression, but there's a long way to go. In the meantime, emotional and psychological trauma is evidence that oppression is real. Thus the most engaged activist students—the ones most fluent in the language of intersectionality—are positively eager to identify themselves as traumatized. It's a sign of being truly woke.

Traumas and Triggers

"Asking for help is a sign of your strength, not of your weakness," read a sign at Arizona State University, which I visited on a gorgeous November afternoon. The sign invited readers to check out the university's wellness website.

I did not have to walk far before I stumbled across another message from ASU's wellness department: "Four tips to overcome anxiety." The tips included "Move your body," "Recognize and accept your feelings," "Interact with someone in person," and "Take a deep breath (or ten)."

Students on skateboards zipped past me as I continued to wander the campus. It happened to be Trans Day of Remembrance, and students had set up a series of portraits of transgender individuals who had died in 2017—many of them by suicide. "Today we remember those victims and continue to strive to make the world safer for the community," read a sign. The display had been organized by the campus's Rainbow Coalition, a female student told me. She wore a T-shirt that said "Scum Fuck Flower Boy," the unofficial title of a rap album by musician Tyler, the Creator.

With its palm trees and endless sunshine, ASU is without a doubt one of the most beautiful campuses in America. (Even the students are good-looking: on its list of colleges with the most attractive girls, *Maxim* magazine ranked ASU third.)[20] But one would be forgiven for thinking all those attractive young people must be suffering from some staggeringly serious mental illnesses, at least according to the endless series of official health warnings.

"Burnout is preventable!" read yet *another* sign referring students to ASU's online wellness portal, in case they had somehow overlooked all the other signs.

Another sign informed readers that "44% of ASU students report having difficulty managing stress." And then there were the constant reminders to keep performing normal bodily functions. "Breathe in. Breathe out. You got this," read another sign. Are ASU students in the habit of routinely forgetting to breathe?

Urban Dictionary, a crowdsourced online database that offers plenty of what young people would call #realtalk, defines ASU as "sort of a college, but not really."[21] That's a joke, obviously. And yet it fits. ASU is sort of a college, but also sort of group therapy.

The destigmatization of talking about mental health has been a good thing, broadly speaking; some people do struggle with depression or other mental illnesses and can benefit from a range of formal remedies provided by a university. If students are struggling, on the outside or the inside, they should seek help. Increasingly, they are more than willing to do so.

"I have seen a level of comfort to talking openly about mental health issues that I've not experienced before," Kayum Ahmed, a doctoral fellow at Columbia University, told me. "And I do see that as a positive. I think that students are now more likely to engage openly with professors and teaching assistants about the mental health challenges that they face, which they may not have been able to do previously."

People who need help shouldn't be afraid to ask for it. But at so many campuses, it has begun to feel like mental instability and trauma are the norm—that students are encouraged to see themselves as sick and vulnerable, and so they do. They have fully appropriated the language of mental illness. When students don't like something, they talk about how it triggers a kind of self-diagnosed PTSD.

Intersectionality provides a partial explanation for why this may be so. Think of an LGBT activist: this individual suffers under just one kind of oppression. A *black* LGBT activist, on the other hand, can claim two. A black LGBT activist with PTSD, though, can claim a *third* type of oppression. This person has much more cultural cachet among the activist crowd, which is probably why online biographies of academic activist types often list the mental issue the person suffers from. Mental disorder–based oppression is much easier to add to one's oppression resume, of course; it's hard to falsely claim to be a person of color and get away with it (though that hasn't stopped some from trying; we'll discuss Rachel Dolezal at a later point), but it's comparatively easier to say that you've been traumatized, or triggered, or made to feel debilitatingly depressed by the suffering you've witnessed.

Kathryn, a UC Berkeley student, told me she wouldn't feel safe attending a meeting of a conservative political group on campus. I asked her if she meant that she worried they might attack her. No, it wasn't that, she said. I then asked if she thought they might say something she found hurtful.

"Yes, exactly," she said. "They're going to trigger me. They know what they're going to do."

To deal with triggers, activists have borrowed an interesting solution from the world of social media. "Trigger warnings" actually originated on the internet, first appearing on feminist websites, where they would warn readers that they were about to encounter an article that could "trigger" a person who had experienced the kind of trauma described in the article: an eating disorder, for instance, or sexual assault. The idea is straight out of mental health psychology: people who have experienced deeply disturbing, traumatic events may undergo intense emotional pain—flashbacks, anxiety, depression—when exposed to stimuli that evoke memories of the initial trauma.

"We have students that have experienced sexual assault that have PTSD," Jacqueline, an Evergreen State College student, told me. "Sometimes if a student gets a warning beforehand that the thing that they're about to read has, say, sexual assault in it, it has a mention of that or it portrays that, then the student can do what they need to do on their own time to prepare themselves to actually handle that work. It's not asking for an exemption from the work, but just providing potential avenues for students."

Unfortunately, triggers are not always as obvious as, say, reading about sexual assault if you are a sexual assault survivor. Colors, noises, and smells can trigger PTSD as well.

"In psychological parlance, a trigger can be any stimulus that transports a PTSD sufferer back to the original scene of her trauma," wrote Katy Waldman in *Slate*. "It might be visual (a red baseball cap like the one an old abuser wore, a gait or facial expression) or aural (a whistle or slamming door). Some people are triggered by the smell of cigarette smoke or traces of a specific perfume. Others react to spoken or written language: words that switch on the brain's stress circuits, bathing synapses in adrenaline and elevating heart rate and blood pressure."[22]

It can prove difficult in practice to forewarn people about the vast swath of potential human activity that could conceivably provoke discomfort. Trigger warnings had already worn out their welcome among some observers as far back as 2010, when the sex blogger Susannah Breslin accused feminists of using them "like a Southern cook applies Pam cooking spray to an overused nonstick frying pan."[23] But years later, the hunger for trigger warnings has spread.

According to the *New Criterion*, some 63 percent of surveyed students supported mandatory trigger warnings. It has become one of the most common requests by students, and is frequently included on their lists of demands. Activist students at the University of Arizona said "potentially problematic" classroom material should come with a trigger warning and an alternative assignment, and that these were "demands, not simply requests or suggestions."[24] I have seen similar demands for mandatory trigger warnings from students at American University, Rutgers University, and countless other colleges. The student government at the University of California, Santa Barbara, approved a resolution demanding trigger warnings, and Oberlin College briefly instated such a policy before cooler heads prevailed.

Flashy, obvious plots to codify trigger warnings invite derision and are frequently torn apart by right-leaning media outlets. But subtler policies survive, often going unnoticed until a professor runs afoul of spoken or unspoken policies. At Drexel University, for instance, the sexual misconduct policy notes that professors are expected to "offer appropriate warning and accommodation regarding the introduction of explicit and triggering materials used."[25]

Jacqueline told me she doesn't want trigger warnings to be mandatory, but she thinks there should be "a way for students to ask for them and feel like that is welcome in their classrooms."

But it bears repeating that there's no real evidence such an approach is beneficial for students' mental health. Psychologists generally recommend gradually exposing patients to psychological triggers—albeit in a controlled environment, rather than a classroom—in order to help them overcome their traumas. If a person is truly in danger of fainting at the first encounter with a trigger, that person needs actual therapy. But for the vast majority of students who are perfectly mentally healthy—despite what they might tell themselves—trigger warnings seem less justified.

Angus Johnston, a historian of student activism at the City University of New York, thinks the negative reaction to trigger warnings is considerably overblown. Johnston uses trigger warnings in his classroom, though he prefers to call them "content notes."

"I basically say at the beginning of the semester that there is going to be some material that we cover in, say, a world history class that some students might find challenging on an emotional level or difficult to deal with in terms of the emotions that it produces," Johnston told me. "We're going to be talking about stuff like lynching and rape and children dying." If any of these subject matters will prove difficult for a student for some reason, that student should talk to Johnston about it beforehand, he recommends.

Johnston gave the example of discussing in class a powerful piece of writing by Charles Darwin in which the scientist attempted to memorialize his ten-year-old daughter, who had died of scarlet fever. "If there were a parent in my class who had had the experience of losing a child in the recent past, I would want to know that before I entered into a conversation about a document like that, because I wouldn't want to cause somebody unnecessary pain," Johnston told me.

Some students, though, have weaponized their triggers to make life difficult for professors who make them even slightly uncomfortable. I have spoken with many academics—even some very far-left ones—who think their students use the language of oppression and trauma in order to get their way.

Take Helen, an acting and theater instructor at a liberal arts college in the Northeast, who told me, "It really feels like teaching in the McCarthy era." Three years ago, she experienced the most bruising semester of her teaching career: her students' passive-aggressive helplessness nearly drove her insane. "By the end, I was so drained and exhausted I wasn't even a good or professional teacher anymore," she said. (Helen spoke with me on condition of anonymity, and I have changed her name.)

Helen's difficulties were eye-popping: her incredibly privileged, mostly white, perpetually offended students made acting class a living nightmare. Their refusal to take on roles that challenged them, their incredible sense of entitlement, and their constant assertions that the material was too traumatizing made it impossible for Helen to teach.

Helen's course is an acting class: students are required to act out different roles and then write reflection papers about the experience. One day, Helen asked a student to play a disabled character—something the student handled with remarkable sensitivity, Helen recalled. But when it was over, half a dozen other students ambushed Helen. They told her the lesson was entirely inappropriate.

"This was six totally able white students," said Helen.

For Helen, the irony was particularly pronounced, given her background. Before transferring to her liberal arts college, Helen worked at a less elite school in a different part of the country. Its students came from humbler origins: many, in fact, were veterans who had just returned from combat in the Middle East.

"They were right on the front lines of Afghanistan, came back, and five days later were sitting in my classroom," said Helen. "Not a single person told me they had PTSD."

Not a single person—until Helen moved across the country and arrived at her new job. She was shocked to discover that the considerably more privileged and wealthy students at the liberal arts college routinely claimed to be suffering from vague mental health issues.

"Ten people have told me they are claiming trauma," she said. "They are getting diagnosed with it."

These were privileged students participating in an acting class. An *acting* class. Once, Helen asked two female students to act out a scene between a husband and a wife. The scene required that the husband, at one point, push the wife onto a bed.

In her reflection paper, the woman who played the husband accused Helen of retraumatizing any survivors of sexual assault who might have witnessed the performance. The student reasoned that no one in an acting class should ever be asked to play such a role. She also revealed that the student playing the wife had later visited the counseling center "to process the trauma it had brought up for her."

Concerned for this student's health, Helen met with her and asked why she hadn't expressed any opposition to playing the part beforehand. The student maintained that she had dropped hints—a statement that exasperated Helen. "I'm being dropped hints by sixteen different people with opposing needs!" she said.

This was not the end of the complaints. The student playing the husband also lamented that the nature of the casting—two women—had essentially forced her to play a lesbian in front of the class, which traumatized her as well. This confession confused Helen, since the young woman had previously talked very openly about having a girlfriend.

One can imagine the difficulty of trying to teach while accommodating the triggers and mental health issues of dozens of different people. And yet this is exactly what teachers are increasingly expected to do.

"Acting is about asking people to step out of their own bodies and into other people's lived experiences," said Helen. "A lot of what we do is trigger people into connecting with things. Those are uncomfortable feelings."

In college, the learning process really does require students to explore troubling issues. There just isn't a reliable way to talk about complicated issues of identity and politics without provoking offense—and if there was, it would not necessarily be to students' benefit. Some lessons should cause discomfort.

That doesn't mean students should always be required to undergo educational ordeals that deeply disturb them. It makes sense to allow someone who has endured a truly traumatic experience to avoid acting out a directly related scene. Limited exceptions can be made for students with special needs. But when all students see themselves as having special needs—and all aspects of the human experience are considered potential traumas—it's simply impossible for the university to function. Teachers need to be allowed to exercise meaningful control over the classroom.

Helen's difficulties, of course, were not confined to the classroom. Her students frequently demanded to meet with her outside of class, for no reason other than their desperate need for validation. In Helen's view, they just wanted her to tell them they were good at acting. (I'm reminded of an episode of *It's Always Sunny in Philadelphia*—the show is basically *Seinfeld* for a younger demographic—where Kaitlin Olson's character, Dee Reynolds, a pathetically incompetent wannabe actress, asks her therapist, "Tell me I'm good, tell me I'm good, tell me I'm good, tell me I'm good," over and over again until the therapist breaks.)

"It's an unlimited well of personal attention for them," said Helen. "And no degree of shame asking for it."

By the end of the semester, anytime Helen received a request for an out-of-class meeting, she would demand an explanation of the purpose for the meeting. She estimated that she had twenty people a week begging her for extra attention.

The students' need for reassurance was exceeded only by their fear of negative feedback. Helen asked one student to change the tone of her voice when acting out a role. In her reflection paper, this student attacked Helen for suggesting that her normal voice wasn't good enough—that there was something wrong with her. Students assigned to play characters unlike themselves accused Helen of invalidating their experiences. Students assigned to play characters too much like themselves felt as though their fitness as actors was being questioned.

Meanwhile, the college continued to stress the paramount importance of accommodating students, and offered training workshops that hit upon these themes. Helen and her colleagues were reminded that racism, classism, sexism, and all the other isms are toxic influences that must be rooted out of the academy.

It's not so much that this view is wrong—racism is, in fact, bad. But according to Helen, the workshop utterly failed to explore the trade-offs and tensions between policing racism and permitting uncomfortable expression. The directives were entirely one-sided.

Helen stressed to me that some students' grievances were legitimate. But signing up for an acting class should require, in some sense, enough mental fitness to, well, study acting. One wouldn't encourage a student who fainted at the sight of blood to become an ER doctor, or a student with a debilitating fear of spiders to become an arachnologist.

Helen is not the first professor to make this complaint. She isn't even the first *theater* professor. The *New Yorker*'s Nathan Heller visited Oberlin College to interview students and professors. His conversation with Roger Copeland, a professor of theater and dance, was illuminating. According to Copeland, in 2014 he criticized a student's performance during a rehearsal for a play. The student went to Copeland's department head and accused the professor of creating "a hostile and unsafe learning environment."[26]

"I'm thinking, Oh, God! I'm cast in one of my least favorite plays of all time, 'The Crucible,' by Arthur Miller!" Copeland recalled to Heller. He then attempted to argue that no reasonable person could have interpreted his actions as threatening, but the department head explained that this did not matter. Intersectionality holds that each individual is the expert when it comes to his or her own oppression, and so the only relevant evidence was that the student did indeed feel unsafe.

The Ouroboros

So far, I have detailed the origins of intersectional theory, explained how certain aspects of Zillennials' upbringing might make them seem fragile, and described the educational environment that weaves these two threads together into one unified narrative—an activist movement that is simultaneously hypersensitive and militant in its approach to rooting out oppression.

But in practice, this movement is anything but unified—in fact, it frequently engages in self-cannibalization. Not all victims of oppression get along, since they are quite often in tension with each other. The intersectional progressive says: *We must fight racism, and sexism, and homophobia, and transphobia, and the Trump administration's immigration policies, and the wealthy, and global warming, and anti-Muslim bigotry, and ableism, et cetera, et cetera.* There are millions of people, though, who want to fight some of these things but not others—and if intersectionality requires them to commit to every single cause at once, they simply won't. Some people might decry racism and sexism without fully understanding or agreeing with the demands of the trans community; indeed, there's even a community of feminists who specifically reject the notion that trans women should be considered women (more about them in Chapters Four and Five). Other people might want economic equality for the poor but hold socially conservative views on gay rights, or oppose Trump's harsh treatment of immigrants but feel ambivalent about climate change. Still others might be strident progressives in nearly all respects but dissent from the notion that Muslims deserve space in the club when Jews do not. (That's not a theoretical example. In modern progressive parlance, Muslims are oppressed and Israel is the oppressor. Thus anti-Islamic bias is viewed as a source of oppression, while anti-Semitism is frequently ignored—even though Jews tend to be much more liberal than Muslims.)

There are three main problems with intersectionality: the education problem, the perfection problem, and the coalition problem.

First, the education problem. One important implication of intersectionality is that the sole authority on an individual's oppression is the individual in question. White men who are heterosexual and cisgender shouldn't try to "mansplain" the struggles of black women or people of color: they aren't oppressed, so they can never understand what it's like, even if they happen to be extremely progressive or well educated about left-wing causes.

At the same time, "it's not my job to educate you" is one of the most frequently recited catchphrases in Zillennial activist circles—I've heard it time and time again in conversation with activists and in their writings on the subject. "It is not my responsibility as a marginalized individual to educate you about my experience," wrote Elan Morgan in a post for *Medium* on this subject, which provided twenty-one reasons this statement was correct.[27] Given what we have learned about the Zillennial activists' relationship with mental health problems, it's easy to see why they believe this to be the case. Answering questions can be exhausting and triggering—a reminder of past traumas.

But here we have an obvious issue: asking people about their oppression—even earnestly, out of a sincere desire to become better educated—is discouraged, and there's no other way to gain this knowledge, since the oppressed themselves are the only experts. This makes it frustratingly difficult to have supportive conversations about oppression, let alone tense ones.

The second problem, which follows logically from the first, is the perfection problem. Very few people can grasp with 100 percent perfection the various requirements of intersectional progressivism, given that they aren't allowed to interrogate the oppressed, who are the only source of knowledge about oppression. I once saw this issue explained perfectly in a blog post, written by a woman complaining about all that was required of her. "As an ally, my job is to not impose my own beliefs of what's 'right,' but instead amplify the voices of the oppressed people that I'm trying to be an ally for," she wrote. "Except that I shouldn't bug them about educating me, because that's not what they're there for. And it's my duty to talk about the issue of oppression in question, because it's the job of all of us, rather than the oppressed people, to fix it. Except that when I talk, I shouldn't be using my privilege to drown out the voices of the oppressed people. Also, I should get everything right, 100% of the time. Including the terminology that the oppressed people in question themselves disagree on."[28]

Even the most well-intended person is bound to slip up. I once saw someone post a note on Facebook asking for help finding shelter for a wheelchair-bound neighbor.[29] The immediate reply was this: "The only resource I have for you at the moment is in regards to the words wheelchair bound," accompanied by a link to a *Huffington Post* article titled "Stop Saying 'Wheelchair-Bound' and Other Offensive Terms." You probably didn't know "wheelchair-bound" was offensive terminology—I certainly didn't—and in any case you shouldn't ask someone in a wheelchair what the *correct* terminology is, because it's not that person's job to educate you.

In the *Daily Beast,* Kristen Lopez described the 2018 Marvel superhero film *Ant-Man and the Wasp* as ableist—that is, disparaging of people with disabilities—for including a character who suffers from chronic pain and is attempting to cure her condition. "Instead of helping Ava find a way to cope [with] (and not necessarily eradicate) her disability, the film seeks to provide a cure." That's a bad thing, wrote Lopez, because not all disabled people want to overcome their disability.[30] Who knew you could run afoul of disability activism by making a movie in which a character who suffers from chronic pain tries to overcome said pain?

The writer, academic, and activist Freddie deBoer once described an event he witnessed: "A 33-year-old Hispanic man, an Iraq war veteran who had served three tours and had become an outspoken critic of our presence there, [was] lectured about patriarchy by an affluent 22-year-old white liberal arts college student."[31] The veteran had committed a crime of the "wheelchair-bound" variety: he had called on other veterans to "man up" and denounce the war. What he did not and could not have known, since he had spent part of his adult life on a battlefield rather than in a feminist studies classroom, is that "man up" is a gendered term, and thus unacceptable.

According to deBoer, these incidents frequently resulted in would-be allies growing disheartened with the cause. Nobody's perfect—and that's an issue for intersectionality, since it demands total adherence to all facets of its approach.

The third problem, which grows out of the first two, is the coalition problem: it's extremely difficult to form strategic relationships with groups outside the progressive left for the purpose of advancing a single issue. Take any cause—legalizing marijuana, for example. There are a lot of Americans who subscribe to a diverse range of ideologies, with some interest in the issue. There are liberals and leftists who think using marijuana is no big deal, there are libertarians (like myself) who think the government has no right telling consenting adults what they can put in their own bodies, and there are even some conservatives who think enforcing federal marijuana prohibition is a waste of law enforcement resources and a blow to states' rights. People from all three of these groups could and should work together to advance marijuana decriminalization, despite their myriad differences on other issues. But intersectionality gets in the way, since the intersectional progressive only wants to work with people who oppose *all* the various strains of oppression—not just the ones relevant to the narrow issue of marijuana legalization.

It's difficult to imagine, for instance, that one of the crowning achievements of recent single-issue advocacy—gay marriage—would have gone as relatively smoothly had intersectionality been as ubiquitous a decade ago as it is today. Gay marriage was in some sense the last non-intersectional leftist cause: activists who supported the issue were extremely disciplined and specifically avoided tying it to other, more fringe causes. Adherents of gay marriage, in fact, worked tirelessly to bring conservatives into the movement, stressing that gay people only wanted legal equality and sought to form the same kind of family arrangements that social conservatives believe are desirable for society. The marriage equality movement turned to Ted Olson, a Republican and former solicitor general under President George W. Bush, to represent it in the lawsuit against California's Proposition 8, which had banned gay marriage.

Consider Andrew Sullivan making the case for gay marriage in a 1989 *New Republic* article. "Marriage provides an anchor, if an arbitrary and weak one, in the chaos of sex and relationships to which we are all prone," he wrote. "It provides a mechanism for emotional stability, economic security, and the healthy rearing of the next generation. We rig the law in its favor not because we disparage all forms of relationship other than the nuclear family, but because we recognize that not to promote marriage would be to ask too much of human virtue. In the context of the weakened family's effect upon the poor, it might also invite social disintegration."[32] It's a fundamentally conservative argument, crafted specifically to appeal to conservatives. In my lifetime, support for gay marriage has increased from 27 percent in 1996 to 67 percent two decades later, and gay marriage is legal everywhere in the United States.[33] This extremely happy development is in large part due to the work of a coalition that would be much harder to put together in the age of intersectional activism.

Contrast the triumph of gay marriage with some examples of the setbacks and infighting that occur within an intersectional framework. During the June 2017 Chicago Pride Parade in recognition of gay equality, organizers asked Laurel Grauer, a Jewish lesbian, to leave. Grauer had dared to carry a flag bearing a rainbow (the symbol of the LGBT community) *and* the Jewish Star of David.[34] She was told her display made people feel unsafe. One might expect everybody who supports equal rights and dignity for LGBT people to be welcome at pride events, but from the standpoint of the organizers, the march was intended to be intersectional—meaning it was both pro-LGBT and "anti-Zionist." (Anti-Zionists oppose the state of Israel's existence.)

For the modern left, Jews are outranked by minority groups whose oppression is considered more serious than, and to some degree at odds with, their own. The incident at the Chicago Pride Parade is not a one-off. Linda Sarsour, an activist and a leader of the Women's March, has made the dubious claim that anti-Semitism is "different than anti-black racism or Islamophobia because it's not systemic."[35] Sarsour and fellow Women's March leaders Tamika Mallory and Carmen Perez have drawn criticism for their ties to controversial Nation of Islam leader Louis Farrakhan, who is widely considered to be an anti-Semite.

Or consider an illuminating episode involving the Democratic

Socialists of America, the left-wing faction of the Democratic Party that got a huge boost from Bernie Sanders's 2016 presidential campaign. In January 2018, the DSA tweeted that it would be unveiling its Medicare for All campaign, an effort to extend the national health insurance program to everyone in the country. This was an unsurprising development—empowering the government to provide more comprehensive health care coverage is a fairly standard goal of liberal activists, not just the far left. More surprising was the furious blowback the DSA received from many of its own members who identified as disabled. The DSA's Medicare for All committee had apparently failed to consult the Disability Working Group about the campaign's rollout, which led the latter to protest that they were being left out of relevant decision-making. Since disabled people are especially affected by health care policy, the Medicare for All group had essentially failed to let disabled people be the experts on their own oppression—an intersectionality no-no. Amber A'Lee Frost, a Medicare for All activist and prominent DSA member known for appearing on the left-wing *Chapo Trap House* podcast, hit back, accusing her critics of trying to sabotage the movement with their "pathological anti-social behavior." This made matters much worse: the comment was perceived as an attack on the autistic community.

Frost had committed an ism: ableism. Several dozen DSA members signed a petition demanding "that Amber A'Lee Frost immediately remove herself from any involvement, official or unofficial, with DSA's Medicare for All campaign, and should she not, that she be removed."[36] Because intersectionality means casting suspicion on organizing efforts if these efforts do not make the marginalized the center of attention.

College campuses, where the grievances are significant but the stakes are low, play host to some of the most farcical examples of intersectionality-induced bickering. A particularly revelatory crisis emerged at Evergreen State College in Washington during the spring 2017 semester. Every year, activist students organized a Day of Action during which students of color would deliberately leave campus as a means of protest against racism. But in 2017, the activists decided to try something new: they would ask students of color to remain, and white people to leave. This tactic didn't sit well with Bret Weinstein, a biology professor at Evergreen. Weinstein was a fellow progressive—he supported Sanders over Hillary Clinton—and sympathized with the activists' goals, but felt that the new plan for the Day of Action was unsound.

"There is a huge difference between a group or coalition deciding to voluntarily absent themselves from a shared space in order to highlight their vital and under-appreciated roles, and a group or coalition encouraging another group to go away," Weinstein told an administrator. The latter, he contended, "is a show of force, and an act of oppression in and of itself."[37] In response, activists surrounded Weinstein outside his classroom and accused him of being a racist. "This is not a discussion!" they told him. A student activist, Hadley, later explained her actions to *Vice* correspondent Michael Moynihan: "You [Weinstein] don't get to spread this problematic rhetoric."

A subsequent dialogue between the activist students and college president George Bridges similarly spiraled out of control. During the meeting, activist students repeatedly belittled Bridges, a meek, bow-tie-wearing white man—even instructing him to keep his hands at his sides and stop pointing at people. "Fuck you, George!" said one student. "We don't want to hear a goddamn thing you have to say." When George asked the students to let him leave the room so he could use the lavatory, they told him to hold it. Hadley told Moynihan that Weinstein should go be a "racist and a piece of shit" somewhere else. The campus police told Weinstein they could no longer guarantee his safety on campus; he eventually resigned.

Each of these examples shows how activists who worship at the altar of intersectionality felt compelled to turn on people for committing venial sins. It's not enough to share the intersectional progressives' goals relating to a specific issue: one must also support their tactics, speak their language intuitively, defer to the wisdom of the oppressed without either speaking on their behalf or expecting them to speak for themselves, and commit to every other interrelated cause.

The intersectional approach often seems petty and performative. The symbol of the gay equality movement, the rainbow flag, was designed by the activist Gilbert Baker in 1978: its colors were pink, red, orange, yellow, green, turquoise, indigo, and violet, which represented sex, life, healing, sunlight, nature, magic, serenity, and spirit. In 2017, the city of Philadelphia debuted a new rainbow flag to celebrate Pride Month—this flag included brown and black stripes, in recognition of people of color. Many members of the LGBT community—particularly younger ones, according to *BuzzFeed*—liked the new intersectional flag, which takes a stand against homophobia *and* racism.[38] But many older LGBT activists were confused, since none of the original colors reflected ethnicity at all. Will the flag eventually have to add stripes for Latinos, Asians, and Native Americans? What about the disabled community, and those who languish under the oppressions of sizeism?

The thinkers who first defined intersectionality probably hoped that by linking all kinds of oppression together, they would force people to fight against a wider swath of bad things. Patricia Hill Collins hinted at this when she wrote, "Many African Americans deny the existence of sexism, or see it as a secondary concern that is best addressed when the more pressing problem of racism has been solved. But if racism and sexism are deeply intertwined, racism can never be solved without seeing and challenging sexism." Collins wanted to tie sexism together with racism, so that everybody fighting racism would have to fight sexism, too.

But the more isms added to the pile, the more tenuous this approach becomes. It's all well and good to say that sexism is as pervasive a problem as racism, but the intersectional activist of 2018 is reaching much further and making many more demands. From the standpoint of this movement, a woman marching against Trump, against the Republican Party, against police brutality, against war, against sexual violence, and *for* Israel's existence is not an ally or potential ally: she is an enemy. She is part of the problem. She has failed the test of intersectionality—she is not, as anti-Trump poet (yes, poet) Elisa Chavez put it, "intersectional as fuck."[39] She might as well have voted for Trump.

The rest of the book will put this understanding of intersectionality's pervasive influence to good use as we focus on the various contingents of Zillennial activism, beginning with the anti-Trump resistance.

TWO

NAZI PUNCHING

ANTI-TRUMP, ANTI–FREE SPEECH, ANTIFA

A day before the Women's March, spectators and activists of all stripes descended on Washington, D.C., for the inauguration of President Trump. Supporters of the new president wore "Make America Great Again" baseball caps and toted "Trump-Pence 2016" signs. Detractors were more colorful.

"Trump is the symptom, capitalism is the disease, socialism is the cure," read one sign, wielded by a woman with a T-shirt depicting a clenched fist.

Others were at least funny: I spotted a man holding a sign featuring a cartoon Batman slapping Trump in the face with the caption "Stop tweeting!"—a parody of a drawing from the *Batman* comics, in which the caped crusader slaps Robin. (The image has become a popular meme—for all you less-savvy tech users, a meme is a funny picture accompanied by text and circulated on social media websites.)

The demonstrations were mostly peaceful. Mostly.

Masked protesters known simultaneously as the "black bloc" (because they wear black clothes and hoods to mask their identities) and "antifa" (as in anti-fascist) smashed the windows of a local

Starbucks and a Bank of America. They also set a limousine on fire. How these acts of property damage were intended to undermine Trump remains a mystery, given that the CEO of Starbucks and many Bank of America employees were financial supporters of the Hillary Clinton campaign. The limo driver, we learned, was a Muslim immigrant.[1]

A rioter knocked a friend of mine, the journalist Philip Wegmann, to the ground, causing him to briefly lose consciousness—even though, Wegmann told me, he was wearing credentials that clearly identified him as a member of the press.[2] Wegmann is a writer for conservative news outlets the *Washington Examiner* and the *Daily Signal,* however, and one of the main principles of the new activist left is that unfriendly media organizations should not have the right to cover their activities, even on public property. But it isn't just conservative media outlets that bear the "unfriendly" designation; many activists are equally dismissive of mainstream news sources. One activist told me that she hates CNN just as much as Trump supporters do. "I don't trust CNN," she said. "I don't trust any mainstream media." Only explicitly leftist media organizations are permitted to cover the antics of the #Resistance.

Of course, the most famous victim of Inauguration Day violence was alt-right leader Richard Spencer, a white nationalist with some positive feelings about Trump. An Australian news channel was interviewing Spencer when a masked protester walked up to him and punched him in the face while the cameras were rolling.

One can—and should—strenuously object to Spencer's racist opinions while still acknowledging his right to hold them. As a strictly legal matter, his speech is quite obviously protected by the First Amendment. The Supreme Court has carved out a few exceptions in two hundred years of jurisprudence, but none of them would apply here. In the 2011 decision *Snyder v. Phelps,* for instance, the Court held 8–1 that the virulently anti-gay Westboro Baptist Church could picket military servicemembers' funerals, waving signs that read "God hates you" and "Fag troops." The fact that the church's message was objectively offensive and emotionally damaging to the families of deceased soldiers was not enough to strip it of constitutional protections. If such speech is protected by the First Amendment, you can bet Spencer's is, too.

But this did not stop members of the left from defending—even praising—the antifa activists who struck Spencer. Natasha Lennard, an activist and journalist who participated in black bloc activities in D.C. that day, described the attack as "pure kinetic beauty" in *The Nation*.[3] The window-smashing, trash-can fires, limousine-burning, and Spencer-punching "should be celebrated as an opening salvo of resistance in the era of Trump," she wrote. Mob violence is only a problem "if you think there are no righteous mobs, or that windows feel pain, or that counter-violence (like punching Richard Spencer) is never valid."

The most extreme members of the anti-Trump resistance have taken up the banner of antifa, a continuation—in their minds—of a movement that arose in Germany in the 1930s to counter the rise of Nazism. In the nearly one hundred years since, antifa movements have sprung up in a variety of countries, often opposing Nazis and Nazi sympathizers while also promoting general far-left politics of the Marxist and communist variety.

Modern antifa is decentralized and relatively leaderless; many of its members are anonymous and unknown. Though they are known for wearing black masks, bandanas, and black clothing and for committing acts of destruction, antifa itself is an ideological position and does not prescribe any specific tactics. One can be opposed to fascism without endorsing black bloc tactics, property destruction, censorship, or violence.

In practice, however, antifa groups tend toward illiberal means to achieve their ends—both historically and at present. In *Antifa: The Anti-Fascist Handbook*, Mark Bray writes that antifa explicitly rejects "the classical liberal phrase incorrectly ascribed to Voltaire that 'I disapprove of what you say, but I will defend to the death your right to say it.'" According to Bray, "Anti-fascism is an illiberal politics of social revolutionism applied to fighting the Far Right, not only literal fascists."

Thus antifa often must embrace violence. In their view, their enemies started it—by making statements that serve to further marginalize people who languish under some form of oppression. Caring about intersectionality means that an attack on one disadvantaged group is an attack on all. And if it is wise to stop people on the right from speaking against any member of the coalition, then it must occasionally be necessary to silence them when they try to speak. If they will not be silenced willingly, then violence is the only alternative.

"The inherent contradiction of antifa," wrote Carlos Lozada in his fair-minded but ultimately critical review of *Antifa: The Anti-Fascist Handbook,* "is that, if America is indeed so irredeemable and hypocritical that violence is the answer, then what exactly are you fighting to preserve?"[4]

Those who defend the validity of mob violence claim that it is justifiable to the extent that it unnerves the powers that be. But do the powerful really feel threatened by a smashed Starbucks window or Richard Spencer taking a punch? The evidence strongly suggests the opposite: when leftists resort to explicit violence, they make regular people more sympathetic to governmental authority and a conservative worldview. Princeton University's Omar Wasow studied protest movements in the 1960s and found that violent upheaval tended to make white voters more conservative, whereas nonviolent protests were associated with increased liberalism among white voters. "These patterns suggest violent protest activity is correlated with a taste for 'social control' among the predominantly white mass public," wrote Wasow in his study.[5]

This is something that President Richard Nixon understood quite well. In March 1969, he received a memo from an aide warning him to expect increased violence on college campuses in the spring. The president grabbed a pen and scrawled a single word across the document: "Good!" He knew something many activists failed to grasp: law-and-order policies become more palatable to the silent majority when leftists are punching people in the streets.

In contrast, "nonviolent movements succeed because they invite mass participation," Maria Stephan, a director at the United States Institute of Peace, told the *New York Times*.[6] Violent resistance, on the other hand, is incredibly divisive. Stephan and Erica Chenoweth produced a book, *Why Civil Resistance Works,* that found nonviolent resistance movements were twice as likely as violent movements to achieve their aims in the twentieth and early twenty-first centuries. "A campaign's commitment to nonviolent methods enhances its domestic and international legitimacy and encourages more broad-based participation in the resistance, which translates into increased pressure being brought to bear on the target," they wrote. According to Stephan and Chenoweth, governments have little trouble justifying brutal crackdowns on violent protesters, but *non*violent protesters engender greater sympathy from the public, reducing the likelihood of repression.[7]

Based on these findings, it's hardly surprising that Spencer himself isn't wholly opposed to violence. "The fact that they are excusing violence against [me] inherently means that they believe that there's a state of exception, where we can use violence," Spencer told the *Atlantic*. "I think they're actually kind of right."[8]

When asked by a fellow traveler, Gregory Conte, whether members of the alt-right should support free speech as a general principle for the long term, Spencer responded, "No, of course not."

To drive the point home, I asked Spencer about his attitude toward free speech (and much else; read Chapter Eight for the rest of the interview). He told me he was certainly not for absolute free speech, and he thought the state should have "at least some involvement" in promoting a better society by suppressing dangerous ideas.

In any case, the idea that certain people do not deserve free speech protections is now as popular among the far left as it always was among the far right. But it didn't used to be this way: leftists were once firm defenders of free speech for all, even for Nazis. In fact, when the Nazis came to campus in the 1960s, they did so at the left's invitation.

That Was Then

Yes, you read that last part right: in May 1964, a progressive student group called SLATE brought the leader of the American Nazi Party's Western Division, Ralph P. Forbes, to the University of California, Berkeley, to speak. According to Nathan Glazer, a sociology professor who taught at Berkeley at the time, Forbes spoke in the men's gym, which was the largest indoor space on campus.

Even more shocking, the students promoted the event by donning Nazi uniforms and handing out leaflets at the entrances to campus. "The young Nazi-clad figures were not really Nazis, but adherents of the liberal-progressive Slate, who had hit upon this as a clever way to publicize the meeting," wrote Glazer.

SLATE also invited a member of the far-right John Birch Society to campus. Malcolm X, Communist Party leader Albert J. Lima, and conservative commentator William F. Buckley spoke as well. Hosting these speakers was a way for students—including the very liberal students of SLATE—to assert their "absolute belief in free speech," according to Glazer.

Neither the administration, the rest of the student body, nor the people who actually showed up for the talks tried to shut down controversial speakers. Even Forbes, a literal Nazi, enjoyed a well-behaved audience.

"They were greeted politely," wrote Jo Freeman, a feminist scholar who studied at Berkeley during the 1960s. "Malcolm X was applauded. Capt. Forbes heard silence relieved by occasional laughter. At the end of their talks, the audience dispersed. What these people said, not whether they should have had a University forum in which to say it, dominated student bull sessions for days."[9] Imagine that: young people arguing about a speaker's actual message rather than whether letting him speak was a form of violence.

Note that these were not quiescent students. They were true leftist radicals. Many were sympathetic to communism. Others were leaders of the civil rights and anti-war movements. They were passionate about left-wing causes. But they viewed free speech—even for Nazis—as one of those causes.

According to Freeman, appearances by objectively offensive speakers such as Forbes produced "neither riots nor mass conversions to politically unacceptable ideas." The students were emotionally capable of inviting harmful people to campus, considering their ideas, and then rejecting them as they saw fit.

Free speech rights were so important to students at Berkeley in the 1960s that they formed a movement uniting people of all ideological stripes for the purpose of pressuring the university administration to stop coddling them. Indeed, Malcolm X, Lima, and Forbes were permitted on campus only after student activists successfully convinced administrators to rescind paternalistic policies that placed strict limits on who could say what at Berkeley.

Chief among these policies was the unofficial "speaker ban," which came into existence during the reign of Robert Gordon Sproul, who served as president of the University of California from 1930 until 1958. No outside group or person was allowed to speak on campus without the president's approval, and Sproul retained the right "to prevent exploitation of the university's prestige" by denying a platform to any person with whom he disagreed. In practice, the policy was most often used against communists, though not exclusively. Since any and all outside political activity was unwelcome at the university, political figures Richard Nixon and Adlai Stevenson both were denied speaking opportunities on campus in the 1950s.

Ironically, Nixon later commented favorably on the speaker ban, and made it a feature of his 1962 campaign for governor of California. Nixon vowed to expand the ban to exclude more undesirable perspectives from public university campuses if elected governor. (Modern-day student leftists' position on free speech is arguably closer to Nixon's position than to the position of their radical forebears.) But Nixon was defeated by incumbent Democratic governor Pat Brown, who supported the efforts of Sproul's successor, University of California president Clark Kerr, to end the ban entirely. Those efforts came to fruition on June 21, 1963, when the California Board of Regents voted 15–2 to open the campuses to controversial speakers.

But the speaker ban was just one onerous restriction on students' free expression rights. Another was the university system's prohibition against on-campus political activity of any kind. Students were not allowed to organize for the purposes of political activism, set up tables, or hand out flyers in support of political causes. In theory, this ban applied not just to communists but to all political organizations, including the Young Democrats and conservative students.

Indeed, it was an incident involving the College Republicans that kicked off the official Free Speech Movement (FSM) at Berkeley in the summer of 1964. According to Freeman, moderate Republicans were working to recruit students to oppose the archconservative Republican senator Barry Goldwater of Arizona, who was running for president. They were doing this in a small plaza, Bancroft Strip, which was believed to be city property but was actually owned by the university. This meant the recruiters, as well as many others who had placed political flyers on the pillars in the plaza, were technically violating the campus ban on political activity, which irked a vice chancellor.

Both President Kerr and Berkeley chancellor Edward Strong were away from campus at the time, so the vice chancellor appealed to the dean of students, Katherine Towle, to enforce the ban. But student organizers, primarily but not exclusively those involved with the progressive group SLATE, refused to leave the Bancroft Strip. The sudden enforcement of the rules against organizing made strange bedfellows of various student groups, with both left-leaning and right-leaning activists joining forces to oppose the administration.

The police eventually arrested one person, a Berkeley alumnus and civil rights activist, and gave everyone else twenty-four hours to leave the area or face arrest. Brown and Kerr intervened, and the demonstration ended peaceably. It was, however, just the opening salvo in a war to liberalize Berkeley.

On October 3, the students—now led by a charismatic twenty-one-year-old from New York City named Mario Savio—officially formed the Free Speech Movement. "In the person of Savio, the movement speaks with a voice that has been heard in America since the beginning, the voice of an exalted, quasi-religious anarchism," wrote Henry F. May, a historian who taught at Berkeley.

During the summer, Savio had gone to Mississippi to help register black people to vote. He returned to Berkeley in the fall, intending to help raise money for liberal causes—and was livid that the administration had decided to crack down on such activities. Savio was possessed of an absolute faith in reasoned argument to win debates, if only advocates were permitted the right to make their case. He wasn't afraid of contrary opinions; he was afraid of what would happen if the administration held the power to punish them. Savio agreed with the Greek philosopher Diogenes that the most beautiful thing in the world was freedom of speech. "Those words . . . are burned into my soul," said Savio.

"Mario Savio supported the right of speakers from all political perspectives to speak on campus," wrote historian Robert Cohen in *The Nation*. "Rather than ban speakers he disagreed with, Savio debated them, whether they were deans, faculty, the student-body president, or whoever."[10]

This was what the leader of the Berkeley activist movement in the 1960s looked like. This was the model leftist ideologue: someone wholly dedicated to free expression.

And Savio wasn't alone. On December 2, six thousand students attended a rally in the plaza in front of Sproul Hall in protest of the administration's efforts to punish FSM leaders, including Savio. Some eight hundred of them followed Savio inside Sproul Hall and engaged in a sit-in. While the administration had agreed to let students organize on campus, officials were unwilling to grant full freedom of speech. The sticking point was this: administrators wished to continue to deny students the right to advocate in favor of any activity that was illegal off campus. FSM's leaders rejected this compromise, and Savio warned fellow activists that they should all be prepared to go to jail.

Over the course of twelve hours, the police proceeded to arrest everyone occupying Sproul Hall. A general student strike followed, and within a month, Berkeley's new chancellor, Martin Meyerson, granted full free speech and political organizing rights to all students. The activists had won, and free expression was saved.

What motivated these students to risk expulsion and jail time? Above all, a unifying respect for, and belief in, the First Amendment. Savio thought that only this law, as interpreted by the courts, could be used to judge him. He did not favor free speech just for the safe, or the innocent, or the uncontroversial.

"The First Amendment exists to protect consequential speech," wrote Savio a semester later. "The Free Speech Movement demands no more—nor less—than full First Amendment rights of advocacy on campus as well as off: that, therefore, only the courts have power to determine and punish abuses of free speech." It couldn't be any clearer: he thought the only authority with the power to curb speech was the courts. Not administrators, or police, or other students.

The students' stand for free speech continued to irk authoritarians and busybodies for years to come. In June 1965, the California State Senate's Subcommittee on Un-American Activities released a report that concluded: "It is our considered view that to throw wide the portals to any controversial speaker who wishes to utilize the opportunity to harangue a college audience, is to put curiosity and entertainment above the educational process, and to appeal to the morbid and emotional rather than to the scholarly and the intellectual."

The above statement could have been written by a campus official in defense of shutting down the right-wing provocateur Milo Yiannopoulos, something Mario Savio certainly would have protested if he were alive today (he passed away in 1996, though his widow, Lynne Hollander, has defended Yiannopoulos's First Amendment rights). But half a century after the successes of the Free Speech Movement, Berkeley activists are the ones most concerned about "controversial speakers who wish to harangue a college audience"—and are willing to use violence to stop them.

This Is Now

All is not well at Berkeley today. When I visited the campus, I found the steps where Mario Savio initiated the Free Speech Movement walled off by police barricades.

This was the fall of 2017—the day of Yiannopoulos's planned return to Berkeley—and perhaps a hundred police officers patrolled the nearby area. No one could gain access to Sproul Plaza without first passing through a metal detector. Women with purses were turned away, as were men with backpacks. No bag of any sort was allowed through. I met up with a friend and fellow journalist; she had packed a bag stuffed with the tools of a true millennial reporter—spare cellphone, battery pack—and we had no choice but to ask a student to watch our stuff while we entered the plaza. (My friend offered money, but the student, who was an employee of a nearby copy shop, kindly agreed to stash our bags for free.)

The line to enter the event was long. The man standing in front of me, a Trump supporter and fan of Yiannopoulos, carried an American flag; the police told him he couldn't bring it into the plaza because it could be used as a weapon. They also made him leave his studded motorcycle gloves behind.

Indeed, the university purportedly spent more than $800,000 on security measures for the Yiannopoulos event, which were so cumbersome that by the time Milo appeared, only about twenty people had actually made it past the barricades. Instead of speaking, he signed autographs—and at least one fidget spinner (a spinning toy for children that is increasingly popular with Zillennials because it's, bafflingly, intended to reduce stress)—for a few minutes and then disappeared. Whether or not such security measures were actually necessary, there is just one reason the university put them in place: antifa, whose promises of violence impose a steep cost on institutions that are duty-bound to secure the physical safety of unpopular speakers. This is the explicit rejection of the values the previous generation of radicals worked so hard to enshrine. In another era, Berkeley activists fought to protect the free speech rights of every single person against the aggressions of authority figures. Now free speech needs protection from the activists.

"It's one of those great historical ironies, the fact that Berkeley was the foundation of the Free Speech Movement in the modern era," Alice Dreger, a historian and former professor of bioethics at Northwestern University, told me in an interview. "The students have absolutely no knowledge of that."

A problem, it seems, is that activist students increasingly see free speech as a tool for harming some aspect of the intersectional agenda. Speech wielded by the powerful against the marginalized is not desirable, whether or not it's "free."

"Free speech is not dead. It was never alive," wrote Juniper, the trans student at Berkeley, in a May 2017 op-ed for the student newspaper, the *Daily Californian*. She continued: "I am not here for free speech."[11]

Juniper wrote this in response to Yiannopoulos's first visit to campus. Trouble seems to follow Yiannopoulos, a former editor at the pro-Trump conservative news website *Breitbart* and author of the book *Dangerous,* about his favorite subject (himself). But much of that trouble is self-inflicted. Yiannopoulos first made national headlines back in 2014, when he became one of the best-known defenders of the GamerGate movement, a public awareness campaign undertaken by (mostly male) videogame players who were annoyed by left-leaning media coverage of the industry. For these gamers, some developers and journalists were ruining the gaming experience by injecting social justice themes into games or deriding the lack of politically correct representations. A favorite target of the GamerGate movement was Anita Sarkeesian, creator of the Feminist Frequency YouTube channel, which called out sexism in videogames like Super Mario Bros., Metroid, and The Legend of Zelda. GamerGate activists frequently resorted to nasty tactics to convey their irritation at Sarkeesian and other "social justice warriors"—a term of derision leveled against particularly pro-PC individuals—sending harassing tweets and even death threats.

Whatever legitimate grievances the GamerGaters had were more than cancelled out by their obnoxious and abusive behavior, but they found a powerful champion in Yiannopoulos. As a young, out, and proud gay man, Yiannopoulos was a perfect vehicle for countering the argument that GamerGaters were mean-spirited, backward jerks. *How can we be right-wing assholes if the flamboyantly gay Milo Yiannopoulos supports us?* the argument went. And Yiannopoulos was happy to equip them with this defense, as long as it made him the center of attention.

Indeed, Yiannopoulos's shtick had always involved putting the personal before the political. Before he was GamerGate's staunchest ally, he was actually a *critic* of gamer culture.[12] In February 2013, prior to his reinvention as emperor of the nerds, he was making japes at gamers' expense. "Few things are more embarrassing than grown men getting over-excited about video games," he tweeted. Later, he tweeted a link to an article about the social habits of gamers, with the colorful caption "Are online gamers as overweight, awkward, and lazy as we think they are? Writer trying to be nice but answer is yes." He even said that the only people present at videogame launches are "pungent beta-male bollock scratchers and twelve-year-olds." But then Yiannopoulos had a change of heart—probably because there were millions of clicks to be mined from attacking the enemies of said pungent beta-male bollock scratchers.

Yiannopoulos gradually transitioned from attacking the Sar-

keesians of the world to attacking liberals and political correctness more generally—as well as defending the avatar of resistance to
political correctness, Donald Trump. When I interviewed him during the 2016 campaign, he told me that Trump—whom he affectionately refers to as "Daddy," a term with both parental overtones and
pseudo-sexual connotations in the gay world specifically—is "becoming an icon of irreverent resistance to political correctness.
It's why people like him." Yiannopoulos noted—correctly, in my
view—that a lot of young people on the right were excited about
Trump not because of his policies but because he was reliably,
militantly anti-PC.

It was this base of young, right-leaning, anti-PC students that
helped catapult Yiannopoulos to national notoriety. He soon
undertook a campus speaking tour, at the invitation of student
Republican organizations at various colleges and universities. The
events gave Yiannopoulos what he wanted, attention, and they gave
the young conservatives what they wanted—also attention. They
provided an opportunity for Yiannopoulos to make ridiculous and
offensive statements, like calling for women to eschew engineering
jobs, suggesting that lesbians may not exist, downplaying sexual
abuse, and excusing Trump's behavior.

The scheme would have failed if only the left had decided to
simply ignore Yiannopoulos's provocations. Instead, they turned
out in droves to protest Yiannopoulos's speeches, shout him down,
and even attempt to revoke his platform or cancel his events.

For conservatives, this was the entire point of bringing Yiannopoulos to campus in the first place. The Republican groups knew
they could drum up publicity—national publicity—by inviting a
speaker who was sure to provoke the ire of the left. Keep in mind
that many conservative student groups already bear the brunt of
censorship on campus; bringing Yiannopoulos and watching the
spectacle unfold must have seemed like a surefire way to prove the
point that yes, the campus left *is* intolerant and eager to shut them
down. Yiannopoulos wasn't particularly well versed in conservative philosophy, or even much of a conventional Republican

(beyond his support for "Daddy" Trump, another unconventional Republican without much of an interest in conservative philosophy), but that didn't matter to them.

Writing for the conservative Trump-skeptic magazine *National Review*, former Stanford University student Elliot Kaufman described a scene he had witnessed at a meeting of the university's conservative student paper, the *Stanford Review*, when someone suggested bringing Yiannopoulos to campus.

"'Someone should sponsor his lecture—it's a matter of free speech,' argued a confused fellow editor," Kaufman recalled. "Soon, other editors made different arguments: 'This will create a huge stir,' said one. 'It will drive the social-justice warriors crazy,' offered another. That is, the left-wing riots were not the price or downside of inviting Yiannopoulos—they were the attraction."[13]

So it was at Berkeley, the site of the most infamous Yiannopoulos event. Invited by the Berkeley College Republicans—with the support of Berkeley's administration, which wisely upheld its free speech commitments (this time)—Yiannopoulos attempted to deliver his usual shtick. Two hours before the event was scheduled to begin, antifa struck.

Protesters surrounded the building where he was supposed to speak, tearing down the metal barriers erected by the police. They started banging on the walls of the building, smashing several windows. Then they began to light fires: one particularly large blaze consumed a nearby tree (lighter fluid helped). Police smuggled Yiannopoulos out of the building before he could say a word. Hence the beefed-up security measures months later, when Yiannopoulos attempted his return: no one wanted a repeat of the Battle of Berkeley.

Assuming Berkeley's Republicans had the same goals as Stanford's Republicans, the event was successful nonetheless: it proved the campus left was just as censorious, violent, and destructive as advertised.

"They're just making him more famous," a freshman student, Kevin, told me.[14]

The intolerance was not primarily the work of students—according to reports, some of the masked vandals who lit the fires and smashed the windows were local activists. But many students supported these efforts, because letting Yiannopoulos speak would be tantamount to unleashing actual violence on the sorts of people that Yiannopoulos criticizes: people of color, trans people, immigrants, feminists, and others.

It was against this backdrop that Juniper wrote her op-ed taking issue with free speech. I asked her why she did so. "The premise of the op-ed was basically discussing the importance of prioritizing student safety over abstract concepts like free speech," Juniper told me. "The intention was not to diminish free speech as a right or a privilege, but more so to refocus conversation on the lives of marginalized students."

Another Berkeley student, Kathryn, who is majoring in rhetoric and African American studies, told me she was furious at the administration for providing a platform to speakers who make her feel threatened. "I came here to learn," said Kathryn. "I didn't come here to feel threatened or violated or oppressed. I came here to further my knowledge and I can't even do that because of who they're inviting to come speak and who they're protecting."

Turning Against Free Speech

Clearly, modern Zillennial activists feel differently about free speech than their predecessors did.

"When we're dead, when people die, and you're sitting here like, 'Well, at least they got to practice their free speech,' I'm so sorry, your free speech is not more important than the lives of black, trans, femmes, and students on this campus," Jamil, a student and activist at Evergreen State College, told *Vice*.[15]

The question, of course, is, *why*? How did the left stray so far from Mario Savio's ideals?

To the extent this newfound hostility toward speech is philosophical, the widespread influences of intersectionality and safety culture—as discussed in Chapter One—help shed light on what's happening. An extra sensitivity to harm, coupled with a drive to find more and more—and smaller and smaller—sources of oppression, might have made shouting down the Milos and Murrays suddenly seem much more important to activists.

Indeed, many of the academics who teach and promote intersectionality come out of a tradition of new leftism that emphasizes language itself as a form of oppression. During the 1950s and 1960s, the German-born sociologist Herbert Marcuse—famously described as the "father of the New Left"—held a variety of teaching positions at Columbia University, Harvard University, Brandeis University, and finally the University of California, San Diego. In his most famous essay, "Repressive Tolerance," Marcuse argued that the government would be perfectly justified in abridging the freedoms of right-wing movements, and that capitalism had undermined democracy to the point that society could no longer trust social equality to triumph in the marketplace of ideas.[16]

"Liberating tolerance, then, would mean intolerance against movements from the Right, and toleration of movements from the Left," wrote Marcuse. "It would extend to the stage of action as well as of discussion and propaganda, of deed as well as of word."

Marcuse even used a familiar metaphor: "The traditional criterion of clear and present danger seems no longer adequate to a stage where the whole society is in the situation of the theater audience when somebody cries: 'fire.'" In context, Marcuse meant that an act of right-wing political expression was akin to shouting "fire" in a crowded theater, and should be prevented on public safety grounds.

Marcuse's project was making Marxism palatable for a new century. Marxism, of course, refers to the older leftism of nineteenth-century socialist thinker Karl Marx, who viewed class struggle as the overarching source of human oppression. Marxist thinking dominated the left in the second half of the nineteenth century and first half of the twentieth century, culminating in the Russian Revolution and global ascendance of communism. (I'll have much more to say about Marxism in Chapter Six.) But by Marcuse's time, Marxism seemed hopelessly naive; Marx had hypothesized that the world would inevitably progress beyond capitalism, but capitalism was more entrenched than ever, and undeniably more successful than Stalinist Russia or Maoist China.

"In the West, the Left has failed to generate significant socialist parties, and many socialist parties have become moderate," argued Stephen Hicks, a professor of philosophy at Rockford College, in a 2002 essay. "Major experiments in socialism in nations such as the Soviet Union, Vietnam, and Cuba have been failures."[17]

In the 1960s, 1970s, and 1980s, leftist thinkers assailed Marxism as too scientific: postmodernists such as Michel Foucault and Jacques Derrida were skeptical of Marx's grand claims about history and economics. It's difficult to make generalizations about postmodernist thinkers, since their writings are often inscrutable, esoteric, and filled with contradiction. But broadly speaking, these thinkers were hostile to Enlightenment ideas about using reason and science to arrive at objective truth. Postmodernists understood that objectivity was a lie—that the interplay of language, power, and oppression served to obscure the truth.

"To my mind, the high-water mark of academic postmodern theory, at least in its political form, was the 1990s," wrote Matt McManus in an essay for *Quillette*. "Many of the pioneers of postmodern theory were at the height of their fame and influence."[18]

That doctrinaire Marxism and leftist postmodernism are in significant tension with each other may surprise readers who are familiar with the term "postmodern neo-Marxism" (occasionally called "cultural Marxism," often by those on the far right who dabble in conspiracy theories, as this term is anti-Semitic and anti-gay in origin), which is something that many right-of-center thinkers have recently pilloried. Canadian psychologist Jordan Peterson, an infamous critic of the left whose attempts to speak on campuses have frequently resulted in shutdown attempts, has claimed that postmodern neo-Marxism is the ideology of the modern left and leads to totalitarianism, as it squelches free expression and tramples individual rights. Peterson's critics often ridicule this analysis, pointing out there's no group of leftists who call themselves postmodern neo-Marxists. What's more, hard-line Marxists should view postmodernists with suspicion, and vice versa. Marxism is a rationalist system that purports to explain how certain social and economic phenomena arise, whereas postmodernism assails the very idea that phenomena have rational explanations.

But despite this inconsistency, a kind of postmodern neo-Marxism does appear to exist in the wild. Francis Fukuyama, the influential author of the 1992 book *The End of History and the Last Man,* briefly studied under Derrida in the 1970s. In a recent interview with the *Chronicle of Higher Education,* Fukuyama described a philosophy that sure sounds a lot like postmodern neo-Marxism to me.

"They were espousing a kind of Nietzschean relativism that said there is no truth, there is no argument that's superior to any other argument," he recalled of the postmodernists. "Yet most of them were committed to a basically Marxist agenda. That seemed completely contradictory."[19]

Call it what you will—Peterson likes "postmodern neo-Marxism"; I, on the other hand, am attempting to coin the phrase "neo-Marxist in the streets, postmodernist in the sheets"—but it does seem like the left proceeded from Marxist assumptions about the oppressive nature of capitalism, swallowed Marcusian ideas concerning the power of language to thwart social change, embraced the postmodernist approach to eschewing the Enlightenment in favor of radical subjectivity, and let intersectionality endlessly expand the circle of grievances. Sprinkle in the new cultural understanding of safety as requiring emotional protection, and the portrait of a suddenly speech-critical left is complete.

FOR THIS CROWD, free speech is not an absolute, or a moral good in and of itself. It's a means to an end—and a flawed one at best.

Free speech is good if the people exercising it are saying the correct things. If they are using free speech to say hateful things, their speech shouldn't be protected, according to Zillennial activists.

This view has been spreading and reproducing itself for the past few decades, and has clearly found a home among Zillennials. Some young people now even believe—quite wrongly—that hate speech is already outside the protection of the Constitution, for reasons that would certainly impress a streets/sheets leftist philosopher.

"Our country's free speech amendment says, 'Free speech except for hate speech,'" Jessica, a white female student at historically black Howard University in Washington, D.C., casually informed me. "It's very clear that when people practice the right of 'free speech' to use hate speech that it incites violence."

I spoke with Jessica at a protest on the steps of the Lincoln Memorial in summer 2017; her small group of demonstrators had gathered to oppose a nearby alt-right rally. Some of Jessica's friends carried signs bearing the message "Hate speech does not equal free speech," which echoed her comments.

"A good analogy I like to use is that in Nazi Germany, after the Holocaust, Germany did not allow the fascists and the Nazis to continue to organize, rally, and spread propaganda and indoctrinate people with hate speech," said Jessica. "We should not allow the same in the United States. Only fifty years ago was interracial marriage even legalized."

The implication, then, is that it would be wrong to allow racist speech, since the United States has only recently granted full legal rights to racial minorities. Immediate post-Nazi Germany, which vigorously policed speech in order to root out fascists, should serve as a role model.

Jessica was not alone in thinking that free speech was a good thing only if it excluded hate speech. Take Rose, a seventeen-year-old high school student wearing a shirt bearing the text "Feminist A.F." I asked her to explain what all the free-speech-is-not-hate-speech signs meant to her.

"Free speech is allowing people to express themselves in a way that doesn't put other people down," she said. "It doesn't oppress people and damage our society."

Speech is "free," according to Rose, only if it *doesn't oppress people or damage our society.* But speech is just words. Believing that speech itself (rather than, say, the effects of such speech) is oppressive or damaging is, I gather, exactly the kind of thing the Petersons of the world are concerned about.

It's worth remembering that the new activist approach to speech is completely at odds with legal norms. The First Amendment to the U.S. Constitution reads, "Congress shall make no law respecting an establishment of religion, or prohibiting the free exercise thereof; or abridging the freedom of speech, or of the press; or the right of the people peaceably to assemble, and to petition the Government for a redress of grievances." Nowhere in the text of the First Amendment, or anywhere else in the Constitution, does it mention the words "hate speech."

In fact, the Supreme Court has never recognized any sort of hate speech exception to the First Amendment. On the contrary, the Court has repeatedly noted that so-called hate speech enjoys the same legal protection as other kinds of speech. As recently as 2017, the Court ruled 8–0 that the First Amendment explicitly protects offensive statements. The case before the Court was *Matal v. Tam*, in which an Asian American musical group applied for a U.S. trademark for the name of their band, the Slants. "Slant" is a derogatory term for an Asian person, but the group wanted to reclaim the word, following a proud tradition of minority groups reappropriating offensive language used against them. The U.S. Patent and Trademark Office disapproved, rebuffing the band's efforts on the grounds that the name was offensive.

The Court sided with the Slants. Speaking for a unanimous court, Associate Justice Samuel Alito noted, "Speech that demeans on the basis of race, ethnicity, gender, religion, age, disability, or any other similar ground is hateful; but the proudest boast of our free speech jurisprudence is that we protect the freedom to express 'the thought that we hate.'"[20]

And in a concurring opinion, Associate Justice Anthony Kennedy held, "A law that can be directed against speech found offensive to some portion of the public can be turned against minority and dissenting views to the detriment of all. The First Amendment does not entrust that power to the government's benevolence. Instead, our reliance must be on the substantial safeguards of free and open discussion in a democratic society."[21]

It would seem obvious, then, that hate speech is vigorously protected by the First Amendment. If it were not protected, the Supreme Court would need to offer a definition of hate speech such that the average person could tell the difference between protected and unprotected speech. But no such distinction exists, and for good reason. The statements "Jesus Christ did not rise from the dead" and "The Prophet Muhammad did not communicate with angels" would certainly constitute hate speech to millions of people worldwide, but for millions of others, they are self-evidently true sentiments, and it is every American's right to express them.

Not all protest-goers agreed with Jessica and Rose. One woman at the protest, Jackie, bore a sign that read: "Freedom of speech does not equal freedom from criticism." She told me: "I'm all for freedom of speech. I would give up my life for [the alt-right to have the right] to wave their flags and have their rally down there. The First Amendment protects your speech from the government. It doesn't protect your speech from your peers and society. You can be told that you're a fucking moron. You can be told that you're wrong. Be kicked off Twitter. All of that's legal. As far as I understand, the government has not done anything to make the alt-right be quiet, which is how it should be, as much as I hate the alt-right."

Jackie's interpretation of the First Amendment is exactly correct, and was widely embraced by liberal activists of years past. She would have fit right in with the Berkeley protesters of the 1960s. Today, her position seems less common. Jackie, at age twenty-eight, is on the older side for a Zillennial. Younger people at the protest—the college-aged Jessica and the high-school-aged Rose—took the view that the First Amendment does not permit hate speech.

Some activists take a broad view of free speech when it comes to their own side—understanding that any crackdown on offensive speech would imperil their advocacy efforts—but muddy the waters when it comes to the other side.

"I am with free speech," said Ma'at, an American University student. "I need free speech to be able to do what I do."

But much like Rose and Jessica, Ma'at believes that there is a "fine line" between free speech and hate speech—and indeed, that the Constitution spells this out explicitly.

"I'm definitely not for censorship. However, when you start threatening identity, that's when it needs to be addressed, because that's past free speech," said Ma'at. The idea that speech posing a threat to identity loses its protection is an interesting implication of intersectionality, though it's obviously nowhere to be found in the law. And yet, Ma'at assured me, "that's in the Constitution. You can't scream fire in a movie theater and expect to have no consequence, because that was dangerous."

Kathryn, the Berkeley student, used an even more colorful metaphor. "Of course people can say what they want and do what they want, but when it intersects with someone's safety, that's where you have to draw the line," she said. "When speakers come and they want to entice violence and subject transgender students to feel embarrassed of who they are and to get people killed and a woman run over by a car and murdered, that's not free speech, that's hate speech, and that's just evoking violence out of people. You can't yell 'bomb' on an airplane because that's going to jeopardize people's lives and safety. It's the same concept."

The fire-in-a-crowded-theater line (and its more modern version, the bomb-on-an-airplane line) is frequently deployed as an example of the kind of speech that is clearly not protected by the First Amendment. According to constitutional law experts, this is a fairly misleading analogy, dating to the controversial 1919 case *Schenck v. United States*. In the Court's unanimous opinion, Associate Justice Oliver Wendell Holmes Jr. wrote: "The most stringent protection of free speech would not protect a man in falsely shouting fire in a theatre and causing a panic."

But consider the case: using the fire-in-a-crowded-theater rationale, the Court held that the U.S. government could arrest a person—Socialist Party secretary Charles Schenck—for distributing leaflets urging able-bodied men to refuse to be drafted into World War I. (Schenck believed that the draft was a form of involuntary servitude and thus unconstitutional under the terms of the Thirteenth Amendment, which prohibits slavery.) Holmes's opinion, therefore, essentially held that denouncing the military draft and the pointless atrocities of World War I was akin to yelling fire in a crowded theater.

It seems obvious that this way of thinking would give the government far too much power to police dissent of all kinds. Thankfully, the Supreme Court subsequently narrowed the scope of the *Schenck* decision. In the 1969 case *Brandenburg v. Ohio*, the Court held that the government could not suppress speech, even speech advocating unlawful activity, unless the speech was inciting "imminent lawless action." In other words, in order for speech to fall outside First Amendment protection, it must consist of a clear call to commit a specific crime in the near future. Said speech must also be likely to *succeed* at inciting criminal behavior. If no one is taking the speaker seriously, the threshold of imminent lawless action is not met. What this means is that when young people cite the fire-in-a-crowded-theater example, they are deferring to a standard that no longer applies.

"Holmes's famous quip demonstrates the pernicious power of slogans to replace serious engagement with legal issues," Ken White, an attorney and First Amendment expert who writes for the legal blog *Popehat*, told me. "First Amendment analysis can be complex, but it's based on specific rules and precedents. It's principled. When people invoke Holmes's rhetorical device, they're abandoning that principled analysis in favor of a visceral, slogan-based generalization pointing to the result they want."

But for the Zillennial activist, hate speech isn't just akin to falsely shouting "fire"—it's akin to lighting the fire yourself in an attempt to hurt people of color, women, trans people, the disabled, the LGBT community, and so on.

To that end, one of the most common demands of student activists is for university administrators to vigorously prohibit hate speech on campus. Activists at Regis University, a Jesuit college in Denver, provide a perfect example. In March 2017, Regis's College Republicans chapter attempted to hold an All Lives Matter rally and bake sale at which students would be charged different amounts of money based on their race, as a protest against the kind of race-based admissions that take place under affirmative action policies. The point of the bake sale event—something conservative groups at colleges have hosted countless times over the years—is to suggest that considering race when making admissions decisions is just as discriminatory as considering race when selling baked goods. But bake sale events typically provoke controversy, and Regis was no exception.

In response, anti-conservative students organized a community dialogue session called "Courageous Conversations: Race at Regis." The event was put together by the campus's Black Student Alliance, the Somos Student Affinity Group, and the Center for Service Learning's Engaged Scholar Activist Program. This last organization is an official activist training module, run by the university, under the guise of an educational program. The students deemed the mere expression of the idea "all lives matter" to be "indisputably immoral and malicious" and a clear example of "hate speech" that made students of color feel "uncomfortable and unsafe in class." They also accused the Republicans of violating the Civil Rights Act of 1964 for good measure.

Regis's administration was also guilty, in the activists' view, both for failing to prevent this hate speech from occurring in the first place and then for making no apology. The activists released a lengthy list of demands, which included the establishment of campus as a "safe space," changes to the curriculum, diversity training for faculty, biweekly meetings of an inclusivity awareness group, and "that hate-speech, as defined by United States regulations and statutes, be included in the Regis University Student Handbook under Prohibited Conduct."

Unfortunately for Regis activists, there aren't any federal regulations or statutes that define hate speech. The student handbook, by remaining silent with respect to hate speech, already reflects the U.S. Constitution's position. But the fact that students believed they could prohibit hate speech merely by bringing the university's position in line with the government's is telling.

Not All Young People

Despite what we've seen thus far, it's important to keep in mind that the entire Zillennial cohort is not responsible for the few truly outrageous instances of censorship on college campuses over the past few years. For instance, it was not a majority of the student population at Middlebury College in Vermont but a small number of young activists who prevented the conservative American Enterprise Institute scholar Charles Murray from debating a liberal professor, Allison Stanger, in the spring of 2017. After successfully derailing the event, the hecklers—who were outnumbered by willing audience participants—pursued Murray and Stanger as they attempted to escape. A scuffle ensued, and a protester actually injured Stanger's neck. She would later call it "the saddest day of my life."[22]

Murray had been controversial for decades because of his 1994 book, *The Bell Curve,* which claimed that there were IQ differences among the races. But Murray was unaccustomed to being shouted down. "In the mid-1990s, I could count on students who had wanted to listen to start yelling at the protesters after a certain point, 'Sit down and shut up, we want to hear what he has to say,'" wrote Murray. "That kind of pushback had an effect. It reminded the protesters that they were a minority." But by 2017, the radical anti-free-speech minority held sway over the majority, and none would denounce them for shutting down the event.

How did we get from the Berkeley of 1964 to the Middlebury of 2017? For most of the years in between, free speech remained a relatively important part of progressive activism. The left and the First Amendment did not always enjoy an easy marriage, though; in 1977, when the American Civil Liberties Union defended the right of Nazis to march through Skokie, Illinois, the organization received significant pushback from its supporters.

"In '77 and '78, the ACLU lost 15 percent of our members over the Skokie case," former ACLU president Nadine Strossen told me.

Even so, the ACLU stood strong. Its board voted unanimously to reaffirm the position that the ACLU would defend the right to engage in hate speech. This drew criticism from Richard Delgado, a civil rights professor at the University of Alabama School of Law, who accused the ACLU of "First Amendment totalism" in a 1994 article.[23]

In the 1980s and 1990s, countless university administrations implemented "speech codes" to punish racist, sexist, and otherwise offensive speech. But these codes were struck down in court time and time again.

During my own college years—2006 to 2010—the *Michigan Daily,* the left-of-center student paper at which I worked, invariably defended the free speech rights of utterly loathsome speakers. When Columbia University president Lee Bollinger (formerly president of the University of Michigan) invited Iranian president Mahmoud Ahmadinejad—a dictator, Holocaust denier, and enemy of the LGBT community—it was the conservatives who objected, particularly Republican senator John McCain. Weighing in on the controversy, the *Michigan Daily*'s editorial board wrote, "Free speech is not only for those whose ideas may be agreeable, but also for those whose opinions are disagreeable. . . . This type of dialogue should be more common in today's society, especially on college campuses and in academic circles."[24]

Free speech has always been under attack—from university administrations, some left-wing professors, Republican politicians, and a variety of others on the right and left. But it seems that it was just in the last few years that free-speech-skeptical leftist students became a significant threat. This is an impression shared by Greg Lukianoff, president of the Foundation for Individual Rights in Education, a free speech organization that defends the First Amendment on college campuses. FIRE keeps a list of notable people who were invited to campus to give speeches and then subsequently disinvited; the number of such disinvitations has steadily increased over the last few years, and conservative speakers are much more likely to be censored, according to FIRE.[25]

For the activist left, illiberal anti-free-speech norms appear to be in vogue; among Zillennials overall, it's not so easy to tell how widely this thinking has spread. The "kids these days" type of generational fatalism is often prone to exaggeration, and when it comes to the speech question, there's a lot of contradictory evidence.

Some surveys of young people do give cause for concern. According to a 2015 Pew survey, just 28 percent of people support giving the government the power to censor statements that offend minorities.[26] More women than men supported government-backed censorship, as did more Democrats than Republicans, and more relatively uneducated people (those with no more than high school degrees) compared with college graduates. But the cohort most likely to support censorship was millennials, 40 percent of whom thought the government should have the freedom and power to suppress offensive speech. Gen Xers and Boomers were respectively just 27 percent and 24 percent supportive of government-backed censorship.

A Knight Foundation study released in the winter of 2016 found that 69 percent of college students thought university administrations should be able to prohibit intentionally offensive language. Sixty-three percent thought "costumes that stereotype certain racial or ethnic groups" could be banned. And 27 percent thought colleges should have the power to restrict "the expression of political views that are upsetting or offensive to certain groups." Twenty-seven percent is a minority, to be sure, but it's still notable that a quarter of students surveyed wanted to give their administrators the power to suppress political views that upset "certain" groups—in other words, anyone.

In 2015, Yale University released a study, conducted by McLaughlin and Associates, involving interviews with eight hundred college students from around the country. The results were striking: 51 percent wanted "speech codes" that would prohibit other students and faculty members from saying offensive things, and 63 percent favored mandatory trigger warnings—they wanted to compel professors to warn them ahead of time if anything in the material would be objectionable.

A few liberal thinkers, including *Vox* writers Matt Yglesias and Zack Beauchamp (the latter is a good personal friend), have pushed back on the idea that there's a Zillennial free speech problem, even going as far as to claim that the purported free speech "crisis" is a myth.[27] Supporting their position is the fact that only a very small number of speakers have actually been disinvited from campuses. "There is limited evidence of a systematic and serious threat to free speech on campus," wrote Beauchamp.

He's not wrong, but that's because it's quite difficult to track these things, and it's virtually impossible to quantify the chilling effect on students and faculty members who choose to keep their mouths shut because of the handful of high-profile shutdown incidents.

Jeffrey Sachs, a professor at Acadia University who has also criticized the crisis narrative, cites the General Social Survey—a widely used data set that goes back to the early 1970s—as offering proof that Zillennials are actually better on free speech than their predecessors.[28] And again, there's something to this: more young people think homosexuals should be allowed to speak in public today than did in 1975. But I would suggest that this probably reflects improving tolerance toward homosexuals, not changing free speech norms. On the question of racist speech—something that is still considered offensive today, unlike pro-gay speech—young people are now more likely to support censorship than they did previously. (The General Social Survey data might also be less relevant than they seem; for instance, the survey does not poll students who live in "group quarters," such as dormitories.)

I think the critics are right to push back on some of the more hyperbolic claims about a free speech "crisis" on college campuses. But current students are, by some measures, more hostile to free speech than just about anybody else. One of the most comprehensive—and depressing—surveys of American attitudes toward free speech was published by the Cato Institute in October 2017. According to Cato, 55 percent of Americans expressed the view that people should be free to disrespect each other, but a slim majority (51 percent) of current college students and graduate students took the opposite position: people don't deserve free speech rights if they are disrespectful. While 64 percent of college-educated Americans said the government should permit hate speech, current students were divided on the question. Which demographic was the most likely to say hate speech constituted violence? You guessed it: 60 percent of the under-thirty crowd thought so.

Cato also asked respondents whether they thought it was morally permissible to punch someone for simply being a Nazi. Most people—68 percent—said no. The breakdown didn't matter much here; a majority of Republicans and Democrats, white people and minority groups, and young Americans and older Americans all opposed Nazi punching.

Just one subgroup offered dissent. Some 51 percent of *strong* liberals, or leftists, said it was morally permissible to punch a Nazi. With this fact in mind, occurrences of far-left violence seem less surprising.

Much Ado About Antifa

Columbia University provides another example of the self-defeating spectacle that arises when young activists succumb to their new censorious impulses. I visited the campus in October 2017, when Columbia's College Republicans (CUCR) had invited Mike

Cernovich, a far-right blogger with ties to the alt-right conspiracy theorist Alex Jones, to give a presentation to students on how the traditional media is failing in the age of Trump.

Cernovich's views fall well outside mainstream conservatism, and indeed, many on the right would deny that the notorious pro-Trump troll deserves a seat at any legitimate table. When Fox News invited Cernovich to come on its program *Red Eye,* conservative writers Ben Shapiro and Ben Howe were apoplectic.[29] (Shapiro: "Granting any legitimacy to a fringe kook like Mike Cernovich ... is close to insane." Howe: "They're giving this motherfucker legitimacy? Oh my God!") But CUCR leader Aristotle "Ari" Boosalis, citing free speech and a need for wider ideological diversity on campus, decided to host Cernovich.

It's perfectly legitimate to question the wisdom of extending a platform to such a figure; like Shapiro and Howe, I would have recommended ignoring him entirely. That was not the approach taken by Columbia's leftist activists, who posted flyers calling out all the board members of CUCR by name and picture. This practice—revealing private information, such as names, phone numbers, and addresses—is called "doxing," and it has become a staple of both far-right and far-left irritants looking to punish members of the other side. In this case, the doxing was the work of NYC Antifascist Action, a representative antifa group. Fearing for his safety, Boosalis filed a harassment complaint with Columbia.

That might strike readers as an overreaction; it did to me, until the day of the event. Cernovich's talk occurred in the basement of Lerner Hall, a building awash in purple concert lights for domestic assault awareness. I arrived early and was the first person to enter the staging area. Only ticketed attendees were allowed entrance, which meant that the event itself was largely civil. A handful of determined activists had been granted access, and though they occasionally heckled—when Cernovich asked the audience if anyone knew a victim of suicide, a voice rang out, "You should try it sometime!"—Cernovich was able to deliver his remarks.

Said remarks mostly consisted of recycled complaints against the mainstream media. It was an unpersuasive shtick. While mainstream media outlets frequently make mistakes, the *New York Times* and *Washington Post* are inarguably more reliable stewards of objective reporting than *The Alex Jones Show,* a program that has advanced the idea that the moon landing was faked, the Bush administration was responsible for 9/11, and the government puts chemicals in the water that turn frogs gay (sad to say, I'm not making this up). As an occasional cohost of *The Alex Jones Show,* Cernovich is in no position to complain about inaccuracy in journalism.

Nor did the CUCR group acquit themselves well. I overheard one member ask a reporter for the campus paper to make sure her write-up of the event included Cernovich's advice to men about how to imbue their semen with magical properties. (Cernovich purports to be a sex and relationships expert, among other things.)

I left the event thoroughly repulsed by Cernovich. Any fair-minded person would have felt the same.

And then I stepped outside, into the cold night air. At least a hundred protesters had gathered—not just to denounce Cernovich but to denounce free speech, capitalism, Zionism, and "whiteness" (as in white people). Intersectionality, of course, requires all good people to oppose each of these things.

"Whiteness is a bomb that incinerates!" intoned one of the protest leaders, a black male wearing a hoodie. His audience then parroted the statement back at him. "And this shit burns!" he continued. This was also repeated by the audience.

Another protest leader, a female student of color, took the mic. "Columbia is the most conservative institution in the fucking United States!" she said. (Fact check: Columbia University faculty and staff overwhelmingly donate to liberal rather than conservative politicians.) She accused the university of emboldening white supremacy and vowed to "scam Columbia" by refusing to internalize the things she was learning as a student. She pledged to return to her community after college and teach "alt-history" rather than "learned history." (A year of tuition at Columbia College costs about $56,000, raising the question of who is scamming whom under this scenario.)

Other students chanted "No justice, no peace" and "If we don't get it, shut them down" ("it" being justice). I saw signs reading "End fascism" and "End apartheid at Columbia," referring to the system of explicit racial segregation that existed in South Africa until 1991. (Another sign, which criticized Cernovich for being against pedophilia, was actually a hoax perpetrated by the alt-right; the sign-maker's intention was to frame antifa as being pro-pedophilia.)

I saw antifa attack a Trump supporter, forcing him to beat a hasty retreat. As he stepped beyond the gate separating the campus from the rest of New York City, an antifa activist snatched the man's cellphone and ran off with it. Toni Airaksinen, a Columbia student and writer for the conservative student publication *Campus Reform,* had a concerning run-in with protesters. She told me several people identified her as a member of a right-of-center news media group and yelled "Follow her" and even "Attack her." "They then started advancing towards me," Airaksinen told me. "I backed away and asked a security guard about what I should do, who shrugged me off."

In his book about antifa, Bray traces their current tactics to the Autonomen, a 1970s West German militant group consisting of antifascists, feminists, antinuclear groups, and squatters' rights activists. They "dressed in black," writes Bray, "with their faces covered by motorcycle helmets, balaclavas, or other masks to create a uniform, anonymous mass of revolutionaries prepared to carry out militant actions, sometimes involving weapons such as flagpoles, clubs, projectiles, and Molotov cocktails."

But even Bray notes, "Some have argued, however, that the 'incessant invocation' of the specter of fascism by the Left diluted its rhetorical value." He later provides an example of the kind of thing one imagines could have had such an effect: in November 1989, just days after the fall of the Berlin Wall, an antifa activist, Cornelia Wessmann, died after she was hit by a car while fleeing from riot police in Göttingen, Germany. "In retaliation, her comrades in thirty cities unleashed a coordinated wave of targeted property destruction against department stores, banks, and government buildings—appendages of the capitalist state responsible for her death in their eyes," wrote Bray.

Waves of "targeted property destruction" seem unlikely to convince the moderate masses that the anti-fascists are the good guys. But it is the position of antifa that fascism is on the verge of its ultimate triumph—or is already triumphant, given Trump's ascendance to the White House—and so the time for half-measures has long since passed.

Nowhere is this strategy more evident than in Berkeley (one of the main hubs of antifa activity, alongside Portland, Oregon), where antifa protesters—many, though not all of them, young people—routinely assault attendees at right-leaning rallies. The violent predilections of antifa were most obvious during the last weeks of the summer of 2017, when a Portland-based political group called Patriot Prayer attempted to hold a series of "pro–free speech" and "anti-Marxism" rallies in the San Francisco Bay area. Patriot Prayer is a difficult group to classify; many would call it far-right, alt-right, or at the very least pro-Trump, though its founder and leader, Joey Gibson, describes himself as a defender of liberty who makes efforts to exclude extremists and white nationalists from his movement. The Southern Poverty Law Center defines "hate group" broadly when it comes to the right, but it lists neither Gibson nor Patriot Prayer as an advocate of hate. The SPLC even noted in an article that Gibson denounced white nationalists and neo-Nazis at one of his events.

Careful distinctions, though, are not a hallmark of antifa counterprotests. The *Weekly Standard*'s Matt Labash reported in person on the mayhem that erupted during the weekend of August 27. He titled his piece "A Beating in Berkeley" and described the events as "the Crips vs. the Bloods for white people."[30] The rallies were formally canceled due to threats of violence from antifa, but Gibson and his friends made a public showing anyway at the

Martin Luther King Jr. Civic Center Park—and the left was there, waiting for them.

"A hundred or so masked-up antifa ninjas and affiliated protesters seem to simultaneously turn," wrote Labash. "It looks like we've interrupted al Qaeda tryouts."

Someone smacked Gibson in the face. Then another black-clad antifa member cracked a flagpole over his head. He was pepper-sprayed by the mob at least five times, by his count. Eventually the police intervened—to arrest Gibson and his bodyguard. The police later claimed this was done for their own protection, to get them out of the area; Gibson and his bodyguard were let go without being charged. Labash confronted some of the antifa activists and asked whether the beating of Gibson and his friends was justified. The answer, according to Labash, was "Hell yeah."

"I ask them to cite anything Joey has said that offends them, as though being offended justifies this," wrote Labash. "A coward in a black mask says: 'They're f—ing Nazis. There's nothing they have to say to offend us.'"

Gibson later vented his frustration during an appearance on Fox News. "We just want to be able to exist in America, we want to be able to exist in the middle of a public park in Berkeley," he said.

But antifa does not believe coexistence with a pro-free-speech and anti-Marxist group is desirable. Either you are part of the revolution or you are an enemy of it.

I witnessed this firsthand when I came to Berkeley two weeks later, for the second Yiannopoulos event. Having triumphed utterly in their goal to shut down the planned speaking series, antifa took to the streets to harass whichever fans of Yiannopoulos remained. This time the police were prepared: dozens of them followed the demonstrators and counterdemonstrators wherever they went, stepping in whenever violence broke out between the two groups. I saw one antifa protester tackled and arrested by police for taking a swing at a Milo fan. Many alt-right attendees were just as eager for a scuffle, proving the symbiotic nature of the leftist and rightist versions of illiberalism.

I made my way through the throngs of protesters, choosing to approach a young man wearing a black bandana and sunglasses over his face. I identified myself as a journalist and asked him what he was hoping to accomplish by participating in the protest. "We don't talk to the press," he said, pushing past me. I heard this over and over again; there was no interest in a discussion. The next day, I returned to campus just as an antifa-aligned group occupied the steps of a campus building, led an impromptu chant, and distributed literature. I approached them for comment and was once again rebuffed.

In a guest post recapping the scene at Berkeley for It's Going Down, an anarchist news website that routinely runs content written by and for an antifa audience, an anonymous contributor described free speech as "a concept that has never truly protected meaningful dissent." The title of the article was "Behind Every Liberal, a Fascist." "As anti-authoritarian, anti-capitalist and autonomous individuals, we are all we got, and we will continue to fight the fascist creep in all its forms, on and off campus, through protest, disruption and community support and self defense," wrote the author.[31]

Antifa is well aware that this is an anti-liberal idea. But liberalism—by which we mean a representative democracy where all ideas are permitted and the best ones prevail—has failed to contain fascism, in their view.

"At what point do you say enough is enough," said Bray during an appearance on Democracy Now!, "and give up on the liberal notion that what we need to do is essentially create some sort of regime of rights that allow neo-Nazis and their victims to co-exist, quote, 'peacefully'? And recognize that the neo-Nazis don't want that, and that also, the antifascists are right in not looking at it through that liberal lens, but rather seeing fascism not as an opinion that needs to be responded to respectfully but as an enemy to humanity that needs to be stopped by any means necessary?"

The chaos at Berkeley is as good an argument as any against this position. Antifa purports to oppose the kind of police militarization that is common to fascist societies. "The police serve as an occupying force," claims another anonymously written article on It's Going Down.[32] But when I came to Berkeley, I saw a city and a university that were teeming with law enforcement personnel *because* of antifa's threats of violence. Perhaps a hundred police patrolled the streets, maintaining order and ensuring that neither the far left nor the far right could kill anyone.

There are historical examples as well. The Battle of Cable Street, an anti-fascist riot in the East End of London in 1936, is widely but incorrectly remembered as a successful mass movement against Oswald Mosley's British Union of Fascists. Mosley attempted to march with thousands of his "blackshirts" but was prevented from doing so by twenty thousand anti-fascist counterdemonstrators, some of whom attacked the police as cops attempted to clear the streets for Mosley's march. In the end, Mosley gave up and sent his supporters home.

Antifa remembers the event fondly. Bray wrote that the Battle of Cable Street successfully mobilized "broader society to confront fascists" and "became a powerful model for collective anti-fascist resistance that has inspired many to this day." That's one view. Bray, to his credit, makes mention of the other: as historian Daniel Tilles persuasively argued in *The Myth of Cable Street*, Mosley's fascist party "was able to convert defeat on the day into longer-term success and to justify a further radicalisation of its anti-Jewish campaign." It is estimated that the fascists gained an additional two thousand members—which is quite a figure, considering that the party was only three thousand strong before Cable Street. According to Tilles, the fascists "thrived off the publicity that violent opposition produced. The national media, under pressure from the government, largely avoided reporting on Fascist activity other than when disorder occurred."[33]

Similarly, Spencer's alt-right movement appears to have grown—in numbers and attention paid to it, if not in actual influence—at the same time it has become fashionable to punch Spencer himself on sight. The historical parallel is obvious: without the violence of antifa, Spencer, like Mosley before him, would find it much more difficult to recruit readers, fans, and followers.

It would not seem to be the case, then, that antifa is preventing fascism. Rather, it appears Nixon may have been right all those years ago when he welcomed far-left violence as a boon to his administration: antifa creates the conditions that spread the thing it claims to oppose. Yiannopoulos, Spencer, and Cernovich are loathsome—and we will further explore the alt-right's particular brand of loathsomeness in Chapter Eight—but it's harder to fixate on their ugliness when the people who protest them are setting cars on fire, smashing windows, and throwing punches.

One more example. In August 2018, a man named Paul Welch attended a Patriot Prayer event as a counterprotester. Welch, a liberal who voted for Bernie Sanders in the 2016 Democratic presidential primary and Hillary Clinton in the general election, brought an American flag with him in an attempt to reclaim the symbol from the far-right group.

Antifa showed up as well. Two masked agitators spotted Welch's flag, explained to him that it was a "fascist symbol," and demanded that he hand it over. When he refused, antifa attacked him. One of the agitators begun to beat him with a metal rod, finally striking him in the head. Welch slumped to the ground—he would need four staples to repair the three-inch head wound.

Welch wasn't a fascist by any stretch of the imagination. But antifa both endorses violence and defines fascism very, very broadly. If you're not with them, you're against them—and people who are against them don't have rights, in their view. It's easy to see how this is a recipe for total disaster.

Thankfully, many in the liberal coalition are increasingly becoming aware that sacrificing norms of free speech is a terrible strategy for the anti-Trump resistance, as it plays directly into the forty-fifth president's persecution narrative. Barack Obama himself has repeatedly warned liberals not to shut down people with whom they disagree. In a July 2018 speech, the former president criticized the left for doing just that.

"You can't [change minds] if you just out of hand disregard what your opponent has to say from the start," said Obama. "And you can't do it if you insist that those who aren't like you because they are white or they are male, somehow there is no way they can understand what I'm feeling, that somehow they lack standing to speak on certain matters."[34]

Obama's remarks were an indirect rebuke of one of the paramount tenets of the intersectional activist framework: that only the marginalized should be permitted to speak about matters pertaining to their oppression. Let's hope the #Resistance was listening.

THREE

OFF TO THE RACES

IDENTITY, CULTURE, AND BLACK LIVES MATTER

It was the middle of October in Ann Arbor, and a particularly long summer had finally come to an abrupt end. The day I visited my alma mater, the University of Michigan, was dreary, rainy, and cold.

The campus felt uneasy: chilly, but not chill. And it wasn't just the weather. The fall semester had seen a series of racially charged incidents. Someone spray-painted the Rock—a campus landmark that's exactly what it sounds like—with the message "Fuck Latinos." (The *Michigan Daily* reported the message as "anti-Latinx," using the gender-neutral parlance preferred by activists who think the terms "Latino" and "Latina" make gender-nonconforming Hispanics feel marginalized.)

Just two weeks later, a black student named Travon Stearns returned from lunch to find that someone had scrawled the *n*-word under the name tag on his dorm room door. What made the incident particularly disturbing, Stearns told the *Daily*, was that it took place inside West Quad, the dormitory that houses the Michigan Community Scholars Program, in which Stearns is a participant. The Scholars Program is thought to be even more of a safe space than the rest of campus.

"Maybe people do those things as a joke but they don't realize what psychological impact that can have on a person," said Stearns, who found it difficult to concentrate on his studies after the incident. "Especially since I am at the University to study and get an education. But then I have to worry about the feeling of oppression and not being accepted. I have to watch my back at all times. And that just puts extra pressure on me on top of regular college life."[1]

Next came the flyers, appearing in various corners of the campus. "Make America white again," read one. Another insisted that black people were less intelligent, on average, than white people.

University president Mark Schlissel condemned these displays of racism but could do little else. Despite threats from activists on social media—"If y'all don't check West Quad cameras & get to the bottom of this . . . we rioting," wrote one person on Twitter—the police failed to apprehend any of the perpetrators. They had no idea who was responsible, and could only guess at the true motives of the vandals. Most students, though, understandably accepted the evidence on its face: these actions were the handiwork of an abominable racist.

This was the backdrop of Charles Murray's October 11, 2017, visit. Murray, a resident scholar at the American Enterprise Institute (AEI), is the author of the 2012 book *Coming Apart: The State of White America, 1960–2010*, and was invited by conservative students at the University of Michigan to discuss his work, which describes the economic and cultural conditions that helped make Trump's victory possible. But Murray is *also* a coauthor of *The Bell Curve* (the controversial 1994 book mentioned in Chapter Two), which argues that intelligence is partially heritable and there are differences in average IQ scores among the races.

In the more than two decades since its publication, *The Bell Curve*'s findings have provoked criticism from other researchers and thunderous anger from many on the left. There was no question

Murray would face a hostile mob at Michigan—the only question was whether things would turn as ugly as they had at Middlebury, when Murray and his debate partner, Allison Stanger, were not just censored by the mob but assaulted as well.

At 4:00 p.m., I headed to the Diag, the campus's central outdoor green space, for the planned protests. The area symbolically separates Church Street from State Street (get it?). Important buildings—Angell Hall, the Hatcher Graduate Library, and Randall Lab—surround the Diag on three sides; the fourth side is open and offers a view of Rackham Graduate School in the distance. The square at the foot of the library steps contains the famous brass block letter *M*, embedded in the ground. Chalking is permitted here, and student groups frequently scrawl announcements on the ground, though the rain had washed the area clean of chalk on this particular day. The block *M* itself is considered sacred—church and state notwithstanding—and fraternity members take turns guarding it to prevent rival football teams from vandalizing it before big games. Three weeks before Murray's visit, a male student of color, Dana Greene, knelt at the block *M* for twenty-one hours straight, in protest of racism on campus. Schlissel was out of town at the time but made a statement of support, while the university's Counseling and Psychological Services distributed yoga mats to Greene and other kneelers who had joined him.

"It really was just like a spontaneous thing," Greene told me much later. He was sick of encountering racist messages everywhere—messages that seemed to become more common in the wake of Trump's election. "This stuff happened continuously or has been happening continuously on campus. I kind of just felt like I was tired of feeling tired, if that makes sense. There was this sense of helplessness, like this was something that we had to accept now."

As I entered the Diag, a student activist affiliated with BAMN—the Coalition to Defend Affirmative Action, Integration & Immigrant Rights and Fight for Equality by Any Means Necessary—handed me a flyer. "Protest white supremacist Charles Murray: defend our campus community against racism and immigrant-bashing," it read. But the flyer called for more than mere protesting. It continued: "Statements from the University logically refuting these theories are not sufficient to fight racism. There is no reasonable debate to be had with white supremacists. They must be shut down."

I asked Kate Stenvig, a local BAMN coordinator who has been active at UM for at least ten years (I remembered her from my time as an undergrad), whether she would like to see Murray shut down. "Yeah," she replied. "With the threat of violent, racist attacks on [students of color], immigrant students, Muslim students, we've been demanding that this campus be a sanctuary for immigrants, and also that the university will stand against racism in action. And that means not giving a platform."

BAMN was not the only group organizing a protest. The local anti-fascist club, Young Democratic Socialists of America, and Science for the People's UM chapter had arranged for several faculty members to give speeches on the Diag inveighing against Murray. John Vandermeer, a professor of ecology and evolutionary biology, criticized some of Murray's work. Notably, Vandermeer did not go overboard; he pointed out that *The Bell Curve* actually made fairly weak claims about the heritability of intelligence. One of the organizers of this particular event told me they had no intention of shutting down Murray. Their only goal was dialogue.

Other protesters were less circumspect. "Charles Murray, get out of town! By any means necessary, shut him down!" chanted one activist. Others soon joined him. They led a march to a different area of campus—closer to the building where Murray would be speaking—and passed out sign-making materials. (Most of the finished signs bore some version of the message "Charles Murray is a white supremacist.") "Let's go get him," shouted another activist as the appointed time drew near.

I watched an argument between a protester and a student in a Washington Capitals jersey—the only student, it seemed, who thought Murray should be allowed to speak without interruption.

The protester, also a student, disagreed. He referenced the "paradox of tolerance": the idea, first described by philosopher Karl Popper in 1945, that in order for a society to remain tolerant, it might have to place restrictions on intolerance, lest the intolerant gain too much power and overthrow the tolerant. As Popper wrote in *The Open Society and Its Enemies:* "If we extend unlimited tolerance even to those who are intolerant, if we are not prepared to defend a tolerant society against the onslaught of the intolerant, then the tolerant will be destroyed, and tolerance with them."

It's easy to see, based on this passage, how one might conclude that revoking the rights of intolerant people is justified under Popper's worldview. However, Popper hedged it just sentences later, saying, "I do not imply, for instance, that we should always suppress the utterance of intolerant philosophies; as long as we can counter them by rational argument and keep them in check by public opinion, suppression would certainly be unwise."

Popper probably never meant to suggest that we ought to suppress intolerance via illiberal means; rather, he believed liberal society could choose violence as a last resort if that's what is required to battle the intolerant.

"To Popper, intolerance is not to be deployed when the utterance of intolerant ideas might make you uncomfortable, or when those ideas seem impolite, or when they get you really mad," wrote Jason Kuznicki, a research fellow at the Cato Institute, in an article expounding Popper's views. "It was only in a footnote that he considered the possibility of using violence, and he did so with obvious disdain."

I struck up a conversation with the student protester who had referenced the tolerance paradox as justification for shouting down Murray. I'll call him Stanley. He was white, with short brown hair and the scraggly beginnings of a beard. He wore a red jacket over a plaid shirt, and he smoked a cigarette as we talked. He told me he had recently transferred to the University of Michigan from a college in the Pacific Northwest. (This might have explained why he apparently didn't know that smoking was prohibited on university property, as it had been since the start of my senior year, in 2009; one of my earliest triumphs as a professional libertarian was persuading my colleagues on the *Daily*'s editorial board that the paper should come out against the smoking ban.) I asked Stanley if he thought the protesters had the right to shut down Murray.

"I think they have a right to go in there and make a big fucking noise until nobody can hear him and he leaves," he said.

His one caveat, he said, was that he hoped the protest didn't turn violent. But that was only because he didn't consider Murray extreme enough to be deserving of violence. The alt-right, on the other hand, was different. By endorsing explicit white supremacy, this group was already attacking people of color—any violence in response would be self-defense.

"If I say I'm going to fucking beat your ass unless you leave this country, you can punch me in the fucking face," he explained.

I asked Stanley what he, specifically, was doing at the protest. He said he was waiting for antifa to show up: he "loves" what they are doing and was hoping to get involved with them. He hated how the media was covering antifa and equating the movement's actions with the alt-right. The two groups couldn't be more different, he said, and antifa wasn't engaged in nearly as much destruction as reported. Even so, I asked whether he thought antifa's extreme behavior—overstated though it may be—ran the risk of scaring away the moderate majority of Americans.

Stanley shrugged. "They weren't winnable, anyway," he said.

Perhaps a hundred protesters marched to Palmer Commons, where Murray was slated to speak. Event organizers had limited attendance to students only, but I was permitted entrance as a member of the media. While in line, I overheard a protester explaining to his friends that free speech hadn't been of any use to German citizens confronting Nazism in the 1920s.

No one was allowed inside the auditorium with a water bottle, the fear being that someone would throw a liquid at Murray. That wasn't a problem, but the cops also stopped attendees from carrying in umbrellas, and nearly everybody had one. The process of checking umbrellas at the front desk took forever, but at least two hundred people stuck with it, because every chair in the auditorium was filled.

A student named Ben Decatur—the short, sunny-dispositioned student coordinator for AEI's Michigan chapter, who looked a tad too young to be in college—took to the podium. He began by reciting a "free speech pledge" and asked the audience to respect Murray's right to speak, reserving questions and remarks for the question-and-answer period. The audience, which consisted of perhaps one or two dozen conservative students, genuinely curious neutral parties or reporters, and about 180 sign-wielding activists from BAMN, Black Lives Matter, Students of Color of Rackham, and the DSA, laughed.

Next up was Murray himself. Keenly aware of what was likely to happen, he implored the mostly hostile audience to hear him out. The response was not an explosion but a slow boil. These villagers constructed quite the pyre before setting their witch on fire.

First a cellphone alarm went off. Then another, and another. Several were going off at once. The smirking faces of the young activists revealed that the prank was planned well in advance.

Then a student flipped the light switch and the room fell dark, revealing text on the wall behind Murray's head—someone in the audience was using a projector. "White supremacist," read the message. So there could be no mistake, the text included an arrow pointing at you-know-who. Another protester began playing the "Imperial March" from *Star Wars* (the Darth Vader music). As the din reached a crescendo, a student wearing a bright red turtleneck and jean jacket leapt out of his seat.

"I'm a child of Iranian immigrants," he declared. "Charles Murray wants me dead! He wants me dead!" He continued: "They are killing us! They are killing us! Anyone who has a suit and is a Republican is killing us! You, sir," he said, pointing at Murray, "you are killing us." I counted ten police officers standing in the room; none took any action to deter or eject the heckler.

Murray then spoke uninterrupted for a minute and a half before another student, a young Asian woman wearing a Michigan sweatshirt, stood up and declared that the audience would rather hear her speak. She then shouted a prepared statement denouncing Murray's work. Afterward, the dam broke, and students began to chant, "Charles Murray, go away! Sexist, racist, KKK!" Murray was drowned out, and it seemed likely the remainder of the event would be canceled.

But it wasn't over yet. Rick Fitzgerald, a member of the university's public affairs department, ascended the stage and spoke into the microphone.

"I am going to ask you to please be quiet," he said.

This irritated a student, a black woman with long braided hair, who shouted at Fitzgerald, "Stop silencing students of color!"

A brave audience member seated near this woman, a young man who identified as Muslim, stood up to argue with her. He asserted that he had come to the event to hear from Murray and make up his own mind whether he agreed with what the scholar had to say. After arguing with him for a time, the woman with the braids finally gave in, asserting that she was being put through "too much emotional labor," and she and her friends took their seats.

What followed was a solid ten minutes of actually thoughtful discussion and debate. A graduate student with knowledge of statistics and Murray's work was invited to present his argument against *The Bell Curve,* and then Murray responded. It was an actual exchange of ideas—the audience could make up its own mind about whose points were more persuasive.

It didn't last long. Exactly forty minutes into the evening's programming, the activists engaged in a coordinated mass walkout. This had been the backup plan: if they failed to shut down the event entirely, they would simply jump ship at the chosen time. From a free speech perspective, a walkout isn't nearly as destructive as a shutdown, since it doesn't prevent the rest of the audience from continuing to enjoy the event. The problem, however, was that the auditorium could only fit two hundred, and many interested students who had failed to find a seat had gone home long before the walkout. By taking up space in the room, despite having no intention of sticking it out, the protesters had in some sense denied other students the opportunity to hear Murray speak.

The event was a disappointment but not a total disaster. The administration asked the protesters to be civil, and one or two vocal students challenged them to let Murray speak; those tactics actually worked, forestalling a complete shutdown. By challenging the power of the hecklers, they reduced it.

After the walkout, the group of protesters gathered outside the building. Tensions were running high, and that's when the only act of true aggression took place: Nathan Berning, a conservative student representing the right-leaning Leadership Institute, attempted to record video footage of the protesters on his phone, and one protester snatched the phone out of his hands and tossed it off a balcony.

Someone announced the next phase of the evening: activists were invited to head to the Rackham Graduate School building for a post-protest pizza party. Curious, I followed the crowd to a room in the basement of Rackham.

The Iranian man in the red turtleneck was there, as was the black woman with the braids, and a few dozen others—mostly though not exclusively students of color. A graduate student remarked that this was a place to "take a breath and de-stress." Someone turned on some music—soul music—and pizza was served.

There were enough new faces present that I wasn't immediately singled out, but eventually a young black woman came up to me and politely asked if I was a graduate student. Later I struck up a conversation with a bearded graduate student. He had evidently caught wind that I was a journalist, and appeared slightly unnerved by my presence; I said I would leave willingly, but his manners got the better of him, and he invited me to have a slice of pizza.

We started chatting about the Murray event and what was happening on campus. I told him I thought the walkout was preferable to a shutdown, because Murray's free speech rights would have been violated much more manifestly in the latter case, and also because a full shutdown would make the students look fragile and afraid of disagreement. I asked the graduate student whether he agreed with me that outright censorship of a speaker deemed offensive was likely to backfire, create a martyr, and engender sympathy not for the student protesters but for their opponents.

Perhaps, but that wasn't his concern, he told me. "I'm worried about people feeling safe and comfortable on campus," he said.

The next day was just as cold and gray, but less rainy. I went back to the Diag, taking notice of several things I had missed during the bustle of the protests the day before. Advertisements for university programs hung in designated flyer-posting areas. One showed the picture of a pretty female student and the words "IT'S ABOUT EQUALITY" in all capital letters. Another asked, "What does social justice mean to you?" It was an advertisement for the School of Education.

Then there was the block *M* itself, surrounded on all sides by four separate but identical messages: "Black lives matter," thrice in white and once in pink. The messages were written not in chalk—chalking is of course permitted, as Rick Fitzgerald confirmed for me when I asked him—but in spray paint.

A Double Wrong

Historically, the fight for racial justice has been synonymous with the defense of free speech. Those who wanted to abolish slavery, repeal Jim Crow, desegregate schools and the civil service, end discrimination, and defend the voting rights of black Americans typically understood that the First Amendment was a tool that empowered them to make arguments for equality and liberty. It's no accident that Mario Savio and his friends were proponents of racial harmony and free speech: these principles were morally and practically indivisible.

In the nineteenth century, there was no more passionate advocate for the rights of black people than Frederick Douglass, a gifted orator who escaped slavery and became one of the leaders of the abolitionist movement.[2] His memoir, *Narrative of the Life of Frederick Douglass, an American Slave,* was indispensable to the anti-slavery cause.

But Douglass was also a fierce defender of free speech. In December 1860, a mob shut down a public discussion of the question "How shall slavery be abolished?" Douglass responded with an impassioned defense of the First Amendment, his "Plea for Free Speech in Boston." Douglass defended speech as the first and foremost right of a free citizenry. "Liberty is meaningless where the right to utter one's thoughts and opinions has ceased to exist," he said. "That, of all rights, is the dread of tyrants. It is the right which they first of all strike down. They know its power." He predicted that free speech would eventually mean the end of slavery—it was the slaveholders and their supporters who were most eager to quell discussion of the subject.

Describing censorship as "a double wrong," Douglass was unequivocal. "Equally clear is the right to hear," he said. "To suppress free speech is a double wrong. It violates the rights of the hearer as well as those of the speaker. It is just as criminal to rob a man of his right to speak and hear as it would be to rob him of his money."

A century later, civil rights activists such as Dr. Martin Luther King Jr. and John Lewis were by necessity free speech advocates as well. They had to be: the authorities routinely violated their free speech rights in order to oppose their movement. Lewis went to jail for carrying a sign outside a courthouse, and King was arrested for praying outside city hall in Albany, Georgia. In retrospect, the local policies prohibiting demonstrations, signs, prayers, and the distribution of literature on public property were certainly violations of the First Amendment. The day before his assassination, King implored America to "be true to what you said on paper" and recognize First Amendment rights for all.[3]

Indeed, civil rights activists' efforts were aided by court decisions that reaffirmed the universality of free speech rights—even for people who were militantly opposed to civil rights. In 1969, the Supreme Court overturned the conviction of Clarence Brandenburg, a Ku Klux Klan leader who had been arrested for making inflammatory speeches against black and Jewish people. *Brandenburg v. Ohio,* a landmark free speech case, held that authorities could not criminalize speech merely because it was inflammatory. This decision, in support of a white supremacist's speech, became essential to the struggle for equal rights and liberal causes in general. Later, Charles Evers, a black civil rights activist and secretary of the National Association for the Advancement of Colored People, led a boycott of stores in Claiborne County, Mississippi; this resulted in a civil suit against the protesters. The Supreme Court of Mississippi ruled against Evers and the NAACP, but that decision was reversed—after more than ten years—by the U.S. Supreme Court, which applied the *Brandenburg* standard. *Brandenburg* was also referenced in a 1973 decision that struck down the conviction of an anti-war activist for threatening to "take to the fucking streets."

"The history of modern incitement jurisprudence begins with a KKK leader's free speech rights and extends to a Vietnam War protester and a great civil rights icon," Lee Rowland, a senior staff attorney at the ACLU, noted in an article for the civil rights organization's website.[4]

Pauli Murray, a civil rights and women's rights activist, would have appreciated this irony. She was a law student at Yale University in 1963 and would later become the first black woman to receive a J.S.D. from the school. That year, the Yale Political Union invited Alabama governor George Wallace, an explicit segregationist, to speak on campus. The administration was not pleased. According to the *New York Times,* "The provost and acting president of Yale,

Kingman Brewster Jr., advised the students to withdraw their invitation. Mayor Richard C. Lee said Wallace was 'officially unwelcome' in New Haven."[5]

One could scarcely find two people with more dissimilar views than Murray and Wallace. And yet Murray petitioned the administration to allow Wallace to come speak on campus. "The possibility of violence is not sufficient reason in law to prevent an individual from exercising his constitutional right," she wrote in a letter to Brewster.

But many of today's young radicals don't have much reverence for the struggles of generations past. When I asked Ma'at, the American University student, whether she felt a connection with sixties activists, her answer was an unequivocal no.

"That's not where we're coming from anymore," she said. "That was very male dominant, very preachy, very religious, and I just don't think as many millennials are that religious."

She complained that previous activist movements had been "co-opted by black men," something her intersectional generation—with its increased focus on gender, sexuality, and other forms of oppression that aren't exclusively built around race—is determined to prevent.

"As a black woman, I don't want a black man speaking for me when I'm very much capable of speaking for myself," she said. "So I think that in terms of just civil rights activism, I think that that's not what we're doing here."

Ma'at is representative of a new crop of activists much too young to feel a kinship with the sixties. The galvanizing event for her movement wasn't Selma in 1965, or even Rodney King in 1991—it was a series of deaths beginning with the killing of Trayvon Martin in 2012. Martin, a black seventeen-year-old, was fatally shot by a Hispanic neighborhood watch volunteer named George Zimmerman in Sanford, Florida. Martin had committed no crime, but Zimmerman, a wannabe lawman, spotted the teen and thought he looked suspicious, and approached him after calling the police. Zimmerman later claimed he had acted in self-defense, and the cops—having no reason to disbelieve this—declined to arrest him. He was charged with murder after Florida governor Rick Scott appointed a special prosecutor to handle the case. Ultimately, Zimmerman was acquitted, to the considerable consternation of those who thought—not unreasonably—that anti-black racism was at play.

On July 17, 2014, a tall, heavyset black man named Eric Garner was illegally selling loose cigarettes on the streets of New York City when police approached him. Garner, who had had dozens of run-ins with police over the years, pleaded with the cops to leave him alone. "Every time you see me, you want to mess with me," he said. "I'm tired of it." Officer Daniel Pantaleo, a white man, then approached Garner from behind and put him in a chokehold, an unauthorized maneuver. Garner was thrown to the ground, and—after muttering "I can't breathe" no fewer than eleven times—died, a victim of both overzealous policing and New York's absurdly high cigarette taxes. A grand jury declined to indict Pantaleo.

Less than a month later, a white police officer, Darren Wilson, fatally shot a black teenager, Michael Brown, after an altercation following the latter's alleged theft of some items from a convenience store in Ferguson, Missouri. Wilson fired a total of twelve shots at Brown; the officer later claimed he was acting in self-defense and that Brown had tried to grab his gun. The Obama-era Department of Justice reached a similar conclusion after investigating the case, and a grand jury declined to indict Wilson.

But the protesters who took to the streets of Ferguson in the days following Brown's death bought into a different narrative, which held that the teen had been in the process of peaceably surrendering when Wilson opened fire. "Hands up, don't shoot" became the rallying cry of the protesters, based on the idea that Brown had had his hands up and uttered the plea "Don't shoot" just before Wilson shot him dead. (The *Washington Post*'s "Fact Checker" section would later award this idea a full four Pinocchios.)[6]

In November, twenty-six-year-old Cleveland police officer Timothy Loehmann shot and killed Tamir Rice, a twelve-year-old boy, at a public park. Loehmann and his partner wrongly believed Rice was armed; the kid had actually been playing with a toy gun. Video footage of the encounter showed Loehmann driving up to Rice and shooting him immediately, without taking any time to assess the situation. A subsequent investigation revealed that Loehmann had been fired from a previous police job for emotional instability and incompetence with firearms.[7] But this didn't matter—Loehmann, too, avoided indictment. Given that Rice had done nothing wrong, and the police had unnecessarily escalated the situation, this was a particularly galling miscarriage of justice, in my opinion.

Five months later, Baltimore police officers arrested Freddie Gray, a black man, for carrying an illegal knife. They put him in a police vehicle, where the perfectly healthy twenty-five-year-old somehow suffered neck and spine injuries, slipped into a coma, and eventually died. Police failed to adequately explain how a man in custody for a trivial offense could have sustained such egregious injuries. A medical examiner ruled the death a homicide resulting from failure to properly restrain Gray during the rough ride. As with the previous cases, none of the involved officers would go on to suffer formal consequences.

Riots began following Gray's death, and intensified after his funeral on April 27. In anticipation of possible violence, police shut down a public thoroughfare, which prompted some students from a local high school to throw rocks and bricks at officers. The violence spread from there: rioters lobbed a Molotov cocktail at police, looted and set fire to a nearby CVS, destroyed a senior center, and injured fifteen officers. The mayor's office reported 144 vehicle fires, fifteen other fires, and nearly two hundred arrests, according to the Associated Press.[8] Another riot took place the following night.

In response to these and other instances of the government denying justice to the families of black people who were wrongly killed, the Black Lives Matter (BLM) movement came into being. It started as a hashtag—a way to label a statement on the internet, essentially—on social media sites: #BlackLivesMatter. The group is broad-based, is informally run, and possesses little in the way of an official hierarchy, though three self-described "radical black organizers," Alicia Garza, Patrisse Cullors, and Opal Tometi, are credited as its founders. According to the group's website, under a heading called "Herstory" ("*His*tory" would be improperly gendered, one gathers), "The space that #BlackLivesMatter held and continues to hold helped propel the conversation around the state-sanctioned violence they experienced. We particularly highlighted the egregious ways in which Black women, specifically Black trans women, are violated. #BlackLivesMatter was developed in support of all Black lives."[9]

Garza, now thirty-seven, has long black braids and a septum piercing. When I interviewed her, she ended our conversation with an exhortation to "stay strong woke."

She was the one who came up with the phrase "Black lives matter," she told me. "What I was intending to do was just express my own feelings about the aftermath of [the George Zimmerman] verdict," she said. "What we found was that we weren't alone in that anguish, and in that rage, and in our desire to actually get organized with other people. To figure out how we can get to a place where we're not having mothers losing their children before it is their time."

According to Garza, too many people trip themselves up trying to interpret her movement's actions and parse its goals. She favors a literal approach. "When I say black lives matter, I mean black lives matter," she said. "I don't mean all lives matter, I don't mean black and brown lives matter. I mean black lives matter. I'm very intentional about why. It doesn't mean I don't think all lives matter. But when we say black lives matter, it means just that."

Garza disputed my characterization of Zillennial activism as fundamentally different from what came before it, preferring to see intersectional progressivism as an extension of the past. "None of these tactics are new," she said. "It's just a new time."

Even so, Garza echoed the sentiments of other activists, asserting that the movement *must* be intersectional. "In order to build a movement for and by black people, we have to include all black people," she said. "So we can't just say, 'Only black people that are this gender and heterosexual.' Because that leaves out black people who are queer, black people who are trans; it leaves out a whole bunch of people."

What does Black Lives Matter want? The movement opposes police brutality, racial profiling, and the kinds of criminal justice policies that have led the Unites States to jail vastly more people, proportionally speaking, than any other country in the world. These aren't exactly new demands, but the greater media attention to and public awareness of wrongful police killings of black people have given the issues a sense of heightened urgency in recent years.

"Black Lives Matter has provided the first truly large-scale political mobilization against police violence and mass incarceration since the War on Drugs began," wrote Jacob Levy in an article for the liberal Niskanen Center. Levy went on to praise the kind of identity politics that BLM represents as "one of the most significant political mobilizations in defense of freedom in the United States in my lifetime."[10]

By no means are these merely left-wing causes. Liberals and libertarians have supported criminal justice reform since well before BLM came into existence, and even many conservatives were increasingly willing to question mass incarceration, the war on drugs, and the efficacy of increased police militarization in the last decade. High-profile Republicans including Senators Mike Lee and Rand Paul have joined their Democratic colleagues in sponsoring legislation that would reform mandatory minimum sentencing— laws that obligate judges to impose unnecessarily harsh penalties on convicted criminals. As recently as 2014, congressional passage of significant criminal justice reform legislation seemed all but inevitable, since the issue is truly bipartisan.

Several developments—most notably, the election of straight-forwardly pro–law and order Republican president Donald Trump and the elevation of reliably pro-cop Senator Jeff Sessions to the attorney general position—muted the expectations of many who support criminal justice reform (including the author of this book).

"Last year, despite significant bipartisan support in Congress, criminal justice reform crashed on the shoals of an election year, the opioid crisis, and ongoing and escalating tensions between police officers and the communities they serve," wrote the Heritage Foundation's John Malcolm and John-Michael Seibler at the end of 2017.[11]

The next year was more encouraging. Sessions lost his job, and Trump endorsed the bipartisan First Step Act, which would make it easier for judges to impose lenient sentences. Incidentally, Trump's proximity to the world of reality TV means that he occasionally takes his cues from people like Kim Kardashian and Kanye West, both of whom visited the White House to sell the president on backing criminal justice reforms.

Even so, candidate Trump ran hard on the idea that law enforcement officers, rather than innocent black citizens, were the true victims of injustice—and he won. Despite Levy's contention that BLM has been "one of the most significant political mobilizations in defense of freedom," we must consider the possibility that BLM's arrival on the scene in 2013 and 2014 actually *harmed* the cause of criminal justice reform, by associating policies that had been gaining popularity on their own (sentencing reform and drug decriminalization) with appeals to race-based identity politics. When criminal justice reform was about fairness, big government, and the unaffordability of locking everybody up, its advocates were making strides. After the issue became more explicitly about race, the nation elected Trump in response.

This, of course, is a chief failing of intersectionality: framing a specific issue in identitarian terms makes it less appealing to people who do not identify with the category of marginalization in question. This in turn results in the issue coalition being less diverse and thus prone to tactical errors, such as engaging in performative acts that confirm the wokeness of the in-group but scare off others.

A good example unfolded at William and Mary College in October 2017. The college had invited Claire Gastañaga, executive director of the American Civil Liberties Union in Virginia, a graduate of William and Mary, to come speak on campus. The subject of her talk, ironically, was "Students and the First Amendment." She planned to discuss the legal rights of student protesters.

That's not what happened. Gastañaga had scarcely said hello to the audience before a group of students calling themselves Black Lives Matter at W&M marched to the front of the room. Gastañaga attempted to mollify the mob by declaring her sympathy with the protesters—"Good, I like this," she said—but to no avail. The shouting soon drowned her out.

"ACLU, you protect Hitler too," chanted the protesters, many of whom were white. This was the least colorful of their slogans; they continued with "The revolution will not uphold the Constitution," "Blood on your hands," and "Shame, shame, shame" (which I took as an ode to Queen Cersei Lannister's dehumanizing abuse at the hands of the Faith Militant during the fifth season of HBO's *Game of Thrones*—although it turns out that this particular chant predates the show).

Most notably, the activists also shouted "Liberalism is white supremacy." Such a statement will strike many readers as incoherent—it was incoherent to me as well, at least at first. As an ideology, white supremacy is a staple of the far, far right, and associated in America with the KKK and neo-Nazi movements. These groups are not exactly conservative—which is why their newest incarnation needed to invent a term, "alt-right," as in an alternative to the right as it is currently understood—but they are in direct opposition to liberalism. Liberalism in all its forms (classical, New Deal–era, modern, neo-) is the ideology of individual rights and anti-racism. Whatever their differences with mild, plain old liberalism, surely the leftist activists did not actually view it as equivalent to white supremacy.

In fact, they did.

"This is about liberals' use of the concept of free speech in the furthering of White Supremacy," one of the protesters told the *Black Voice*, a campus publication run by students of color, and one of the few media outlets with which the activists were willing to speak (probably because its writers and editorial team were themselves activists). "Our goal is to silence white supremacy, to not allow it a platform like the ACLU has done for a long time."[12]

Historically, the ACLU has defended the First Amendment rights of *everyone*, including neo-Nazis, the alt-right, and the Westboro Baptist Church—but also communists, gay activists, and racial and environmental equality organizations. The ACLU believes that when one group's free speech rights are threatened, the entire principle is endangered. That's why, in 2017, the ACLU sued the Washington Metropolitan Area Transit Authority for viewpoint discrimination, alleging that in preventing certain groups from advertising on the Washington, D.C., Metro system, the transit authority had violated the First Amendment. In order to make the point that free speech is a universal right, the ACLU selected a wide range of candidates for the suit, choosing to represent Carafem (a nonprofit that supports abortion), People for the Ethical Treatment of Animals (PETA), and Milo Yiannopoulos himself. It's not about Carafem's views, or PETA's, or Milo's: it's about the free speech protections that all Americans enjoy under the First Amendment.

But for the activists at William and Mary, the issue is black-and-white: you are with them or you are against them. And in taking the side of white nationalists in free speech cases, the ACLU had declared itself an enemy of the left, in the young protesters' view. Intersectionality, of course, does not concern itself with an individual right such as free speech: it is concerned with rights for the marginalized and their allies. The intersectional left will not defend free speech as a good thing in and of itself—it's good for intersectional progressives to have it, and bad otherwise.

Unlike at the Charles Murray event in Ann Arbor, William and

Mary's administration provided no pushback whatsoever. On the contrary, one of the students who had helped organize the ACLU event handed the protesters a microphone, encouraging their leader to speak.

"We know from personal experience that rights granted to wealthy, white, cis, male, straight bodies do not trickle down to marginalized groups," said the leader of the protest, a black female student preaching intersectionality. "We face greater barriers and consequences for speaking."

But these protesters faced no formal consequences. The university released a mild statement—"William & Mary must be a campus that welcomes difficult conversations, honest debate and civil dialogue"—and that was that. Having successfully prevented the event from taking place, the activists approached Gastañaga, the thwarted speaker. Some in the audience attempted to have a private conversation with her; the activists closed in, continuing to drown her out. Eventually those students departed, no longer willing to defy the mob.

I emailed Camryn, editor in chief of the *Black Voice*, asking for clarification regarding the protesters' motivations. She declined to put me in touch with any of the other activists, claiming that "we have recently become familiar with your work and frankly do not find that it reflects the views of this publication." I countered that of course *my* views did not reflect those of her publication but that I was open to being persuaded if she put forth an argument for why I was wrong. Her response was polite, but she steadfastly refused to defend—or simply explain—why her circle of friends thought censorship was the best path to ideological victory.

In the end, Camryn would answer only one of my questions: she confirmed that "shame, shame, shame" was *not* intended as an homage to *Game of Thrones*.

In any case, I submit that chanting "Liberalism is white supremacy" is not a good tactic for a movement that needs to win over some liberals, moderates, and conservatives in order to succeed.

Hate or Hoax?

One defense of the campus Black Lives Matter group's illiberal actions is that desperate times call for desperate measures. Students have witnessed a disturbing and unprecedented rise in overtly racist incidents, acts of vandalism, and hate crimes, this line of thinking goes. White supremacists are openly recruiting on campuses, the anti-immigrant and anti-black alt-right is ascendant, and President Trump's racially charged rhetoric has provided cover for racist forces to act more brazenly.

"Consider the climate of hatred that's taking place across the United States," Columbia University doctoral fellow Kayum Ahmed told me. "Consider what has happened in previous locations where alt-right speakers and fundamentalist speakers have spoken and then the subsequent violence that emerges."

At first blush, it seems surprising that this staggering and sudden surge in racism is most apparent on college campuses, which are (on paper, at least) the most liberal, tolerant, accepting, non-racist, politically correct places on earth. But it could be the case that Trump's election made racist students feel safer making their odious views known (thus one #Resistance slogan: "Make racists afraid again").

On its face, the recent string of racist incidents on campuses would seem to vindicate the left: *We said America is a rotten, racist place, and here is the proof.* If even progressive university campuses contain a fifth column of students posting racist flyers, spray-painting swastikas, hanging nooses, and throwing bananas at students of color, who could disagree that the extreme and frequently off-putting tactics of Black Lives Matter are a necessary antidote to the poison American voters swallowed on November 8, 2016?

Many on the left predicted Trump's rise would produce a corresponding increase in hate crimes and bias incidents. Less than a month after Trump's election, the Southern Poverty Law Center already claimed vindication, releasing a report titled "The Trump Effect: The Impact of the 2016 Election on Our Nation's Schools."[13]

The fact that it was far, far too soon to measure said impact eluded the SPLC's experts, whose report was based on unscientific data collected from email subscribers and website visitors—in other words, people who may have already shared the SPLC's incredibly broad definition of hate. (Note that the center counted Maajid Nawaz, an Islamist turned liberal reformer who works to deradicalize the Islamic world, as an "anti-Muslim extremist."[14] The SPLC later admitted this characterization was erroneous, though it took Nawaz threatening a lawsuit to make the center relent.)

A large majority of respondents said the Trump effect was real: Trump's election had negatively impacted their schools' climate or made students feel more anxious. The SPLC report also produced plenty of incidents of supposedly Trump-related bullying: students yelling "Go back to Mexico" and "Build the wall" at Latino kids on the playground, for instance. It certainly could be the case that kids who are paying attention to the news are repeating what they hear from Trump and his supporters, or feel emboldened to be racists and sexists and xenophobes because of all the excuse-making on the right for Trump's bad behavior.

The SPLC is a widely respected organization that has done a lot of terrific work tracking racist hate groups. But data from the Federal Bureau of Investigation, which publishes yearly updates on the frequency of hate crimes, tell a less depressing story about what's happening in the country right now. According to the FBI, there were 6,121 bias incidents in 2016. In the previous year, 5,850 incidents were reported to the FBI. That's an increase—yes, an increase—of 271. But here's the catch: 257 more law enforcement agencies reported data to the FBI in 2016 than in 2015. If each of those agencies notified the FBI of just one additional hate crime, it would make up the difference almost entirely.

Did the FBI uncover slightly more hate crimes in 2016 than 2015 because Trump unleashed a wave of hate, or because the agency did a better job of gathering accurate information than it had in previous years? The latter seems more likely.

Looking further back, the idea of a 2016 spike seems even less credible. In 2007, the FBI reported 7,621 bias incidents, a thousand more than in 2016. White Americans—the population most at risk of being motivated by Trump to engage in racist activity—represented a whopping 63 percent of all perpetrators in 2007, according to the FBI. By 2016, just 48 percent were white.

The data showed a slight increase in the number of anti-Hispanic incidents since 2015, but still fewer total incidents than in 2012, 2010, 2008, or 2006. Anti-Jewish hate was on the rise relative to 2015, but still down compared with 2012. Anti-black animus was unchanged since 2015, and substantially down since 2006. An uptick in anti-Muslim hate in 2016 was probably the result of the FBI changing the way it classified such incidents. As my colleague at *Reason* magazine, associate editor Elizabeth Nolan Brown, put it, "Obviously, small upticks can turn into big ones over time and are worth keeping an eye on. But looking at a decade's worth of FBI hate crime data shows the folly in making too much of year-over-year fluctuations."[15]

According to Bureau of Justice Statistics data, the rate of hate crime victimization in 2015 "was not significantly different from the rate in 2004." What's more, "the absence of statistically significant change in rates from 2004 to 2015 generally held true for violent hate crimes both reported and unreported to police."[16] This information doesn't include the Year of Trump, and it's always possible things are about to get a lot worse. But the data we have tend to show that the hate crime rate has stayed basically the same, or even dipped a bit, over the long term. This is in keeping with trends relating to plain old not-necessarily-motivated-by-hate crime, which has plummeted massively since the early 1990s.

I experienced a lightbulb moment when I testified before the U.S. Commission on Civil Rights in May 2018.[17] (Disclaimer: I am a member of the D.C. Advisory Committee to the U.S. Commission on Civil Rights, an appointed volunteer position.) The other members of my panel were local law enforcement officers who work in task forces specifically designed to track and combat hate crimes. These panelists conceded that the vast majority of police municipalities—88 percent—report zero hate crimes. Some of these include very large municipalities. Baltimore County, for instance, reported just one hate crime in 2016, for a population of 831,000 people.

Is Baltimore County blessedly hate free? Probably not. The authorities there just don't compile good hate crime information. And here's the important thing: if Baltimore County did a better job with its reporting in 2017 and 2018, it would appear that hate was increasing in Baltimore County. (Just two reported hate crimes would mean a 100 percent spike in hate!) Better reporting of a problem can disguise itself as a worsening of said problem. Over time, as various law enforcement agencies get better at tracking hate crimes, it will appear as though there are more of those crimes— but this just means they were undercounted in the first place.

But what about all the recent incidents of racist, sexist, and anti-LGBT hate on college campuses specifically? Focusing just on college campuses, the picture seems at first glance pretty dark.

BuzzFeed, for instance, reviewed more than four hundred alleged bias incidents reported to the Documenting Hate project since Trump's election. Describing the data as revealing "a shock of hate speech," *BuzzFeed*'s writers "confirmed" (*BuzzFeed*'s word) 154 of the incidents, which occurred at more than 120 different university campuses. "More than a third of the incidents cited Trump's name or slogans; more than two-thirds promoted white supremacist groups or ideology," wrote authors Mike Hayes, Albert Samaha, and Talal Ansari. The piece was titled "'Imagine Being Surrounded by People Who Hate You and Want to See You Dead,'" a quote from a University of Virginia student recounting what it felt like to watch the alt-right marching in Charlottesville in August 2017.[18]

One of the frustrating things about trying to understand hate crimes on campuses is that the perpetrators are almost never caught. In *BuzzFeed*'s review, just 5 percent of the cases involving vandalism or threats were solved. What's more, "at least three investigations led college officials to conclude that a racist incident was a hoax," wrote the authors. I emailed the authors to clarify whether the three hoaxes were among the 5 percent of solved cases; that was the only interpretation of *BuzzFeed*'s counting that makes sense to me, as it would suggest that a very large proportion of the cases where we actually know what happened were something other than what they appeared to be. None of the authors responded. As I wrote in an article for *Reason* at the time, that's a shame: "If *BuzzFeed* is going to run the deliberately inflammatory headline 'Imagine Being Surrounded by People Who Hate You and Want to See You Dead,' its writers should be able to answer questions about whether the data support this nightmarish fantasy."[19]

I've written about hate crimes and bias incidents on college campuses for years. I cannot underscore this enough: we usually have no idea who's responsible. I've seen enough verified cases to make the assertion that some of them are genuine acts of malice perpetrated by racists—often nonstudents. A panic at the University of Missouri in 2015, for instance, is confirmed to have been the work of far-right racist troll Andrew Anglin, who used social media to trick students into thinking the KKK was coming to campus to gun down student activists.[20] And at American University in the fall of 2017, a middle-aged man was caught on camera sneaking into a campus building in order to post racist flyers. This was just the latest in a series of racist incidents at American: earlier in the year, some male students allegedly opened a black freshman's dorm room door and threw a banana at her. This perpetrator was never publicly identified, nor were motives disclosed in any of the cases.

I spoke with Jenna, an American University sophomore of color who wants to be a journalist after she graduates, about the banana incident. I asked her whether the instances of racism felt out of place to her.

"I think you could find this in almost any sort of predominantly white space," said Jenna.

Jenna was one of twelve students who met with American

University administrators about the racist incidents. Activist students rattled off a list of demands, and administrators committed to meeting most of them.

"I was actually really surprised that the administration was really willing to work with us," said Jenna. "But I kind of feel as if there's really no other option, seeing as how the very last protest . . . we pretty much blocked off the entire school garage, so cars were completely backed up."

Indeed, in May 2017, activists blocked traffic from escaping the Bender Arena tunnel, trapping cars in place for over an hour until the administration agreed to their demands.

"There was a pregnant lady who was trying to get out," Ma'at, one of the activists, told me. She confessed that the presence of the pregnant woman gave her pause. "At that moment, I was like, 'Dang, we should let her out.' But activist Ma'at was like, 'Nah, if we let her out, we're about to be here till midnight.'"[21]

She ultimately decided that if the woman really needed to go somewhere, she could get out of her car and call an Uber. "We weren't preventing her from leaving," said Ma'at. "With big risk comes big reward."

One of the students' demands was for the university to designate a certain café, the Bridge, as a "sanctuary" for students of color. Administrators demurred, but offered up a different room for a sanctuary instead.

Activists also asked administrators to grant exam extensions— not just for the student who had allegedly been on the receiving end of the thrown banana but for any student of color who asked.

"I took my last final today," Jenna told me. "It was extended by four days, which I was very grateful for. And the school made that a very easy process."

Another of the activists' demands: racial sensitivity training for faculty members, facilitated by an activist group that calls itself the Darkening.

"They usually are working with different clubs on campus and they hold Darkening trainings where they try to make new clubs really racially sensitive, and just educate them and things like that," said Jenna.

Another banana incident generated an outcry of a different sort. During a fall retreat for Greek life students at the University of Mississippi, Makala McNeil, a leader of a historically black sorority, spotted a banana peel hanging from a tree outside the window of her cabin. The sight of the banana peel had students of color in tears, owing to the historical legacy of racists using bananas to suggest that black people deserve the same status as apes. Officials canceled the retreat; an administrator, Alexa Lee Arndt, told a local newspaper, "I felt it was imperative to provide space immediately to students affected by this incident to allow them an opportunity to voice their pain and concern." It turned out the safe space was unnecessary: the misplaced banana peel was not intended as an act of malice. A student, Ryan Swanson, eventually admitted that he had eaten a banana, and—failing to find a trash can—placed the remains in the tree.

"Although unintentional, there is no excuse for the pain that was caused to members of our community," said Swanson in a statement. "I have much to learn and look forward to doing such and encourage all members of our community to do the same."

Another accidental bias incident unfolded at Michigan State University in the fall of 2017, when someone allegedly hung a noose on a stairwell door handle. This was taken as an attempt to remind black students of extrajudicial lynchings. The police leapt into action, and MSU president Lou Anna Simon (who has since resigned in the wake of the Larry Nassar sexual abuse scandal) released a statement.

"I want to be clear: This type of behavior is not tolerated on our campus," she said. "No Spartan should ever feel targeted based on their race, or other ways in which they identify. A noose is a symbol of intimidation and threat that has a horrendous history in America."

But the "noose" was actually just a misplaced shoelace. The

person who hung it on the door handle was hoping its owner would claim it. That was all.

Another alleged noose, hung from a tree at Duke University in the spring of 2015, was similarly debunked. The student who hung it was foreign-born and unaware of the symbol's racist connotation. His explanation made perfect sense: he had tied a piece of yellow cord around a tree branch, snapped a photo of it, and texted his friends a picture of it with the request to "hang out."

"If there was ever a pun with unintended consequences, this was certainly one," said the student, who came forward to explain the noose's origin and profusely apologize.[22] Duke administrators initially expelled the student, but after he provided the explanation, they relented and said they would allow him back on campus.

At least one activist student was perturbed by the light punishment. Henry L. Washington Jr., a male student of color, complained about the "astonishingly lax sanction" and said it was a slap in the face of "black students and their allies." He continued: "You may have delegitimized the claims of our outcries. It may appear that you have actually disregarded black students' concerns. . . . As a community, we need you to decide that black lives matter, and to do so expeditiously, unreservedly, and permanently, for we still cannot breathe."[23]

But all these cases were accidental bias incidents. There's another category: outright hoaxes.

In late October 2017, Andrew Hammond, a journalism student at Kansas State University, noticed a vehicle covered in painted-on racial slurs like "White's Only" and "Date Your Own Kind." The car belonged to a black man, Dauntarius Williams, who filed a report with the police. The police swiftly caught the perpetrator: it was Dauntarius, who had defaced his own vehicle as some kind of Halloween prank. Authorities decided not to charge him with filing a false report.[24]

A worse hoax struck the U.S. Air Force Academy Preparatory School in Colorado Springs in the fall of 2017, when someone wrote racist messages—"Go home niggers"—on the doors of the rooms where five cadets of color lived.[25] The incident shook the school; Lt. General Jay Silveria, the superintendent, delivered a fiery speech instructing anyone who could not treat others with dignity and respect to "get out" of the school. His remarks quickly went viral and were viewed on YouTube more than a million times.

The school was *again* shaken after investigators discovered that the perpetrator was one of the five victims, whose goal had been to distract from misconduct charges pending against him.

At Eastern Michigan University, the person who spray-painted "KKK" and "Leave niggers" on the wall of a building was . . . a twenty-nine-year-old student of color. He was charged in connection with a separate crime, and is serving one to five years in prison. At the University of Maryland, people initially suspected a spray-painted swastika was the handiwork of a genuine racist, but unexpectedly, police arrested a fifty-two-year-old ex-employee in connection with the crime. (He was black.) And at the University of Michigan, a student claimed a man had threatened to set her on fire for wearing the Muslim hijab. She later admitted to police that she had invented the story.

The hijab hoax occurred just a few days after the election, and was unraveled some weeks later. Kinsey, the *Michigan Daily*'s editor in chief, remembered hearing about the alleged hate crime during the night of her own election to the top editorial position. At the time it seemed to fit with the feeling among minority students that they were under attack.

"I was in this class on the history of Africa," Kinsey told me. "Everyone in that class was black, except for a few people. The class was canceled the day after the election." Black students, according to Kinsey, wondered how anyone could vote for Trump "'while also saying that you're my friend or that you have no malice towards me.' People really felt personally attacked, and their identities attacked. Then there were these literal attacks, or alleged [attacks]."

Two other incidents stuck in Kinsey's mind: a dark-skinned non-Muslim young woman was allegedly pushed down a hill by men who thought she was Muslim. Kinsey believes this crime, unlike the hijab hoax, was genuine—it even inspired her parents to buy her pepper spray. The police failed to identity the perpetrators.

Another incident involved a twenty-one-year-old student, Halley Bass, who claimed a stranger had attacked her with a safety pin and cut her face. Bass said the assailant was retaliating against her for making a statement of support for immigrants. She filed a police report and penned a widely shared Facebook post about her ordeal. Later, Bass admitted that she had scratched her own face. "I was suffering from depression at the time," she said in court.[26]

"It ended up being self-inflicted and she lied about it, but at the time it was scary," Kinsey recalled.

In recounting these hoaxes, I do not mean to suggest that all or even most hate crimes on college campuses are made up. The frustrating truth is that we have *no idea* what the relative percentages are. The most outrageous cases make the news. But usually the authorities don't catch the perpetrator, and are therefore unable to discern true motivations.

Nor am I implying that being the victim of a bias incident is trivial; I have no doubt that it does indeed cause some emotional pain. But the campus racial justice movement's overemphasis on purported hate crimes doesn't quite hold up as evidence of a rising tide of racism. The case for sacrificing free speech norms in order to combat the oppression of hateful rhetoric is thus less strong than intersectional activists claim.

Black Bodies and Anti-Whiteness

It's worth remembering that the civil rights movement was highly inclusive. Martin Luther King's "I Have a Dream" speech depicted a vision of the future in which not just black people and white people but "the sons of former slaves and the sons of former slave owners" would live together in harmony.

The modern intersectional left, though, is not quite so interested in winning over the center with overtures to equality and is less inclined to imagine a future where skin color doesn't mean anything. Their goal is to fight the interrelated oppressions visited on black people under our white, patriarchal, cis-centric, capitalist society.

"We, as black bodies, are tired of debating about our right to exist, about our right to humanity, about our right to be human beings," Columbia's Kayum Ahmed told me.

I have often heard activists of color refer to the oppressed as black *bodies* rather than black *people*. I asked Ahmed to explain it, and he obliged.

"The invocation of black bodies is a reference to the dehumanization of black people into black bodies," he told me. "The black body is therefore considered as a thing rather than a human being. There is an existential dimension to this idea that is deeply embedded in the historical treatment of black people through slavery, colonialism, and apartheid—we see the current struggle that black bodies face as a continuation of this historical struggle."

One can easily imagine why the *enemies* of the activists might prefer "bodies": it's dehumanizing, and reduces people to objects. Slave owners thought of their property as a collection of black *bodies* rather than black people. Less obvious, though, is why black people would use such terminology.

But the field of sociology has made it so: an increasing focus on the physical—on the *seen*—within the discipline helped give rise to "bodies" as a substitute for people. This was not always the case. According to Chris Shilling, a sociologist at the University of Kent, early sociology—in the person of Karl Marx—gave the concept of the body short shrift.

"It was the mind, rather than the body, which served as the receptor and organizer of images concerned with, and deriving from, social stratification," wrote Shilling in his book *The Body and Social Theory*.[27] "In its most enduring form, this approach is evident in the Marxist tradition's focus on ideology, false consciousness and reification." The body was merely a receptacle for the metaphysical characteristics that made people people. But from about 1980 on, sociologists began paying more attention to the body as a "central object of study," as Shilling puts it. After all, sociology is the study of how groups of people interact with one another, and the most obvious kinds of interactions are primarily sensory: reactions to the different ways other people look, feel, and smell. In this light, it's easier to see why modern sociology might regard the physical presentation of the body as more fundamental to the human experience than the unique set of beliefs and personality traits that characterize the self.

This trend has certainly caught on. Talk to activists and read their thoughts, and you too will pick up on their obsession with people as bodies.

I suspect "bodies" has become a popular term for two reasons. One, it's an ultimate form of virtue signaling. What better way for a young activist to indicate learnedness in the field of social justice than to speak the expert's lingo? An activist who uses the word "bodies" signals that he or she has read the literature, taken Marx to the next extreme, hangs out with the right people, and is thus sufficiently woke.

Two, drilling the word "body" into the public's heads is a subtle way of reinforcing the idea that emotional harms can also be physical harms: they are being done not to people but to people's bodies. This seems like a great strategy for gradually redefining hate speech as literal violence. Ideas, experiences, forms of expression— these are facets of being a body, and bodies can bruise.

Ironically, activists often accuse their opponents—particularly their white opponents—of being the truly fragile ones. (Not without reason when it comes to the alt-right, as we will see in Chapter Eight.) "White fragility" is another subject of frequent discussion. The originator of the phrase—Robin DiAngelo, an author and lecturer at the University of Washington who specializes in "critical racial and social justice"—theorized that white people in America are systematically protected from ever having to reckon with the fact that they possess a racist, institutional power over black people.

DiAngelo, who is white, believes white people can become un-comfortable and even hostile when confronted with their privi-lege; they are so blind to the institutionalized racism from which they benefit that they can react with extreme emotional negativ-ity when the subject of race is broached.

For example, picture an out-of-work fifty-year-old white man who never attended college and lives in the Deep South in a town where jobs are disappearing, and imagine he is being told that he is complicit in white supremacy, from which he benefits. He refuses to see this, of course, instead blaming his lot in life on affirmative action, immigrants, and other factors.

"White fragility," though, doesn't just apply to folks who are truly racially insensitive. This should come as little surprise to readers at this point, but DiAngelo reserves some of her harshest criticism for—you guessed it—white liberals.

"White moral objection to racism increases white resistance to acknowledging complicity with it," DiAngelo wrote.[28] That sort of sounds like she's saying *people who aren't racists are the real racists,* but it's a bit more complicated than that. She continues: "In a white supremacist context, white identity in large part rests upon a foundation of (superficial) racial toleration and acceptance. Whites who position themselves as liberal often opt to protect what they perceive as their moral reputations, rather than recognize or change their participation in systems of inequity and domination."

White supremacy, according to this thinking, "rests upon a foundation of superficial racial tolerance and acceptance." There-fore, even if a society appears tolerant and accommodating, it could still be racist to its core. In fact, the more accepting the society appears, the more likely it is to be a white supremacist so-ciety! Tolerance is thus understood as a characteristic of white supremacy—someone should call this the tolerance paradox 2.0—and liberalism, which holds tolerance as one of its crowning values, as the ultimate expression of white supremacy. It is this thinking that undergirds the slogan deployed by activists at William and Mary who shouted "liberalism is white supremacy."

People who react to this characterization with scorn are proving it to be fundamentally sound, in the eyes of the activist. Such a characterization makes liberals uncomfortable, not because it's wrong but because they're suffering from white fragility, a side effect of their complicity in white racism. As one Twitter activist, a woman who describes herself only semi-ironically as a full communist, put it, the goal is to "shut down more white liberals."[29] Her tweet to this effect included an image of three brown fists.

Student activists occasionally blur the lines between being against white supremacy and being against whiteness itself—and, by extension, all white people. Rudy Martinez, a Texas State University student, wrote an op-ed claiming that white people are "an aberration" and that "white death will mean liberation for all." The piece was explicitly racist; Martinez claims, "When I think of all the white people I've ever encountered—whether they've been professors, peers, lovers, friends, police officers, et cetera—there is perhaps only a dozen I would consider 'decent.'" At the end of the piece, Martinez writes, "I hate you because you shouldn't exist. You are both the dominant apparatus on the planet and the void in which all other cultures, upon meeting you, die."[30]

Martinez lost his job as a columnist as a result of the provocative screed, and various college officials condemned his remarks. But somewhat subtler criticisms are routinely leveled at whiteness itself by activist students and professors. Sometimes these generate a backlash—especially if the conservative media catches wind of them—and other times they don't.

Some examples: Every year for the last fifteen years, California State University San Marcos has hosted a "Whiteness Forum."[31] The forum kicks off a class taught by Dreama Moon, a white communications professor, called Communication of Whiteness. At the 2017 forum, a student performed a spoken-word piece with the lines "Whiteness thrives on the hate of everyone."

Ekow Yankah, a professor of law at Cardozo Law School, penned an op-ed for the *New York Times* confessing that he will teach his young sons "to have profound doubts that friendship with white people is possible"—an admission of racism that would surely be career-ending if the races of the concerned parties were reversed. "I will teach them to be cautious, I will teach them suspicion, and I will teach them distrust."[32]

A Michigan State University student, Maggie DeHart, was walking to class when she spotted a sign that said simply, "It's okay to be white." In response, she fired off a letter to the *State News*, Michigan State's student-run publication. "This seemingly simple statement is aggressive and it's false," she wrote. "It's not okay to be white."[33] That DeHart herself is white is beside the point. It's true that "it's okay to be white" is sometimes deployed as an alt-right talking point, and in *this* context it could be seen as an appeal to white superiority. But, as DeHart pointed out at the end of her letter, alt-right racists thrive off claims that whiteness is under attack.

Readers may recall the tragic death of Otto Warmbier, a white American college student who journeyed to North Korea and was arrested by the government on trumped-up treason charges. He was compelled to confess his crimes, and by the time he was released to American authorities, he had slipped into a mysterious coma from which he never recovered. The U.S. government rightly condemned North Korea's disrespect for human rights; outrage on behalf of Warmbier was universal—or *nearly* universal. Katherine Dettwyler, an anthropology professor at the University of Delaware, wrote on Facebook that Warmbier "got exactly what he deserved" for being a "young, white, rich, clueless, white male." (Yes, she emphasized "white" twice.) *Affinity*, a social justice–themed online magazine for teenagers (known for interesting articles like "In Today's Society, Is It Reasonable for Women to Hate Men?"), retweeted a comment about Warmbier's death with the following additional commentary: "Watch whiteness work. He wasn't a 'kid' or 'innocent' you can't go to another country and try to steal from them. Respect their laws."[34]

In the wake of the Las Vegas mass shooting, George Ciccariello-Maher, a professor of political science at Drexel University whose vocal support for the antifa movement and communism in general has given him a relatively high profile among far-left activist academics, said that whiteness itself is responsible for mass killings. "Whiteness is never seen as a cause, in and of itself, of these kinds of massacres," lamented the professor during an interview on *Democracy Now!* Ciccariello-Maher, who occasionally jokes about guillotining the bourgeoisie, continued: "Whiteness is a structure of privilege and it's a structure of power, and a structure that, when it feels threatened, you know, lashes out. And so, that's the kind of thing that we really need to think about, not only why is it—and I think there's a lot of attention to the fact that we demonize often Muslims or, you know, other people of color when these attacks occur."[35] It would seem that Ciccariello-Maher is not opposed to demonization—he just thinks the wrong group is being demonized.

But Ciccariello-Maher was hardly the only one to blame mass shootings on whiteness; writers for the *Huffington Post, ThinkProgress,* and *Newsweek* and the actor Cole Sprouse (formerly of Disney's *The Suite Life of Zack and Cody*) all suggested that mass shooters are disproportionately white, and thus whiteness itself has something to do with extreme violence.[36] *Slate*'s Daniel Engber and *New York Magazine*'s Jesse Singal have carefully eviscerated this notion: according to the data, white people do not commit disproportionately more mass murders than other groups—and even if they did, it would be no more valid to blame this on whiteness as it would be to blame blackness itself for violence within the black community.

Mount Allison University professors David Thomas and Zoe Luba penned an article in the *Canadian Journal of Development Studies* arguing that white students should address their own white fragility before enrolling in any study-abroad programs.[37]

A professor at Grinnell College teaches a sociology course titled American Whiteness that aims to attack racism by "making whiteness visible." The syllabus quotes David Roediger, a professor of American studies at the University of Kansas and author of *The Wages of Whiteness,* as saying, "White identity has its roots both in domination and in a desire to avoid confronting one's own miseries. Whiteness is, among much else, a bad idea. . . . [I]t is quite possible to avoid hating white people as individuals but to criticize forcefully the 'idea of white people in general.'"[38]

An assistant professor at the University of Iowa claimed that her goal as an instructor was to "dismantle whiteness."[39]

And on and on it goes. Many of the people involved in the above examples suffered consequences when the public became aware of their activities—and some of those consequences were quite ghastly. DeHart, the Michigan State student, initially agreed to be interviewed for this book, but backed out after receiving a series of threats from people who didn't like her letter. Social media is a toxic place, and left-leaning activists are often pilloried on Facebook, Twitter, and other mediums. Sometimes their safety is threatened by alt-right trolls.

Most activists and academics who rail against whiteness don't actually hate white people, of course. That would be ridiculous, since many are white themselves. Anti-whiteness is a performance—a social signaling device. That's because "white people" cannot be subjected to racism, according to the dictates of intersectional progressivism. In intersectional parlance, "racism" does not mean what it means to most people: it is not defined as "prejudice, discrimination, or antagonism directed against someone of a different race based on the belief that one's own race is superior," as it is in the dictionary. For modern leftism, racism requires discrimination *and* systemic oppression. Since white people as an identity group have never been systemically oppressed, there is no such thing as anti-white racism. Individual white people can endure marginalization if they are gay, or trans, or disabled, and so on—but not because of their race. One of the simplest ways to signal wokeness, then, is to make anti-white statements. It's like a flashing a badge that reads "I am an intersectional progressive."

The mainstream media was treated to an unusually straightforward example of this in August 2018, when the *New York Times* announced that it had hired Sarah Jeong, a tech policy journalist, to join its editorial board. It was quickly revealed that years before, Jeong had penned dozens of mean-spirited denunciations of white people on Twitter. (Jeong was born in South Korea.) She claimed that these tweets were satirical; at the time she wrote them, she had been the victim of a vicious harassment campaign, and the tweets were intended to mimic the language of her attackers. But I read through the tweets fairly closely, and it seems dubious to me that she was always, in every case, merely trolling a harasser. I think it's more likely she was doing as the intersectional progressives do: signaling her fidelity to the cause by bashing white people, an identity group whose historically privileged status means they are permanent outsiders from the standpoint of intersectionality.

It's true that white people have generally benefitted from their ethnicity and are often privileged by virtue of not being black, or brown, or Hispanic, or Native American. The history of the United States is the story of white people enslaving, murdering, and otherwise mistreating people of color. I don't mean to suggest that white people are typically victims—they're not.

But attacks on whiteness itself play into a certain victimhood narrative that's become extremely popular on the right. Two-thirds of millennial Trump voters, for instance, believe anti-white racism is more pervasive than anti-black racism.[40] That's obviously ludicrous, but it's no doubt fed by people like Sarah Jeong, who found employment at the *New York Times* despite making statements that would render her unemployable if they were about any other racial group.

DeHart, the Michigan State student, wrote in her letter, "The problem with racism in the modern U.S. is that it doesn't look like a sign posted over a water fountain indicating which one is acceptable to use. . . . It looks like people like Richard Spencer claiming that white culture is under attack." Perhaps one reason Spencer has been able to successfully convince people that white culture is under attack is that the mere statement "It's okay to be white" generates apoplectic denunciation.

A Culture, Not a Costume

There's one more major category of race-related controversy among the young woke set: cultural appropriation.

Melia Bernal, a Native Hawaiian by birth, is an attractive young woman who did her undergraduate studies at Yale University. During her time on campus, she founded a dance group, Shaka at Yale, which performed authentic Polynesian dance routines—including, of course, the hula. Bernal takes dance very seriously: she was a member of a traveling hula and Tahitian dance team. The purpose of Shaka was "to create an inclusive group in which native and non-native Hawaiian and Pacific Islander peoples could learn, be exposed to, and share aspects of Hawaiian and Pacific Islander cultures," she told the *Yale Daily News*.[41]

You might have expected that the Association of Native Americans at Yale (ANAAY)—a campus group that promotes Native American culture—would share this goal and express enthusiasm for Bernal's cause. You would be wrong.

"ANAAY condemns Shaka," student leaders of the association wrote in a statement. "There is no room for compromise on this matter."

From the activists' perspective, Shaka had committed a mortal sin, one of the most serious crimes known to campus activism: cultural appropriation. Though Bernal herself was Hawaiian, she had done the unthinkable: she knowingly allowed non-Hawaiian people—some of the other dancers, as well as the audience—to participate in, enjoy, and learn about Hawaiian culture.

ANAAY demanded that Shaka disband at once and apologize to Native American students for subjecting them to the "emotional labor" of having their culture appropriated. Shaka had also committed "erasure," which is the act of behaving as if a certain group of marginalized people does not exist. This is quite the paradox, of course: by educating people at Yale about Hawaiian culture—through an authentic dance led by a woman who was indeed Hawaiian—Shaka had somehow delegitimized the Hawaiian experience. The group had all but erased Hawaii from the map, according to the activists.

"ANAAY calls for Shaka's abolishment and formal apologies to indigenous students and the greater Polynesian community for sexualizing and homogenizing Native peoples, misrepresenting and erasing histories and political realities, and attempting to depoliticize inherently political cultures and communities and communities under subjugation," read the statement. "Once again, ANAAY must make the clarification that our humanity is not up for debate, and that our cultures are not costumes."[42]

Suffice it to say that no one in Shaka, and presumably no one else at Yale University, suggested that indigenous people were anything less than human. But in daring to practice hula—even in a learned, authentic way—for a mass audience, the dancers had essentially engaged in violence against Hawaiian culture.

If that sounds insane to you, consider this: cultural appropriation is one of the most common charges leveled by campus race activists. "A culture, not a costume" is the refrain of black, Asian, Latino/Latina (often supplanted by the activist-invented gender-neutral "Latinx"), Two Spirit (a variant third gender recognized in many Native American cultures), and countless other activist groups on every campus in the country. Few campus issues provoke as much consternation from race-based identity groups—and confusion from everyone else—as cultural appropriation.

What *is* cultural appropriation? Simply put, it's the idea that customs, traditions, clothing, songs, and food belong to the descendants of the race that invented them, and that other groups should essentially stay in their own lane when it comes to these traditions. When white people enjoy aspects of black, Latinx, Asian, or Native American culture, they are appropriating—stealing—something that doesn't belong to them.

The term was invented in sociology departments in the 1970s and 1980s as part of the critiques of colonialism and imperialism. White people didn't just conquer and destroy minority societies—they conquered and destroyed their cultures as well. Today, many activists think of modern cultural appropriation as the latest in-carnation of the kinds of atrocities white societies have perpe-trated against minority societies throughout history. It's twenty-first-century subjugation.

"Cultural appropriation's been going on for thousands of years with colonialism," Andres, a student at the University of Chicago, told me. Andres was entering his second year at Chicago when I spoke with him. He is the leader of a "Chicanx" group for Mexican American students. "It's just the idea of eradicating or undermining entire populations, either economically or politically or both, while, in my opinion, sort of stealing their objects, stealing their culture, while trying to also undermine the population where that culture actually comes from. It really echoes imperialism once again when you have this sort of cultural appropriation where you take what you like from the culture but what you don't like are the people that are of that culture you're undermining. [It] just seems unfair and unjust. It repeats a history, a narrative of imperialism within this country and within the world itself."

Critics of the concept of cultural appropriation—and there are many—dispute that borrowing a cultural tradition is necessarily wrong or diminishes the minority group. Cultural appropriation can even promote empathy for other peoples, enhance cross-cultural understanding, and lead to new, blended cultural touchstones. As the libertarian writer Cathy Young wrote, "Peoples have borrowed, adopted, taken, infiltrated and reinvented from time immemorial. The medieval Japanese absorbed major elements of Chinese and Ko-rean civilizations, while the cultural practices of modern-day Japan include such Western borrowings as a secularized and reinvented Christmas. Russian culture with its Slavic roots is also the product of Greek, Nordic, Tatar and Mongol influences—and the rapid Westernization of the elites in the 18th century. America is the ulti-mate blended culture."[43]

But the issue is hardly up for debate among young leftists, and any display of cross-cultural pollination—even a harmless or obviously desirable one—could be subject to scorn.

One of the most infamous of these battles took place at Oberlin College in December 2015, when the liberal arts college's exceedingly privileged students accused the cafeteria workers of serving culturally inauthentic Asian cuisine. "When you're cooking a country's dish for other people, including ones who have never tried the original dish before, you're also representing the meaning of the dish as well as its culture," student Tomoyo Joshi complained to the *Oberlin Review*. "So if people not from that heritage take food, modify it and serve it as 'authentic,' it is appropriative."[44]

The students' lack of self-awareness was jarring. Freddie deBoer, a left-leaning writer and academic who often criticizes the misplaced priorities of fellow activists, said on Twitter, "When you're defending the cultural authenticity of GENERAL TSO'S CHICKEN, you're a living Portlandia sketch," referring to *Portlandia,* a show that often makes fun of Zillennial leftism.

I wrote about the Oberlin cafeteria cultural appropriation controversy for the *Daily Beast;* the widely read article was picked up by dozens of major media outlets—including the *New York Times*—most of which heaped much-deserved criticism on the students. But this did not deter activists from continuing to fixate on cultural appropriation. At Pitzer College in 2016, a residential adviser sent a campus-wide email forbidding white female students from wearing hoop earrings because they "belong to the black and brown folks who created the culture. The culture actually comes from a historical background of oppression and exclusion. . . . Why should white girls be able to take part in this culture (wearing hoop earrings just being one case of it) and be seen as cute/aesthetic/ethnic?"[45] A student, Jaqueline Aguilera, took credit for spray-painting "White girl, take off your hoops!!!" on a campus wall. She later clarified that only intersectional feminists deserved to don those specific earrings.

College kids said some stupid things. Who cares? you might be thinking. But cultural appropriation has even been ground for violent reprisal. At San Francisco State University, a black female student named Bonita Tindle accosted and *attacked* a white male student named Cory Goldstein. Why? Goldstein was a white dude with dreadlocks, and dreadlocks, according to Tindle, don't belong to white people. Goldstein responded that he was going for an "Egyptian" look, at which point Tindle demanded to know whether he was Egyptian.

"You're saying I can't have a hairstyle because of your culture?" asked Goldstein. "Why?"

"Because it's my culture," Tindle replied. When Goldstein attempted to break off the conversation, Tindle grabbed him and began pushing him around.

Portland-area activists have targeted white-owned restaurants for serving ethnic food. Two white women, Kali Wilgus and Liz Connelly, shuttered their burrito business after a local alt-weekly newspaper, the *Portland Mercury,* accused them of appropriating Mexican culture—even though the pair had previously traveled to Mexico to learn the art of the burrito.

A student even targeted a yoga class for disabled people at the University of Ottawa. Yoga comes from India and should not be practiced by Western colonizers, this student argued. The instructor cleverly changed the name of the class from "yoga" to "mindful stretching," but to no avail: administrators still suspended the problematic course.

The surest way to get in trouble is to wear a culturally appropriative Halloween costume: cowboys and Indians, ninjas and samurai, et cetera. That may seem easy enough until you consider that so many beloved costume-friendly characters come from other cultures: Pocahontas, Aladdin, Zorro, and so on. Would lefty culture warriors really tell a little girl she can't dress up as Moana, the eponymous protagonist of Disney's wildly popular 2016 film?

In fact, they would. Both *Redbook* and *Cosmopolitan* published a column by "race conscious" mom blogger Sachi Feris, who hoped to dissuade her daughter from dressing up as the Polynesian Disney princess Moana for Halloween.[46]

Rarely addressed is the fact that Halloween itself was appropriated from Irish culture. Dressing up *at all* is in some sense an act of cultural appropriation of the Gaelic holiday.

By Any Means Necessary

"Given the historic abuses African Americans have suffered at the hands of police and the disproportionate ways they are affected even today by racist or inept police officers, many find the racial framing of Black Lives Matter is essential," wrote the *Atlantic*'s Conor Friedersdorf. "Unfortunately, its explicitly racial focus has been alienating to others, including those who don't believe that racism is a significant factor in police killings; those who put fighting racism low on their priority list; and anti-black racists."

Friedersdorf makes note of a horrific case of police brutality: a cop killing a defenseless hotel guest, Daniel Shaver, in Mesa, Arizona, for absolutely no reason.[47] The incident, described in Friedersdorf's article "A Police Killing Without a Hint of Racism," generated little public attention, in part because both the victim and the officer were white. For Friedersdorf, cases like this are evidence that all people, white Americans included, ought to be more concerned about the abuses of law enforcement, and I agree with him. But by making the cause of criminal justice system solely about race—by blaming whiteness itself for the subjugation of all black bodies—Black Lives Matter may have turned what should be a broadly popular agenda into a fringe crusade. No wonder it's floundering in the era of white identitarian backlash.

I do not mean to suggest that BLM is uniquely radical or pernicious, or to paint an overly rosy portrait of the civil rights movement by comparison. It's easy to romanticize its best elements, like the inspirational message of Martin Luther King, while forgetting about groups like the Black Panthers, a black nationalist fringe group that advocated—and practiced—violence against the police and others. Eldridge Cleaver, a leader of the Black Panther Party, wrote in his memoir *Soul on Ice* that he was guilty of serially raping white women as "revenge." Black Panther founder Huey P. New-ton was accused of numerous crimes, including murder, assault, and embezzlement. And their group was much more obviously radical in that the Panthers had an explicitly socialist ideology. In his essay "On the Ideology of the Black Panther Party," Cleaver wrote that Marxism-Leninism was their guiding ideology, and black people who didn't grasp that were "like crabs that must be left to boil a little longer in the pot of oppression before they will be ready and willing to relate."[48]

At its best, BLM is calling attention to the fact that certain injustices—police abuse, poverty, discrimination—are more likely to be visited upon people of color. If your neighbor's house is on fire, you shouldn't throw up your hands in frustration and declare that actually, all houses matter—you should try to help your neighbor. The statement "Black lives matter" is not an assertion that *only* black lives matter, or that black lives matter more than other lives. It's just a recognition of an unfortunate reality: historically, black lives have not mattered as much as they ought to.

But explicitly identity-based appeals can backfire. And inter-sectionality might make them more likely to backfire, by lump-ing together a bunch of not-necessarily-related identity-based appeals.

When I asked Alicia Garza whether she thought the rise of white nationalism was in part a backlash against her own move-ment's activism, she responded, "I do. I think it is a response to the changing demographic in this country, and globally, with the decline of white people in the U.S. and around the world. But," she went on, "I also think it is a response to an increasingly suc-cessful movement to actually get closer to the ideals that this country was founded under."

FOUR

BURN THE WITCH

FOURTH-WAVE FEMINISM AND #METOO

Before there was the #MeToo movement, there was Emma Sulkowicz and her mattress.

And when Sulkowicz graduated from Columbia University in the spring of 2015, the mattress—a symbol of female perseverance in a violent patriarchal world—went with her: she carried it across the stage, with help from several friends, as she walked up to receive her diploma.

Over her years on campus, Sulkowicz—an attractive young woman with a streak of purple hair, a millennial hipster's sense of fashion, and an interest in performance art—had become the figurehead of the sexual violence awareness movement on college campuses, which held three truths to be self-evident: (1) that one in five women on campus would be raped, (2) that only between 2 and 8 percent of women lied about rape, and (3) that most campus rapists were serial predators who attacked over and over again. The first and most important of these self-evident truths—that the sexual violence rate for college women was somewhere between 20 and 30 percent—became a rallying cry for young feminists in the 2000s, drawing its staying power from a series of surveys that purportedly testify to its accuracy (more on that later). Taking the statistic seriously meant taking seriously the notion that American women not only are threatened by rape but live in a culture that explicitly condones it: a *rape culture*. The movement demanded not just that the broader public recognize the existence of rape but also an acknowledgment that rape is omnipresent: in schools, in homes, in the workplace, in politics, in Hollywood, and everywhere else.

Sulkowicz's journey to the national spotlight began during her freshman year at Columbia University in 2011. (She initially responded to my request to interview her for this book, but failed to answer subsequent emails.) Among her circle of friends was Paul Nungesser, a German student. According to text and Facebook messages sent between the two that were later obtained by the press as part of Nungesser's lawsuit, Sulkowicz first broached the subject of sex with respect to her then boyfriend, who was sleeping with other girls. She asked Nungesser, a friend of her boyfriend, to persuade him to use condoms when he slept around. Their conversations became increasingly intimate after that, and Sulkowicz was not shy about showing interest in Nungesser.

By the end of the year, they had entered into what the kids still refer to as a "friends with benefits" arrangement. According to Nungesser's lawsuit, they had vaginal sex and, at Sulkowicz's insistence, anal sex. (Sulkowicz's text messages suggest, though do not confirm, that she expressed interest in this.) During summer break, Nungesser returned to Europe but stayed in touch with Sulkowicz, who graphically relayed her sexual adventures while maintaining that Nungesser was her true object of affection. She frequently told him that she loved and missed him.

On their first day back together at Columbia, on the night of August 27, 2012, the two again engaged in vaginal and anal sex. But they drifted apart after that, with contact between the two becoming less and less frequent. In his lawsuit, Nungesser maintained that Sulkowicz became "vicious and angry" over time as she realized that Nungesser did not feel the same way about her as she did about him.

Half a year later, in April 2013, Sulkowicz reported Nungesser to Columbia's Office of Gender-Based and Sexual Misconduct. She claimed that the encounter began consensually but that Nungesser failed to obtain consent to have anal sex with her. She also said that he choked her.

The university investigated the matter, consistent with its obligations under a federal statute known as Title IX (more on that later). Nungesser maintained that the sex had been consensual, and a panel of administrators cleared him of wrongdoing the following November. Neither party was happy with the proceedings. Nungesser, for his part, had not been allowed to show the administrators the friendly Facebook messages Sulkowicz sent to him just hours after the alleged assault. Sulkowicz, of course, was dissatisfied with the results of the investigation and decided to go public. In the spring of 2014, she named Nungesser as her attacker—the details of the alleged crime were reported in major media outlets—and vowed to carry her mattress with her to class until he was brought to justice. "My rapist still goes to my school and is still on campus," she said.

The young woman had unleashed a tidal wave.

Awareness about the twin problems of sexual harassment and sexual assault is where progressive activists have left perhaps their most visible mark over the past decade. The landscape for gender activism and anti-rape activism has fundamentally changed both explicit rules and informal norms, and not just on campus. The #MeToo movement—which inspired so many women (and some men) to come forward and publicize their mistreatment at the hands of exploitative and abusive figures such as Harvey Weinstein, Kevin Spacey, and even Donald Trump—might not have been possible without intersectional fourth-wave feminism. This brand of social-media-savvy female empowerment dates to about 2010 and is distinguished from previous waves of feminism by its laser focus on sexual harassment and violence. (For comparison, the dominant issue of first-wave feminism was women's suffrage.) Fourth-wave feminism owes its existence to people such as Sulkowicz, anti-GamerGate crusader Anita Sarkeesian, and online feminist commentary sites such as *Jezebel*, *Feministing*, and *Everyday Feminism*. Julie Zeilinger, a twenty-four-year-old feminist writer and author of the book *A Little F'd Up: Why Feminism Is Not a Dirty Word*, told me in an interview that discovering the "feminist blogosphere" was particularly essential to her evolution as a feminist.

"I was just sort of exposed to these hilarious but really intelligent younger women," she said. "It was a perspective and a voice that I never heard before and really resonated with me."

Undeniably positive things have resulted from feminist advocacy. It was certainly a long time coming, but media companies such as NBC, Fox, Netflix, and Amazon Studios are finally holding men in positions of power accountable for mistreating women in the workplace. The public is listening to victims and believing what they say. Fourth-wavers are following in a proud tradition of feminists fighting for equal rights—and eventually achieving them. And though the election of Donald Trump—and rejection of Hillary Clinton—was undoubtedly a blow to feminists, it was tempered by the fact that Hillary's victory would have landed her husband, an accused rapist, back in the White House. Bill Clinton's fraught relationship with feminism finally appeared to come undone in 2016: the *New York Times*' Michelle Goldberg, echoing several other high-profile left-of-center pundits, wrote that the former president "no longer has a place in decent society" because of his behavior toward Monica Lewinsky, Juanita Broaddrick, and others.[1] Even the feminist activist and writer Gloria Steinem, who had famously defended Bill's lechery in 1998 on partisan political grounds—critics accused her of inventing a "one free grope" rule—partly walked back her earlier stance, telling the *Guardian*, "I wouldn't write the same thing now."[2]

Many people forget the role progressives played in defending Clinton from charges of impropriety. The seven-million-member progressive advocacy group MoveOn.org was formed in 1998: it was named for the desire of its originators to persuade the public to move on from the Clinton-Lewinsky episode. Twenty years later, MoveOn.org is gleefully tweeting #MeToo along with everyone else—a gutsy move for an organization that was born of a desire to sweep the president's sexual misconduct under the rug and now reflects the new priorities of the left.[3]

And yet, for all the broader societal good that has resulted from recent gender-related activism, a crusade of the most devout has left campuses reeling from a series of witch hunts that fundamentally reshaped the norms of human interaction for college-aged young people, and not necessarily for the better. In response to a storm of activity from militant young feminists, campus administrators and the federal government enacted a new regime of far-reaching policies. Critics of these policies—the author of this book included—claim that they abrogate the due process rights of students charged with sexual misconduct, threaten free expression as it relates to sex, grow the campus bureaucracy, violate the law, and rest upon bad statistics and junk science.

"This erasing of distinctions between the criminal and the loutish was a central feature of the campus initiatives of the Obama administration and led to many unjustified punishments," wrote Emily Yoffe, a contributing editor at the *Atlantic* and an important critic of leftist feminism's excesses, in an article for *Politico*.[4]

Gender-based activism overlaps substantially with the causes of the movements discussed in earlier chapters. Readers will recall from Chapter One that intersectionality was invented for the purpose of linking the struggle for women's rights with the struggle for black people's rights. Zillennial feminists are consciously and deliberately intersectional, and they are perfectly willing to shame fellow feminists who do not promote racial and sexual equality as well.

"Our identities aren't singular," Juniper, the trans Berkeley student, told me. "Issues are never just a race issue. They're never just a gender issue. So for myself, I'm queer, but I'm also brown, and I'm also super-poor. So all the identities to me just mix up, and that creates my experience."

Intersectionality can make it difficult to separate individual slices of the activist pie. Even so, explicitly feminist activism has notched considerably more victories than the anti-Trump resistance or Black Lives Matter, and thus it's possible to take a close look at the kind of world these activists want to create—they have come closer to realizing it than many of their comrades. And if the subtext of the previous chapters was that illiberal activism can undermine the noble causes it claims to support, the subtext of *this* chapter is that illiberalism itself creates problems.

The Waves

Equal political rights was American feminism's first cause; second-wave feminism, which began in the 1960s, took a broader approach to equality. It was during this decade that the idea of describing feminism as a series of waves first appeared, courtesy of a 1968 *New York Times* article titled "The Second Feminist Wave."[5] (Coincidentally, this same issue of the *Times* contains a profile of Marcuse that brands him the leading philosopher of the "new left" and sympathetically relates his assertion that it is "self-defeating" for society to extend tolerance and free speech rights to everyone.)

The article concerned a new-to-the-scene activist group, the National Organization for Women, and featured interviews with some of its young, radical members—including twenty-nine-year-old Ti-Grace Atkinson, president of NOW's New York chapter, who was quoted as saying she'd grown bored with advocating for legalized abortion; the issue was just too tame. "I'd rather talk about the demise of marriage," she said.[6] Her cause célèbre was abolishing the family as a unit, preferring that children be raised communally—a practice with which some communist countries had experimented.

NOW's president, Betty Friedan, was more conservative than

Atkinson, but her thinking was still revolutionary for the time. In her 1963 book *The Feminine Mystique*, Friedan posited that women not only were oppressed because they had been denied political equality but also were subjugated by culture and tradition in a society that relegated women to domestic roles as wives and mothers.

One of the most important works of second-wave feminism, Susan Brownmiller's 1975 book *Against Our Will: Men, Women and Rape*, focused on the role sexual violence played in the subjugation of women. Rape was a political act, according to Brownmiller, a "conscious process of intimidation by which all men keep all women in a state of fear." The popular though unscientific notion that rape is about power rather than sex, oft-recited by today's gender activists and even ordinary media figures, can be traced to *Against Our Will*; sociobiologists have been arguing with feminists about it ever since.

Second-wave feminism fought for women's sexual autonomy—including access to contraception and abortion rights—but eventually disputes arose within the movement over the hot topics of pornography and prostitution. The sex-positive wing of the movement viewed attempts to restrict pornography, for instance, as infringements on sexual expression and the rights of women, and as a capitulation to religious puritanism. But leading feminists such as Steinem, Andrea Dworkin, and Catharine MacKinnon took a different view. In her 1981 book *Pornography: Men Possessing Women*, Dworkin defined pornography as "the orchestrated destruction of women's bodies and souls." MacKinnon, who today serves as a visiting professor of law at Harvard, took the position that porn was a form of "forced sex" and should be outlawed as sexual discrimination.

Other feminists, describing themselves as individual-rights feminists, fought back against Dworkin, MacKinnon, and Steinem. One such individual-rights feminist, the lawyer Wendy Kaminer, reserved especially harsh criticism for Steinem, given Steinem's associations with the repressed-memory recovery movement, a

1980s-era moral panic in the United States. Younger readers will be surprised to learn that the repressed-memory movement united sex-negative feminists with some conservative Christians, psychotherapists, social workers, and gullible news reporters who all believed that children throughout the country were being sexually abused by Satanic cults; the children, when questioned extensively (read: coached) by agenda-driven therapists, would "remember" their abuse. "The newest category of feminism, personal-development feminism, led nominally by Gloria Steinem, puts a popular feminist spin on deadeningly familiar messages about recovering from addiction and abuse, liberating one's inner child, and restoring one's self-esteem," Kaminer wrote in the *Atlantic* in 1993, as the panic had begun to subside. "The marriage of feminism and the phenomenally popular recovery movement is arguably the most disturbing (and potentially influential) development in the feminist movement today."

On the other side, defenders of the recovered-memory movement insisted that the public must believe the children who claimed to be victims of abuse. This became the movement's mantra; in fact, the people involved in the most visible Satanic abuse episode, the McMartin preschool trial, even named their advocacy organization Believe the Children. The McMartin family, accused of witchcraft, sodomizing the children in their preschool, and magically transporting them to an underground lair to participate in orgies, were eventually cleared of wrongdoing.

Media coverage finally soured on ritualistic Satanic child abuse as the public came to its senses in the 1990s. Debunked as junk science, the recovered-memory movement faded into, well, memory. Also forgotten was the pivotal role second-wave feminism played in motivating the townsfolk to take up pitchforks. According to the *New York Times*, Steinem donated money to the McMartin investigation. *Ms.*, the feminist magazine she cofounded in 1971, ran a cover article with the title "Believe It! Cult Ritual Abuse Exists" as late as 1993.[7]

"In the coalition powering the satanic abuse persecutions

feminists constituted a powerful component, most conspicuously in the form of Gloria Steinem and Ms. Magazine," wrote the journalist Alexander Cockburn in a 1999 article for the magazine *Counterpunch*.[8]

Steinem and her allies largely lost the argument concerning the various moral panics—porn, prostitution, Satanism—that divided their movement. As the 1990s marched on and Gen X came of age, second-wave feminism gave way to third-wave feminism.

In many ways less well defined than second-wave feminism—feminist scholar Elizabeth Evans said that confusion about its definition was "in some respects its defining feature"—third-wave feminism was nevertheless inarguably more laid-back and permissive when it came to vice: very much a reaction against second-wave feminism's Victorian tendencies.[9] Aesthetically, third-wave feminism was heavily influenced by girl-positive punk rock acts such as Bikini Kill and Bratmobile, dubbed "riot grrl" music. The reclaiming of the word "girl" was arguably part of a backlash against second-wave feminism, which had rejected the concept of "girlhood" as patronizing—an attempt by powerful men to put women in their place. Third-wave feminism, though, was more concerned with creating positive, affirmative identities for women than with advancing specific political goals. Second-wave feminists thought bras and makeup were tools of the patriarchal oppressors; third-wave feminists thought women should wear high heels if it made them feel good about themselves, and avoid them if not. Destroying the very idea of family itself was not on the agenda, thank goodness.

But the idea that people should automatically believe the alleged victim of a sexual crime—irrespective of the credibility of the accuser or plausibility of the accusation—did not die with second-wave feminism. Like the spirit of Sauron, it endured in spectral form until conditions were favorable for its return.

In an interview, Kaminer told me that the censorious "therapeutic feminism" of the 1980s "has thrived on college campuses, engendering broad definitions of sexual harassment and assault, restrictions on allegedly misogynist speech and behaviors, and curbs on the due process rights of alleged offenders. Off campus, it spawned the excesses of the #MeToo movement."

Around the same time that third-wave feminism was transitioning into the more energized, rape-culture-fighting fourth-wave feminism of the present day, activists were working tirelessly to broaden the definition of rape. "No means no" gave way to "Yes means yes," the slogan for the affirmative consent movement, which held that it was not enough for men to back off when they heard the word "no"—they should never even move forward in the first place, the new thinking goes, unless they hear the word "yes."

"More and more sexual acts that previous generations might have filed under 'Terrible College Experience' are being reclassified as offenses that can earn banishment from the Ivory Tower," wrote the journalist Vanessa Grigoriadis in *Blurred Lines,* her 2017 book about the millennial generation's changing norms of sex and consent. "The legions of young men and women who have and will come forward to speak on this topic are caught up in one of the greatest cultural shifts to happen on American campuses in decades: a reframing of sexual dynamics."

Sulkowicz's case is an imperfect representation of the new battles over consent, but it was the one that caught the most media attention, generating an abundance of activist activity. After she became a national heroine for the anti-rape cause, feminists at countless campuses carried mattresses to protests in a show of solidarity. Her crusade even served her own academic purposes: Columbia's School of the Arts permitted her to spin the mattress protest as her senior thesis. In carrying her mattress with her wherever she went on campus, Sulkowicz was not just striking a blow against rape culture; she was also completing her degree. (It was this action that later led Nungesser to file suit against Columbia for, in his view, sanctioning Sulkowicz's campaign of harassment, despite the university's finding of his innocence. Columbia settled Nungesser's suit for undisclosed terms.)

Many of the activists who were most passionate about destroying this rape culture were themselves alleged victims of sexual assault, though they preferred the term "survivor," which gave them a feeling of greater agency. The stakes were personal. They had the harrowing stories: Mattress Girl, their own ordeals, and countless others. They had the statistics. Increasingly, they had the attention of the media and the public—even the Obama White House vowed to do something about campus sexual assault. And perhaps most important, they had each other: the power of the internet had made it much easier for activists at Columbia to compare notes with activists at the University of North Carolina, to identify commonalities, discuss tactics, and even catch each other up on the latest lingo.

"Memes, like Sulkowicz's mattress, viral survivors' tales, and the brilliant and merciless tactics of young activists started to turn a tide that had, for decades, flowed only one way," wrote Grigoriadis in her book. "The power of web-based sharing met the power of belief, creating an epistemic certainty among girls about the frequency of assault."

Epistemic certainty creates fertile ground for change, but not always fertile ground for self-reflection. The campus revolution to combat sexual assault has emboldened a lot of young women, but it's also had dire consequences for certain liberal values—free expression and due process chief among them. Like so many revolutionaries, the activists occasionally overreached. In the specific case of recent feminist activism, the government—unbeknownst to most of the public—provided the activists with a powerful weapon: a little-known, seemingly innocuous federal statute called Title IX.

Title IX has been so essential to the fourth-wave feminist cause that Annie Clark and Andrea Pino, two purported survivors of sexual assault and activist crusaders in the vein of Mattress Girl, got the Roman numeral "IX" tattooed on their ankles.

No One Expects the Title IX Inquisition

In the fall of 2016, a University of Tennessee student named Keaton Wahlbon had to take a test in Professor Bill Deane's earth science class. One of the questions—a joke question—asked, "What is your lab instructor's name? If you don't remember make something good up."[10]

Wahlbon did *not* remember his female lab instructor's name, as it turned out, so he followed the instructions and wrote down the first random woman's name that popped into his head: Sarah Jackson.

Sounds like a common name, no? It is. It's also the name of a Canadian lingerie model (something neither Wahlbon nor the author of this book was aware of).

"I had no idea it was the name of a nude model," Wahlbon told me when I interviewed him for *Reason*.

When Wahlbon got his test back, he had received a grade of zero. The grader had written "inappropriate" next to the Sarah Jackson response.

Wahlbon emailed the professor, insisting that he had no idea "Sarah Jackson" was a nude model. Deane wrote back: "I have no way of determining your intention. I can only consider the result. The result is that you gave the name of Sarah Jackson, who is a lingerie and nude model. That result meets with Title IX definition of sexual harassment. The grade of zero stands and will not be changed."

More than a year earlier, in January 2015, administrators at the City University of New York sent an email to faculty instructing them to cease using gendered salutations in their written correspondence: "Mrs.," "Mr.," and the like. When asked why such instructions were necessary, an administrator told the *Wall Street Journal* that the school was only trying to meet its Title IX obligation.[11]

Then there was Matt Boermeester, the University of Southern California (USC) football player expelled for alleged sexual misconduct. The striking thing about Boermeester's case was that his supposed victim—his girlfriend, Zoe Katz—never made any accusations against him. Instead, a neighbor who saw the couple and assumed they were fighting told Boermeester's coach, who then informed the university, consistent with Title IX requirements. The university initiated an investigation, but when it asked Katz about what had happened, she told the investigators in no uncertain terms, "The report is false." The investigators were unmoved by Katz's denials, and Boermeester was expelled anyway.

Boermeester took the matter to court. His expulsion was stayed, but a judge ruled in September 2017 that he couldn't return to campus until the broader matter was decided. This did not please university officials; a lawyer for USC told the court she was worried "that the stay would keep future victims of sexual assault or harassment from coming forward at USC and send the message there was something 'erroneous' about the investigation," according to the *Los Angeles Times*.[12] For the university, the sanctity of the Title IX process was what mattered most.

You're probably wondering: What on earth is Title IX, and why did this law become both an indispensable tool for gender activists and a source of grave concern for civil libertarians?

Title IX is part of the Education Amendments of 1972, the federal law that stipulates the conditions under which educational institutions can receive funding from the government. Title IX itself is just one sentence long, and states: "No person in the United States shall, on the basis of sex, be excluded from participation in, be denied the benefits of, or be subjected to discrimination under any education program or activity receiving Federal financial assistance."

Legislators who crafted the statute intended to prevent schools from discriminating against women's educational and extracurricular activities. In subsequent decades, Title IX was used to ensure that educational institutions were funding clubs and sports teams for women. Schools could not prevent someone from enrolling in a class or using a certain facility because of that person's biological sex. Exceptions were made—for example, schools didn't have to make their locker rooms co-ed—but they did have to *provide* locker rooms to female students if enough of them wanted to start a basketball team. More recently, the Obama administration determined that Title IX's anti-discrimination provision also applied to gender identity, casting doubt on whether a publicly funded school could legally refuse a biologically male student who identifies as female from using the girls' locker room. (This is dealt with in Chapter Five.)

Title IX enforcement falls under the purview of the Office for Civil Rights (OCR), an agency that exists within the Education Department. It's OCR's job to determine whether primary and secondary schools are meeting their Title IX obligations; the agency informs an institution that it needs to make certain changes to be in compliance, the institution reforms itself, and life goes on. Again, the statute OCR is responsible for interpreting and enforcing is just one sentence long.

On April 4, 2011, everything changed. That's the day OCR released its infamous "Dear Colleague" letter.[13] The letter was sent to the University of Montana but was intended as a blueprint for all universities that receive public funds. In the letter, OCR maintained that sexual misconduct, harassment, and violence were forms of sex-based discrimination and thus outlawed under Title IX. "All such acts of sexual violence are forms of sexual harassment covered under Title IX," wrote Russlynn Ali, who was then assistant secretary of OCR, in the letter. In order to continue receiving millions of dollars from the federal government, schools needed to make a concerted effort to root out sexual harassment and rape on campus.

If OCR's letter had merely required colleges and universities to involve themselves in the business of policing rape, the effects would not have been particularly large—colleges and universities already had in place a wide variety of strategies for reducing sexual violence on campus. But the "Dear Colleague" letter also sought to standardize these practices under the auspices of a forty-year-old federal statute.

OCR insisted upon three key changes. First, university administrators would be required to use a preponderance-of-the-evidence standard when determining whether sexual misconduct had taken place. This standard—essentially 50 percent certainty of a wrongdoing plus a feather, or an abstract belief that it is more likely than not misconduct took place—is easier for accusers to meet than the beyond-a-reasonable-doubt standard, which is required in criminal trials. Before OCR released its 2011 guidance, some colleges and universities employed a clear-and-convincing-evidence standard, which holds that a level of about 75 percent certainty is needed for a finding of responsibility. Overnight, this became forbidden. In September 2014, the last holdout in the country, Princeton University, lowered its standard of proof from clear-and-convincing to preponderance-of-the-evidence.[14]

Supporters of the change note that the lower standard of proof is used in civil procedures, and college sexual misconduct tribunals are more akin to civil than criminal procedures, for one big reason: Princeton doesn't have the power to send anybody to jail. Institutions of higher education do have the power, however, to effectively ruin the lives of students found responsible for sexual misconduct: a guilty verdict could mean expulsion, thousands of dollars lost in tuition, and social pariah status.

Of course, it's still possible for administrative boards to make correct determinations, despite a lower standard of proof. OCR's second new requirement, however, further undercut legal safeguards for the accused.

"OCR also recommends that schools provide an appeals process," the letter stated. "If a school provides for appeal of the findings or remedy, it must do so for both parties."

This was no less than an enshrinement of what's called double jeopardy in the criminal justice system. Even if a student was found innocent of sexual misconduct, the complainant—OCR's term for the accuser—could appeal the decision. On appeal, administrators would again be using the lower evidentiary standard.

Finally, the "Dear Colleague" letter explicitly discouraged universities from allowing the complainant and the respondent (OCR's term for the accused) to cross-examine each other. "Allowing an alleged perpetrator to question an alleged victim directly may be traumatic or intimidating, thereby possibly escalating or perpetuating a hostile environment," the letter stated.

This meant that if a student had accused another student of sexual misconduct, the accused would not enjoy the ironclad right to confront the accuser during the hearing. But cross-examination is a fundamental component of due process, and one of the best tools a wrongly accused person has of establishing innocence. With the release of a nineteen-page document, OCR had gutted it.

"What you ended up having and still have today are policies and procedures that I think are incredibly unfair and inequitable toward the accused," Andrew Miltenberg, an attorney who has represented dozens of accused students in campus sexual misconduct cases, told me in an interview. "You have staff members and administrators and investigators that have been hired during, trained during, and put in place to carry out policies that arose and were written during this time immediately following the 2011 'Dear Colleague' letter, which again meant that the view was toward very aggressive prosecution, for lack of a better word, of the accused when it comes to campus sexual assault."

But due process was not the only liberal principle under threat by the "Dear Colleague" letter; OCR's new guidance also raised important free speech concerns.

In its previous correspondence with colleges, OCR had typically cited the Supreme Court's definition of sexual harassment. According to the 1999 decision in *Davis v. Monroe County Board of Education,* the Court had held that offensive behavior could not be considered sexual harassment unless it was "so severe, pervasive, and objectively offensive" that it "undermines and detracts from the victims' educational experience" in a manner that fundamentally denies the victim a right to an equal education. Otherwise, said behavior would be considered free expression under the First Amendment.

"Severe, pervasive, and objectively offensive" is a strict standard. But OCR made no mention of it in its instruction to universities to get serious about sexual harassment. And in subsequent guidance the agency continued to send mixed messages about what kind of conduct amounted to sexual harassment and what kind of conduct was protected speech. For instance, in a letter to Frostburg State University, OCR informed the institution that its sexual harassment policy was in violation of Title IX.[15] The offending policy stated that "in assessing whether a particular act constitutes sexual harassment forbidden under this policy, the rules of common sense and reason shall prevail. The standard shall be the perspective of a reasonable person within the campus community." This phrasing—using "common sense" and a "reasonable person" test—was a problem for OCR.

It's no wonder that OCR's dictates raised red flags with civil libertarians. The Foundation for Individual Rights in Education was particularly concerned. "FIRE worries that schools seeking to comply with OCR's increased emphasis on sexual harassment education and prevention will fail to promulgate and disseminate sexual harassment policies that provide sufficient protection for student speech," wrote FIRE's attorneys in a letter to OCR.

FIRE was right to worry. In the years since the "Dear Colleague" letter, campus after campus has hired a massive bureaucracy of coordinators, investigators, and compliance officers to ensure that the Obama administration's quixotic interpretation of a one-sentence statute is being observed. OCR's standard operating procedure has been to announce an investigation into a university, and then close the investigation by offering the university a chance to adopt all of the agency's recommendations and keep its federal funding.

It did not take long for activists to grasp the punitive powers of Title IX. The raw numbers bear this out: in 2005, 5,335 complaints were filed with the office. Ten years later, 10,392 complaints were filed. In 2005, just 11 of 5,000 complaints specifically mentioned sexual violence (rather than harassment or nonviolent discrimination). By 2015, there were 164 such complaints.[16]

Most of the broader public has probably never heard of Title IX. But it is central to activist life on campuses. In 2013, two survivors of campus sexual assault cofounded an anti-rape advocacy group; they named it Know Your IX. Their goal was to spread awareness of a powerful weapon in the feminist tool kit.

One of the best examples of activists using the new understanding of Title IX to wreak havoc was the inquisition directed at Northwestern University film studies professor Laura Kipnis.[17] In February 2015, Kipnis wrote an essay for the *Chronicle Review* about the new norms of sex and consent on campus. Kipnis contended that millennial feminism was at times worrisomely Victorian, and wrote fondly of her own time as a student, when it was not uncommon for students and professors to engage in sexual relationships. Kipnis also wrote in measured defense of a Northwestern professor, Peter Ludlow, who she believed was being railroaded by the administration. (Ludlow was accused of sexual misconduct and later resigned after Northwestern found him responsible for harassment.)

To say that Kipnis's essay enraged Northwestern's students would be an understatement. First, they protested her—as was their right. They also started a petition asking the university to condemn Kipnis's "toxic ideas . . . because they have no place here." Finally, two students filed formal Title IX complaints against her. Central to these complaints was the idea that Kipnis, in writing things that were critical of the young woman who had accused Ludlow of mistreating her, had "retaliated" against her. And Title IX prohibits retaliation, according to OCR.

"Both complainants were graduate students," wrote Kipnis in a follow-up article. "One turned out to have nothing whatsoever to do with the essay. She was bringing charges on behalf of the university community as well as on behalf of two students I'd mentioned—not by name—because the essay had a 'chilling effect' on students' ability to report sexual misconduct."

What Kipnis has called "my Title IX inquisition"—a reference to the investigations of heretics undertaken by the medieval Roman Catholic church—involved Northwestern flying in a team of lawyers to investigate her alleged wrongdoing. Kipnis herself was not permitted to have an attorney; instead, she was allowed a support person. This person's activism on her behalf eventually generated Title IX accusations as well, and the supporter was removed from the proceedings.

Weeks later, Kipnis was sensibly found not responsible. But consider the message sent to those who would criticize the excesses of modern feminism: *question us, and face the consequences*—the consequences being possible punishment, censorship, and loss of employment.

Kipnis's ordeal is an eye-popping example of activists using the Title IX process to harm a critic, though by no means the only one. In my years writing about campus issues, I've seen Title IX cited over and over again as the pretext for launching an investigation, or muzzling a student or faculty member over an act of clearly protected expression. Criticizing Title IX is itself a possible violation of Title IX, as Kipnis discovered: her essay about the deficiencies of a Title IX proceeding involving a colleague became the grounds for a new investigation with Kipnis as its target. In this sense, the new interpretation of Title IX is a modern example of Catch-22, the fictitious World War II–era edict from Joseph Heller's book of the same name. (From the book: "'Didn't they show it to you?' Yossarian demanded, stamping about in anger and distress. 'Didn't you even make them read it?' 'They don't have to show us Catch-22,' the old woman answered. 'The law says they don't have to.' 'What law says they don't have to?' 'Catch-22.'")

In the more than two years since the investigation, Kipnis has become a leading critic of this strained application of Title IX, and even published a book on the subject, *Unwanted Advances: Sexual Paranoia Comes to Campus.* But not everyone targeted by a Title IX investigation possesses the ability to capitalize on the ordeal and make something positive out of it. Many innocent students—particularly those who are subjected to inquisitions based on alleged sexual violence—suffered steep penalties. Consider the case of Grant Neal, a former Colorado State University–Pueblo student. Like Boermeester, Neal was a football player; unlike Boermeester, he was black. Neal's girlfriend, a student and athletic trainer known as "Jane Doe" in the eventual lawsuit, was a white woman.

Neal and Doe kept their blossoming romance a secret, since sexual relationships between athletes and trainers were frowned upon at Colorado State, though by no means formally outlawed. But a friend of Doe's suspected something and confronted Doe. For reasons unknown, this friend then contacted the athletic department, concerned that Neal had hurt Doe. When Doe found out, she texted Neal, "One of the other Athletic Training students screwed me over! . . . She went behind my back and told my AT advisor stuff that wasn't true!!! I'm trying so hard to fix it all."[18]

Later, Doe told an athletic coordinator, "I'm fine and I wasn't raped."

One might have expected that to be the end of it, but no: athletic department heads informed Doe that they were required under federal law to report her alleged mistreatment to the proper authorities. This federal law was Title IX.

And so, despite the alleged victim's protestations that she wasn't actually a victim of anything, the university's Title IX office launched a sexual misconduct investigation against Neal. While the investigation was under way, officials banned Neal and Doe from seeing each other—a no-contact order that Doe willingly chose to violate, since she did not view Neal as a threat to her safety. Doe sent him messages using the social media app Snapchat; concerned that he could get in even more trouble because of this, Neal approached Roosevelt Wilson, the Title IX officer. Wilson instructed Neal to open the snaps, screenshot them, and send them to Wilson. Neal did this, only to later receive a message from Wilson warning him that by opening the snaps—in order to screenshot them, so as to comply with Wilson's instructions—Neal "could potentially be in complication with your no contact order."

When I interviewed Neal about his ordeal in February 2017 (the investigation took place in the fall of 2015), he told me that had been the moment he first realized the situation was out of his control.

Neal would never appear before a panel charged with determining his guilt or innocence; CSU-Pueblo practiced something called the "single-investigator model," which invests just one administrator with the powers of an entire panel. Under a single-investigator model, a lone Title IX official investigates the allegations of sexual misconduct, decides which witnesses are relevant to the case, makes notes about the evidence he gathers, and produces a report containing a recommendation. This report is then handed off to another administrator, who often endorses its conclusion, whatever that may be.

This model will strike many readers as brazenly unfair—critics have characterized it as essentially designating one person to play detective, prosecutor, judge, jury, *and* executioner—but it is nevertheless the model recommended by the White House Task Force to Protect Students from Sexual Assault, established in 2014.[19]

As the sole investigator, it was Wilson's job—and his alone—to investigate Neal. That meant that no one but Wilson could decide which people to interview and what evidence was relevant to the case.

"He refused to let me see any statements or evidence against me," Neal told me. "All the evidence I brought to him was . . . he said he would—quote, unquote—he said he would deem things as evidence if he would like to."

Wilson eventually submitted his report to Jennifer DeLuna, director of diversity and inclusion at CSU-Pueblo, in December 2015. DeLuna gave Neal twenty-four hours to appear before her. Neal was permitted to bring legal counsel, but his lawyer was not allowed to speak to Neal during the meeting.

"The legal counsel was there as mental and emotional support," Neal told me. "I was allowed to review the documents and investigation against me, but I was not allowed to leave the room. I was not allowed to get up to use the restroom. I was not allowed to take pictures or copies."

Wilson's report consisted of his *impressions* of conversations with the witnesses he had selected to be interviewed. His conversation with Doe, for instance, was not transcribed directly into the report. Neal was effectively denied any means of proving his innocence—DeLuna could do nothing but rely on the evidence deemed fit for her perusal. Neal was found responsible for sexual misconduct based on a preponderance of the evidence made available to DeLuna, and suspended until Doe's graduation.

"It was basically an expulsion," said Neal. "I am not able to transfer to any other university, although my academic and athletic status would allow me to transfer to almost any major university in the nation. I applied to five different universities and all the denials were basically worded in the same way: 'You're a great student, we'd love to have you on campus. You seem to have the athletic ability to be a part of our program as well. But based on the findings of CSU-Pueblo, we can't have you on our campus.'"

It took years for Neal to achieve a measure of justice: in July 2017, his attorney, Miltenberg, announced that Neal had settled with the university. The terms of the deal remain private—it is unknown whether the financial settlement was sizable enough to repair Neal's formerly bright future, or make up for the years he spent living under a cloud of suspicion. As part of the settlement, CSU-Pueblo admitted no wrongdoing in the course of its Title IX investigation.

Who are these administrators situated within the vast bureaucracy that handles sexual misconduct on campus? Many were hired or retrained over the last decade to bring their universities into compliance with Title IX. Some are academics who moonlight on misconduct adjudication panels (in cases where panels are used in place of the single-investigator model). According to attorneys who have been involved in campus sexual assault proceedings, these people are disproportionately drawn from certain academic fields, including gender studies, that might make them more likely to inherently believe female accusers.

Justin Dillon, an attorney who represents accused students in sexual misconduct cases, gave me an example. He said he once had a case at Oberlin College where a student found responsible for sexual misconduct had appealed the decision; the appeal went to a single appeals officer, who ruled against the student. But this appeals officer had once retweeted the sentiment "To survivors everywhere: we believe you" from the group End Rape on Campus. For Dillon this was a clear example of bias: the appeals officer had expressed an enthusiasm for automatically believing sexual assault claims.

Dillon attempted to make Oberlin aware of its appeals officer's bias, but to no avail. "We notified Oberlin of that and they said we don't think that shows that he would be biased in this case," said Dillon. "Which is kind of like saying no one can prove that David Duke is biased against any individual black person."

Over the course of half a decade of robust Title IX enforcement, it became more and more common for campus sexual misconduct disputes to end with lawsuits. Alleged victims whose accusations were discounted could contend that the school had broken federal law, creating a sexually hostile and discriminatory environment. And alleged perpetrators—the truly guilty and the truly innocent alike—could point to a long list of civil liberties to which they should have been entitled but were nevertheless denied under the "Dear Colleague" understanding of Title IX. Some defenders of the rights of the accused, including FIRE, have even claimed that OCR violated the Administrative Procedure Act, a statute that requires federal agencies to publicize proposed new rules and subject them to scrutiny before enacting them. (OCR countered that the "Dear Colleague" letter was not a new rule but rather a clarification of an existing rule.)

Endless lawsuits work to the advantage of no one—except lawyers—and a sense took hold among many skeptics that the Obama-era Title IX approach just didn't work. In 2016, President-elect Trump—empowered to counteract much of the Obama agenda—chose Betsy DeVos to serve as secretary of education. DeVos, an outsider just like her boss, quickly began soliciting input on what, if anything, should be done about perceived Title IX overreach. In the fall of 2017, she formally rescinded the "Dear Colleague" letter and promised to de-weaponize Title IX.[20]

But a withdrawal of the "Dear Colleague" letter has not meant that colleges were required to get serious about due process, or return to an earlier understanding of sexual harassment.

"Most universities have essentially doubled down or reaffirmed their commitment to the pre-DeVos policies," Miltenberg told me. "Which is interesting because you would have thought that, or I think we would have liked to have seen that, the withdrawal of the 'Dear Colleague' letter would have led to, if nothing else, perhaps a more transparent and equitable procedure. But in my view that's very much not what's happened. Very much the opposite."

In fact, nearly all college presidents who reacted to the news publicly signaled opposition to DeVos's changes, and vowed to continue robustly investigating sexual misconduct.

Why? One reason is probably the ongoing pressure from the newly empowered campus activists and their network of allies. *Ms.*, the magazine that had continued to promote the Satanic child abuse conspiracy long past its expiration date, wrote in the wake of DeVos's new Title IX guidance that "DeVos' remarks echo the talking points of men on the so-called alt-right . . . who raise the specter of widespread false rape allegations in order to deny survivors justice and uphold a rape culture."[21] *Ms.* went on to highlight the important work activists were doing to fight DeVos tooth and nail. The Feminist Majority Foundation accused DeVos of sweeping rape under the rug.[22] When DeVos spoke at Harvard University some weeks after her Title IX announcement, student activists in the crowd held up signs accusing her of being a white supremacist—an ironic charge, given that more robust due process protection in campus sexual misconduct cases would probably *help* students of color, who are likely disproportionately represented among the accused.

"I think that this activism has become an intimidation, a tactic of terror, if you will, on many campuses that leaves administrators very frightened," said Miltenberg.

At the end of 2018, DeVos took firmer steps to rein in Title IX, releasing a list of proposed reforms that would eliminate the single-investigator model, mandate some form of cross-examination, and limit actionable sexual harassment to behavior that is severe, pervasive, and offensive to a reasonable person. These are very sensible changes, from a due process perspective, and could re-balance the scales of justice for those accused of wrongdoing on college campuses. Expect fourth-wave feminists to fight the changes every step of the way.

Indeed, campus sexual misconduct exposes another weakness of intersectionality: competing interests among the marginalized. Several critics of modern Title IX enforcement—including the *Atlantic*'s Yoffe and Harvard University law professors Janet Halley and Jeannie Suk—have noted that immigrant students and students of color seem to be accused of sexual misconduct at stunningly high rates. Hard statistics are difficult to come by, but a survey of one institution, Colgate University, found that 50 percent of students accused of sexual assault in the 2013–14 school year were black men—even though they represented just 4 percent of the student population.[23] Anecdotally, I can say that Title IX disputes often involve a white female accuser and a black male.

The history of racism in the United States is a history in which white women falsely accused black men of sexual impropriety. Consider Emmett Till, a fourteen-year-old black male who was lynched by southern racists in 1955 after a white woman accused him of sexual misconduct for whistling at her. Till's murder helped to galvanize the civil rights movement; his casket is currently on display at the National Museum of African American History and Culture in Washington, D.C.

What's happening to men of color on campus is of course nowhere near as horrific. Even so, in today's climate it would be very problematic to point out the legacy of white women wrongly accusing black men of sexual crimes. Gender is a matrix of oppression, as is race. But intersectionality offers no guidance for adjudicating competing claims of identity-based oppression, nor does it recognize that there are circumstances where marginalized status is an advantage (female defendants are generally treated more leniently than male defendants, for instance). When it comes to campus Title IX trials, gender and race are in tension: being black is a handicap, as it is in other matters concerning the criminal justice system, but being a woman is not.

Statistical Violence and Serial Predators

If Title IX was fourth-wave feminism's sword, and "believe the victims" its clarion call, the statistics of sexual assault served as the movement's codex. Zillennial gender activism is grounded in three scientific claims, and every intersectional feminist who joined the movement in college knows them by the numbers: one in five (or one in four), 2–8 percent (sometimes 2–10 percent), and 90 percent. These numbers correspond with statistical findings relating to sexual violence and are beyond reproach, according to the activists. The numbers were run, and run, and run again, and there is no longer any doubt.

One in five women will be sexually assaulted while in college. It's something every left-of-center entity believes, from Alyssa Milano to NARAL.[24] Op-eds in student newspapers that take the university administration to task for failing its Title IX obligation inevitably reference the one-in-five statistic. The Obama White House's Task Force to Protect Students from Sexual Assault even mentioned the statistic in its thirty-four-page report issued on January 22, 2014. President Obama and Vice President Joe Biden both said it in speeches.[25]

"It's a significant fact that one in five women who attends college can expect to experience sexual violence," writer Julie Zeilinger told me.

Some accept the statistic because it jives with personal experience. "I believe in the one in five statistic wholeheartedly because I am a survivor and I remember how many of my friends disclosed that it had happened to them too," Laura Dunn, an attorney and executive director of sexual assault prevention at SurvJustice, told

Inside Higher Ed. "Most women don't doubt this statistic because we are aware in our conversations how common sexual violence is in our experience."[26]

But the statistic is based on much more than mere conjecture. Its originator was Mary Koss, a professor of public health at the University of Arizona, who in 1987 first produced the research that suggested nearly a quarter of college students had experienced rape. Subsequent studies, including a 2015 poll of college students conducted by the *Washington Post* and the Kaiser Foundation, produced a similar number.[27]

Disputes over methodology have prompted pushback against the one-in-five statistic among the broader public. In surveys, many women describe having survived harrowing ordeals that meet the interviewer's definition of sexual assault—and thus count toward the total—even though the women themselves do not identify as rape victims. The *Post*/Kaiser survey defined sexual assault as "forced touching of a sexual nature, oral sex, vaginal sexual intercourse, anal sex and sexual penetration with a finger or object," but only 9 percent of women said they were assaulted in this manner.[28] More women, 14 percent, said they had experienced "unwanted sexual contact" while they were drunk, drugged, or asleep. Being drunkenly groped at a party is indeed bad, but does it really belong in the same category as forcible rape? The one-in-five statistic is composed of a whole lot of problematic sexual behavior, but not all of it was considered sexual assault by the people to whom it happened.

The second statistic has received less scrutiny, even though it's equally important to the anti-rape movement: *only 2 to 8 percent of rape reports are false.* This statistic provides intellectual support for the believe-the-victims mantra: since victims are rarely lying, the public should follow the strategy of automatically believing claims. There just aren't enough liars to make disbelief or caution a reasonable strategy. As Hillary Clinton put it, "Every survivor of sexual assault deserves to be heard, believed, and supported."[29] (In practice, of course, Clinton has made exceptions to this policy in cases where the accused was her husband.)

But much like the one-in-five statistic, the 2–8 percent rate of false reports relies on a shakier foundation than most activists concede. Its most extreme version—just 2 percent of rape victims are lying—is an unscientific, evidence-free conjecture made by a public servant and copied into *Against Our Will: Men, Women, and Rape*, the 1975 book authored by second-wave feminist Susan Brownmiller.

Studies have produced a wide range of false report rates: on the low end, the 2010 study "False Allegations of Sexual Assault: An Analysis of Ten Years of Reported Cases" found a false report rate of 5.9 percent.[30] On the high end, a 1994 study by the sociologist Eugene Kanin produced a false report rate of 40 percent.[31] But the limitations of these and other studies on this subject are striking. In order for the police to label a report as false, they had to produce significant evidence that the accuser lied; otherwise, a possibly false rape was simply listed as unproven. Additionally, researchers could use only the data available to them, which means they ran the numbers on rapes reported to the police. But when it comes to campus sexual misconduct, accusations are often reported to someone other than the police: a professor, a coach, an administrator, a Title IX official.

It's possible that alleged victims are incredibly unlikely to file false police reports but somewhat more likely to embellish a story when talking with a sympathetic professor or administrator. It's also possible the activists are right—the rate of false reports made to *any* authority figure is very low, and the cases labeled as "unproven" were simply insufficiently investigated. Then again, it's also possible that a significant number of unproven police cases and unfairly investigated Title IX episodes represent genuinely false accusations. Unfortunately, as *Bloomberg View*'s Megan McArdle wrote in an article about false rape report statistics, "We don't know. Anyone who insists that we do know should be corrected or ignored."[32]

Last but not least is the serial predator statistic: *most rapists are repeat offenders, and perhaps as many as 90 percent of rapes are committed by serial predators.* This number has not provoked nearly as much controversy as the one-in-five and 2–8 percent statistics, perhaps because it seems comparatively innocuous. Indeed, it even appears to explain the discrepancy between the huge number of alleged victims of rape and relatively small number of accused rapists. Amanda Marcotte, a well-known contributor to the feminist blogosphere, put it this way in an article for *Slate:* "That 1 in 5 college women have been assaulted doesn't mean that 1 in 5 men are assailants. Far from it. A study published in 2002 by David Lisak and Paul Miller, for which they interviewed college men about their sexual histories, found that only about 6 percent of the men surveyed had attempted to rape or successfully raped someone." Her article went on to explain that the "high rates of campus sexual assault are due mostly to a small percentage of men who assault multiple women."[33]

The serial predator theory is indeed the handiwork of one psychologist: David Lisak, formerly of the University of Massachusetts at Boston. His study, "Repeat Rape and Multiple Offending Among Undetected Rapists," released in 2002, supposedly found that most college rapists attacked multiple women—an average of 5.8 each.[34]

It would be difficult to understate just how influential this theory and the man behind it have become over the last decade—and not just among activists. Lisak was cited in the 2014 White House memo on campus sexual assault prevention, and in training materials for university Title IX coordinators. He was referenced more than a hundred times in *Missoula,* Jon Krakauer's 2015 book about sexual assault at the University of Montana.[35] His thinking undergirds *The Hunting Ground,* the Oscar-shortlisted 2015 documentary that argues campus rapists essentially prey upon women (Lisak even appeared in the film). Lisak was paid to give talks at colleges and universities; people who wanted to understand the way rapists think have turned to Lisak, who has repeatedly suggested that he extensively interviewed the serial predators captured by his study.[36] The notion that campuses are scary places filled with serial sexual predators rests on an intellectual foundation built by Lisak, as do activist efforts to reduce due process and make blind faith the only reasonable reaction to an accusation.

But in early 2015, an administrator at Davidson College made an interesting discovery: the survey data for "Repeat Rape and Multiple Offending Among Undetected Rapists" were not collected by Lisak. Rather, he used data collected by his graduate students for four separate studies; these studies were about violence and abuse, but not campus sexual assault specifically.

Linda LeFauve, an associate vice president of planning and research at Davidson, had been surprised to learn that 90 percent of campus rapes were perpetrated by serial predators who committed an average of nearly six rapes each. "That sent up statistical red flags that became more concerning when the claims about premeditation and psychopathic tendencies were added," she later told me in an email. "When virtually all incidents of a complex act are supposedly the result of a rare psychological type, my skepticism goes on high alert."

She read Lisak's paper, but that only gave her more questions. And so in March she telephoned Lisak.

Lisak confirmed that the data were not his own but rather his graduate students'. These feeder studies, Lisak told LeFauve, "may have been about child abuse history or relationships with parents."[37]

Some 1,882 men participated in the studies. Just 120 of them confessed to actions that met the legal definition of rape or attempted rape, and 76 of the 120 were repeat offenders.

"Lisak told me that he subsequently interviewed most of them," wrote LeFauve in an article for *Reason* that I helped edit. "That was a surprising claim, given the conditions of the survey and the fact that he was looking at the data produced long after his students had completed those dissertations; nor were there plausible circumstances under which a faculty member supervising a dissertation would interact directly with subjects. When I asked how he was able to speak with men participating in an anonymous survey for research he was not conducting, he ended the phone call."

A mutual friend put LeFauve in touch with me, and together we published a series of articles about the flawed scientific basis of the serial predator theory. Suffice it to say that Lisak did not respond to any additional requests for comment.

However, I was able to speak with James Hopper, a former student of Lisak's whose dissertation data were included in the 2002 study. "This is not a typical college sample," he told me when I interviewed him.[38]

Not typical at all: UMass Boston, for one thing, is a commuter school, and none of its students live on campus. Nor were the participants in the surveys necessarily all students; researchers set up booths on campus and asked men who walked past them if they would consider participating in a study. The average respondent was twenty-six and a half years old—older than the average student nationwide—and one participant was in his seventies.

Some participants checked a box indicating that they would agree to be interviewed at a later date. Based on my conversation with Hopper, who relayed some of my questions to Lisak, I was able to estimate that this applied to 22 of the 120 participants who were deemed serial predators. The purpose of the follow-up interviews was to double-check whether participants had given truthful answers, not probe the criminal mind for insights into psychopathy.

Let's recap the serial predator theory: it is based on just one study, situated at an unrepresentative commuter school, in which researchers asked men about their histories of domestic and child abuse. They were not asked specifically about violence they had committed on a college campus, at a college party, or inside a dorm room. They were not asked whether their victims were students. They were not asked whether they were students at the time they had committed the violence. They were not interviewed extensively by David Lisak.

And yet the campus serial predator theory is ubiquitous: the anti-rape activist movement treats it as foundational to their cause.

Lisak's work received little scrutiny until LeFauve and I dug into it. Around the same time that we published our investigative series, *JAMA Pediatrics* released a paper taking aim at the campus serial predator assumption's "surprisingly limited" scientific foundation. The paper concluded that "although a small group of men perpetrated rape across multiple college years, they constituted a significant minority of those who committed college rape and did not compose the group at highest risk of perpetrating rape when entering college."[39]

One of its coauthors was Mary Koss, the originator of the one-in-five statistic (not a rape denier, in other words). In an interview with me, Koss accused Lisak of deliberately promoting the idea that his research was relevant to the campus rape issue.[40]

Lisak, one presumes, did not take kindly to the suggestion that his research was out of date. Hopper went so far as to file a scientific misconduct complaint against Kevin Swartout, the lead researcher and Koss's coauthor of the *JAMA Pediatrics* paper. Georgia State University later cleared Swartout of any wrongdoing.[41]

What does it mean if the serial predator theory is false, or inapplicable to campus sexual assault? It dramatically increases the need for fundamental due process, for one thing. If most accused rapists have victimized five other women, the case for speedily ejecting them from campus appears stronger. But if the reality is that the campus sexual misconduct problem runs the full gamut— from obvious forcible rape to one-off drunken hookups that weren't perfectly consensual at all times—we must insist on the full set of legal protections for discovering the truth of the matter.

It's thus no surprise that activists are so fond of the serial predator theory, despite its flaws. As Vanessa Grigoriadis, the *Blurred Lines* author, said in an interview with *Slate:* "One tactic of the young activists who are primarily responsible for bringing sexual assault at colleges to some mainstream media is to make all sexual assault sound extremely violent. To make them sound like they are done by a very small group of serial predators, and to frighten Americans into thinking that if we don't change something at this exact second, people's daughters are in extreme danger."[42] When hunting for witches, first scare the villagers.

Believing Jackie

One of the most horrible sexual assault episodes in recent memory occurred at Vanderbilt University in 2013. Four football players—Brandon Vandenburg, Cory Batey, Brandon Banks, and Jaborian McKenzie—dragged a wholly unconscious woman into a dorm room and proceeded to beat, rape, and dehumanize her.[43] Vandenburg, who had been on a date with the woman before she passed out from drinking too much, slapped her in order to demonstrate to his teammates that she wouldn't wake up. Someone sodomized her with a water bottle. They took pictures of her in compromising positions. They raped her. Batey even urinated all over her hair. (Vandenburg, Batey, and Banks were all eventually convicted of rape; McKenzie received ten years of probation and lifetime sex offender status.)

I make note of the Vanderbilt case in order to dispel any notion that rape is a nonexistent problem. No one should take away from this chapter the idea that the college rape crisis is a myth: sexual assault is all too common, on campus and off. (The data suggest that for all the attention paid to the campus problem, college-aged women who aren't enrolled in school are actually at greater risk of being raped than female students.)[44] The debate is over the size, scope, and shape of the problem—with the activists often taking the most extreme position that patriarchal forces systematically oppress and violate women, particularly women who are, for identity-based intersectional reasons, extra susceptible to marginalization (women of color, trans women, women with mental health problems, et cetera).

But most sexual misconduct cases are thoroughly unlike the Vanderbilt case. Many involve some degree of ambiguity; such is the problem of mixing copious amounts of alcohol, party drugs, and horny teenagers. United Educators, an insurance company that covers universities' financial losses in sexual misconduct lawsuits, analyzed data from five years' worth of its cases. Victims were under the influence of drugs or alcohol 92 percent of the time, and 60 percent of the time were so intoxicated they couldn't clearly recall the assault.

Encounters often begin consensually, but different expectations or an inability to vocalize desires in the manner required by the affirmative consent doctrine make one party feel violated. In some cases, women who suffered through bad sex later recontextualized the experience as assault. "In the claims reviewed, the accuser often did not immediately report the incident, but waited days, weeks, or months before coming forward," United Educators noted in its report. While it's not always easy to draw bright lines between consensual sex and coercive assault, the activist assumption that all accusers are always automatically telling the truth further complicates the matter.

One of the best examples of the folly of this kind of thinking was the infamous *Rolling Stone*/University of Virginia debacle—a gang rape accusation that at first blush seemed even more horrific than the Vanderbilt assault. In November 2014, *Rolling Stone* magazine published a bombshell cover story about "Jackie" (full name withheld), a University of Virginia freshman who claimed that she endured a violent rape at a fraternity party. According to Jackie's account, her date, the pseudonymous "Drew," lured her into a dark upstairs bedroom, shoved her through a glass table, and invited eight or nine of his frat brothers to rape her as part of some kind of initiation ceremony. Jackie was fully conscious—she hadn't been drinking—as guy after guy took his turn. These attackers—monsters, truly—referred to her as an "it." Bleeding profusely from the glass shards digging into her back, Jackie finally passed out from pain.

Jackie came to hours later, bolted from the house, called her friends to rescue her, returned to her dorm room, and collapsed into bed. One friend, concerned that Jackie would develop a reputation as a tattletale and end up blacklisted from parties, advised her not to go to the cops. Jackie eventually told Nicole Eramo, an associate dean at the university, about her ordeal, but the administration's failure to do anything only succeeded in traumatizing Jackie a second time.

Jackie met Sabrina Rubin Erdely, a freelance writer and contributor to *Rolling Stone,* through Emily Renda, a University of Virginia graduate and mutual friend. Renda, who survived a sexual assault during her first year on campus, later became involved with the campus's Women's Center and sexual assault awareness advocacy.[45] She had served as a member of the White House Task Force to Protect Students from Sexual Assault and joined UVA's administration as a coordinator for sexual misconduct prevention. Renda had heard Jackie's story and offered the young woman emotional support; when Erdely called Renda, asking if she knew of any sexual assault survivors who might be willing to share their stories for a major magazine feature, Renda suggested Jackie.

Jackie agreed to speak with Erdely, but she made a major demand: Erdely could only use Jackie's first name, and she couldn't seek comment from Jackie's attacker. These terms were agreed upon by *Rolling Stone*'s editors, and the story went to print.

Jackie's tale, published in *Rolling Stone* as "A Rape on Campus," was horrifying. It was also a lie, and one that unraveled with remarkable speed. Within a few days, several critics—this author among them—began voicing concerns.[46] Erdely conceded that she hadn't sought to question Jackie's friends or attacker, but trusted Jackie implicitly. Privately, Erdely began to panic. She finally persuaded Jackie to provide the real name of her attacker: Haven Monahan. But no one named Haven Monahan had attended the University of Virginia during the semester of the attack.

Jackie's friends—who had, according to Jackie, declined to talk to Erdely—came forward to contradict key parts of her account. They were no longer in contact with Jackie and would have been happy to speak with a reporter, they said. It became increasingly clear that Jackie had had a crush on one of these friends and went to elaborate lengths to gauge his romantic interest in her: she sent him fake text messages from a made-up persona, a practice known as "catfishing." The made-up persona's name was Haven Monahan.

Rolling Stone was eventually forced to retract the article, though its editors waited months to do so. Nicole Eramo, the dean portrayed as unwilling to take Jackie's allegations seriously, sued the magazine and won $3 million in damages.[47] Phi Kappa Psi, the alleged scene of the crime, won $1.65 million in a settlement.[48] *Rolling Stone* initially seemed to have caught a lucky break with the third lawsuit, filed by individual members of the fraternity: a judge tossed out the lawsuit on the grounds that these young men weren't actually named in the story. But an appeals court reversed course, arguing that two of three fraternity brothers could plausibly argue that the article made indirect reference to them and would have caused people who knew them to suspect they were involved in the gang rape.[49] In December 2017, *Rolling Stone*'s founder and publisher, Jann Wenner, sold his controlling stake in the magazine. Erdely has yet to write another article for *Rolling Stone* or any other publication. Renda left her job at UVA and abandoned her work as an advocate for sexual assault survivors. (She did not respond to repeated requests to be interviewed for this book.)

"A Rape on Campus" was a complete disaster for everyone involved in its production, but things turned out *least* bad for Jackie, whose full name is known to reporters familiar with the story (including this one) but was never printed in any reputable news outlet. She kept her anonymity and avoided becoming the subject of a lawsuit. (I reached out to Jackie for comment; she did not respond.) The Charlottesville police declined to charge Jackie with making misleading statements to authorities; they refused to even characterize her claims as false.[50] (As the journalist Emily Yoffe observed in an interview with me for *Reason,* Jackie's unfounded rape accusation would not be counted in any false rape reporting statistic.)[51]

Nevertheless, some activists who count themselves in the believe-all-victims camp were undeterred. Zerlina Maxwell, a political analyst who hosts a progressive talk show on Sirius XM (the show's Twitter bio describes it as "'The Home of the Resistance!' #Resist #GetWoke"),[52] penned an article for the *Washington Post* titled "No Matter What Jackie Said, We Should Automatically Believe Rape Victims." The headline was changed to "Generally Believe Rape Victims" after readers pointed out the absurdity of this position, though the original title is still evident in the article's URL.[53]

"Disbelieving women, then, not only compounds their trauma (often by making them doubt their own stories), but it also lets a serial rapist go free," wrote Maxwell, citing the work of—you guessed it—David Lisak. "The time we spend picking apart a traumatized survivor's narration on the hunt for discrepancies is time that should be spent punishing serial rapists."

Jessica Valenti, the writer and founder of the essential feminist blog *Feministing*, wrote that the inconsistency in Jackie's story "does not mean she wasn't raped at UVA." Valenti wrote, "We already know that trauma victims often misremember details of their attack—but they also might give incomplete information because they are nervous that the full story will mean being blamed or disbelieved."[54]

The idea that victims of sexual assault are especially likely to forget key details because the ordeal was so traumatizing is quite popular among activists. It's even taught to Title IX coordinators as part of federally mandated "trauma-centered" training. The *Atlantic*'s Emily Yoffe spent significant time researching the origins and prevalence of such training. In Yoffe's telling, Rebecca Campbell, a professor of psychology at Michigan State University, is largely responsible for spreading these ideas.[55] Her 2012 talk at the National Institute of Justice, in which she asserted that victims' memories are scattered like "tiny Post-it notes" on a messy desk, is oft-referenced in Title IX training materials.

But there are major problems with this way of thinking about trauma. For one thing, there's a huge danger in telling adjudicators that if alleged victims seem confused, can't remember what happened to them, or misstate the circumstances of their attack, this should be treated as confirmation that they are indeed trauma victims. Under these circumstances, how would Title IX investigators separate actual victims from those who are plainly wrong or lying?

Second, the science is far from settled. Some neuroscience research, including the work of Harvard University psychologist Richard McNally, conflicts with Campbell's position, and suggests that "extreme stress enhances memory for the central aspects of an overwhelming emotional experience." When Yoffe asked UC Irvine psychology professor Elizabeth Loftus about the trauma-centered approach being taught to administrators, Loftus made an interesting point: it is reminiscent of the recovered-memory movement of the 1980s, in which therapists were supposedly able to help vulnerable people—often women and children—"remember" or otherwise dig up their buried past mistreatment. This was the bunk theory that undergirded the Satanic ritual abuse scare—a period of senseless panic and destructive McCarthyism in which second-wave feminism was morally complicit.

This is quite a reckless combination of beliefs, when taken together: (1) all victims should be believed without question; (2) if victims seem unreliable, they are more likely to be telling the truth as a result of their trauma; (3) the man they accused has probably raped multiple women and will continue to do so until he is stopped. And yet it's central to an activist movement that was incredibly successful over the last half dozen years in changing both norms and explicit policy relating to sexual misconduct.

It's easy to see how intersectionality reinforces these ideas. After all, the marginalized are the sole experts on their own marginalization, and it's not their job to educate everyone else. When Title IX activists talk about sexual assault, everyone else is supposed to believe them and not ask questions. Asking questions could traumatize them all over again—words hurt.

At many campuses, key faculty members—often in the fields of sociology or gender studies—have played an important role in circulating these ideas. Occidental College's Danielle Dirks, a professor of sociology, is a prime example. In September 2013, two freshmen became involved in a sexual misconduct dispute. Immediately prior to the encounter, the woman, "Jane," had texted a friend the message "I'm going to have sex now." She also texted her soon-to-be partner, "John," with a request for him to bring a condom. They then had sex.

KC Johnson and Stuart Taylor Jr., two men who have written extensively on campus sexual misconduct from a perspective that is sympathetic to due process arguments and skeptical of Title IX's excesses, wrote about the Occidental case in their book *The Campus Rape Frenzy*.[56] According to their account, Jane confided in Dirks, who "convinced Jane that she had been raped because she had been impaired by alcohol." Dirks also believed that John "fit the profile of other rapists on campus" because he had a high GPA, was class valedictorian in high school, was on a sports team, and came from a good family. Dirks later claimed that Jane had misunderstood her.

Jane eventually filed a police report. The officer investigating the case took a look at the text messages and concluded the evidence "supported a consensual encounter." A prosecutor agreed and took no action against John.

The Title IX proceeding went differently. At a hearing before a single adjudicator—where John was denied access to a lawyer—the young man was found responsible for sexual misconduct on the grounds that Jane had been too drunk to consent to sex. John protested that he had been drinking, too: if Jane was too drunk to have sex, then so was he. This argument did not sway the adjudicator, and John was expelled from Occidental.

But professors are not always so important to student activism, and students have turned on professors who crossed them or otherwise failed to accede to a suitably extreme position. Few have learned this lesson as memorably as Suzanne Goldberg, a professor of law at Columbia University and vice president for student life. In 2014, the administration appointed her to revise the university's sexual misconduct policies. A leading feminist attorney and gay rights hero—she served as cocounsel to the plaintiffs in *Lawrence v. Texas,* the Supreme Court decision that overturned sodomy laws—Goldberg would seem to be precisely the right person to meet the demands of Mattress Girl and the movement she created.

Alas, in the fall of 2017, a group of activists stormed Goldberg's Gender and Sexuality Law class.[57] Led by student Amelia Roskin-Frazee, the activists read a prepared statement denouncing Goldberg's complicity "in Columbia's culture of sexual harassment." According to Roskin-Frazee, "We are here today because despite the repeated efforts of student organizers, survivors at Columbia and Barnard are still endangered by administrators like Suzanne Goldberg." Columbia was a particularly dangerous place for queer students, Roskin-Frazee claimed, and this fact represented a betrayal of Goldberg's stated commitment to LGBT rights. (A generally applicable lesson of intersectionality is *no one is good enough.*)

When I asked Roskin-Frazee if I could interview her for this book, she emailed me back a one-word response: "No." I then pressed her for comment regarding her disruption of Goldberg's class, again asking her to speak with me.

"No means no," she responded.

It's About Power, Not Sex

Everyday Feminism published this on its website in December 2017: "10 Things Every Intersectional Feminist Should Ask on a First Date."[58] The very first question is not "What do you do for a living?" or "Where are you from?" or even "Is the food good here?" It's "Do you believe that black lives matter?" Anything other than an enthusiastic yes is a deal breaker for the author, and white dates should commit to "decenter their whiteness"—or reduce the importance of white people's achievements compared to those of minority communities.

Dates must also swear allegiance to the Boycott, Divest, and Sanctions movement against Israel. (The acronym: BDS, not BDSM!

That's something else.) And they must accept that capitalism is inherently exploitative. (For more on the anti-capitalism at the heart of the activist left, wait for Chapter Six.)

The article came across as parody to many, and non-leftists mocked it relentlessly on social media. But it was intended seriously, and it is in many ways a useful reminder that mere feminism is not enough for activist Zillennials: feminism must also be intersectional.

"Intersectionality is the acknowledgment that oppression, an experience of oppression, is produced by a number of factors based on your identity," Zeilinger told me when I asked her to define it. "Intersectional feminism is just a movement that acknowledges that, and also centers people who do have these experiences of oppression that maybe would make them even more marginalized and being really conscious about sort of correcting for that."

This position is in some ways admirable. Younger feminists are less likely to be content with generic girl-power sentiments, for example. They won't automatically support female candidates; they want candidates who are good on the issues—and not just feminist issues, but the full gamut of progressivism. Millennial feminists didn't unthinkingly vote for Hillary Clinton just because she was a woman: many, in fact, preferred Bernie Sanders, the more pro-gressive candidate. During the 2016 Democratic primaries, a Reuters poll showed Sanders winning the support of 61 percent of young women, versus 28 percent for Clinton. In the Iowa caucus, Sanders beat Clinton among women twenty-nine and younger by a margin of six to one.[59]

The Clinton-Sanders contest highlighted the divisions within feminism: many older feminists desperately wanted to see Clinton, a woman, occupy the White House, while many third- and fourth-wave feminists took an intersectional approach. That wasn't true across the board—one major millennial feminist, the actress Lena Dunham, served as an important Clinton campaign spokesperson, and even published an article in her newsletter that described the former secretary of state as "an idea, a world-historical heroine, light itself."[60] (Dunham declined to be interviewed for this book.)

But older, high-profile feminists formed something of a monolith for Clinton. During an appearance on *Real Time with Bill Maher,* Gloria Steinem herself chided younger feminists for "feeling the Bern," suggesting they were only doing it for boys' attention.[61] Marcotte, the forty-year-old feminist blogger, strenuously attempted to convince the internet that Sanders supporters (nicknamed the "Bernie Bros") were angry, sexist white guys, prone to harassing women who disagreed with them.[62] (From what I saw, Sanders's most vocal supporters were no more obnoxious than those of Clinton, Obama, Trump, Ron Paul, or any other political figure.)

"I saw a ton of second-wave feminists and older feminists support Hillary," Zeilinger told me. "For incredibly valid reasons, and reasons that a lot of [young] women did too, but also because it was very important to them that she was a woman. I heard the phrase 'I just want to see a woman elected in my lifetime' so many times."

It would be a mistake to think that this generational divide has rendered older feminism obsolete, however. Feminist icons like Steinem, Brownmiller, and the writer bell hooks are often quoted in activists' social media posts on Twitter, Instagram, and Tumblr. As with other kinds of activism, emerging feminists learn about the movement primarily from their peers, social media, celebrity influencers, and even family members.

Of all the ghosts of feminism past, it is Steinem who has managed to stay relevant—and strangely so, given her long history of questionable stances (her role in the Satanic ritual abuse panic, the excuses she made for Bill Clinton's mistreatment of women, and her recent bashing of young women who supported Sanders). In 2016, Vice Media aired her TV show, *Woman with Gloria Steinem,* on its network, Viceland. During the 2017 #MeToo uprising, after Vice was accused of fostering a hostile workplace for women, the company formed an advisory committee to course-correct and foster inclusion.[63] Steinem was immediately named to it, prompting palpable relief from many feminists. Bitch Media, another online feminist news outlet, said that Steinem would help Vice "get its shit together."[64]

Steinem has endured, and so has the second wave's obsession with believing victims. It's a belief with consequences: many of them undeniably good, given the number of sexually abusive media figures run out of Hollywood and politics in recent months. But it's also liable to be abused by zealots. I'll never forget a conversation I followed in a feminist Facebook group. One male participant had posted an image of two female news reporters caressing the oiled chest of Pita Taufatofua, the muscular male Tongan flag-bearer at the 2016 Summer Olympics in Rio de Janeiro, Brazil.[65] The guy posting the image asked, in rather trolling fashion, whether this was not an example of female-on-male sexism.

A female graduate assistant replied with a definitive no. "If you understand how the patriarchy works, then you understand how sexism can only be inflicted on oppressed genders," she wrote. "Go do some research please." Much like anti-white racism, anti-male sexism can't possibly exist—because, according to intersectionality, men are not a marginalized category.

FIVE

LGB VS. T

RADICAL TRANS ACTIVISM

"Fuck you, scared bitch," a student shouted at Kimberly Peirce as she took the podium.

Peirce, a filmmaker, had been invited to Reed College in the fall of 2016 for a screening of her landmark 1999 film, *Boys Don't Cry.* The movie tells the true story of a transgender man, Brandon Teena, who was murdered by bigots. For audiences in the 1990s, it was one of the first major films to portray a trans person in a positive light—prior to *Boys Don't Cry,* the most well-known trans character in cinema was probably Buffalo Bill, the psychopathic serial killer in *Silence of the Lambs* (not exactly an inspiring figure). Peirce herself has identified as a lesbian and genderqueer, and her movie contains a message of acceptance.

To say that Peirce was not well received at Reed would be a considerable understatement. Students hung profane posters near the podium; one read "You don't fucking get it." Waiting at the podium itself was a "Fuck you" poster, and students screamed other expletives at Peirce, bringing the event to an early close.

One would be forgiven for presuming that Reed must be some kind of Christian fundamentalist college brimming with intolerant, homophobic students, but alas, no: Reed is among the most liberal campuses in the country, according to the *Princeton Review*.[1] The students who jeered at Peirce were leftists.

In the eyes of these students, Peirce was a traitor. For one thing, she cast the cisgender Hilary Swank in the role of the trans character, a casting choice that marginalizes trans identities and contributes to trans erasure.

For another thing, Peirce profited from the exploitation of a trans person. Her film depicted violence against a trans person. This was unforgivable, in the students' view, even though *it actually happened* and Peirce's goal was to shed light on a tragic, socially significant event. (Recall from previous chapters that the young activist sees no distinction between words and actions and does not recognize important nuances; thus, making a film about the murder of a trans person is itself akin to violence.)

Lucía Martínez, an assistant professor of English at Reed College who identified herself as a "gay mixed-race woman," posted a comment on an article about the Peirce shutdown in which she confessed that these students terrified her.

"I am intimidated by these students," she wrote. "I am scared to teach courses on race, gender, or sexuality, or even texts that bring these issues up in any way—and I am a gay mixed-race woman. There is a serious problem here and at other [selective liberal arts colleges], and I'm at a loss as to how to begin to address it, especially since many of these students don't believe in either historicity or objective facts. (They denounce the latter as being a tool of the white cisheteropatriarchy.)"[2]

The "cisheteropatriarchy" is the intersectional progressive's nemesis. It refers to *cis* (as opposed to trans), *heterosexual* (as opposed to homosexual), and *patriarchal* (as opposed to female-centric) oppression.

Reed's activist students were upset about a lot more than just the cisheteropatriarchy, of course. The activist group Reedies Against Racism launched a continuous protest against Humanities 110, a mandatory first-year course that they say "perpetuates white supremacy" by neglecting to include black authors. (The group did not respond to a request to be interviewed for this book.) But the Peirce incident is illustrative, because it reveals a larger truth: the battles over gender, identity, and sexual violence on college campuses are at least as vicious as the battles over anything else.

Nationwide, the movement for LGBT equality has come a long way in a very short time. During my own school years, the word "gay" was often used as a slur, and people who openly identified as something other than heterosexual faced bullying and harassment. Conservatives successfully made gay marriage a wedge issue in the 2004 election, galvanizing the country's social conservatives. President Bush was reelected, and Republicans picked up seats in Congress.

A dozen years later, gay marriage is legal across the nation, and LGBTQ people enjoy unprecedented social acceptance. Kids find it strange that it was ever acceptable to mock people for their sexuality; it's more okay to be gay—or bisexual, or asexual, or even unsure—than ever before.

Except in the view of religious conservatives who still believe gay people are going to hell—a not insignificant number of Americans, to be sure, but an increasingly outnumbered (and aging) minority—this progress is admirable. Liberals, libertarians, and even many socially tolerant Republicans and conservatives agree that members of the LGBT community deserve the same rights and dignity as everyone else. I, too, celebrate these strides. And I join other libertarians and social liberals in wanting transgender people to achieve acceptance and equality as well.

What does it even mean to be transgender? The terminology and definitions have rapidly changed, keeping pace with medical innovations that give people a much greater ability to change their physical appearance to match how they feel inside. Fundamentally, to identify as trans is to have an internal sense of your gender that does not match your biological sex at birth.

Relatedly, many of the issues most important to the trans community have to do with physical and mental health: hormone therapy, surgery, at what age teenagers should be able to make decisions without parental approval, and more. There are also the increasingly fraught subjects of public restrooms, high school locker rooms and sports teams, what box to check on government identification cards, and whether other people should be compelled to use a trans individual's pronoun of choice.

In many cases, trans goals are perfectly reasonable and will likely come to pass as the country becomes more sympathetic toward them. But, as the incident at Reed shows, there's an illiberal streak within trans activism that might make the movement's goals seem less reasonable to the average person. The tendency of some trans activist leaders to make hyperbolic statements could be undermining a worthy cause—and putting them at odds with potential allies. Many of the loudest trans voices, particularly on social media, routinely decry all criticism of their activism as not just wrong but a form of assault. Nowhere else has the distinction between words and actions been so thoroughly eroded; people who criticize the trans community are accused of literal violence.

This strain of illiberalism occasionally puts radical trans activists in tension with other members of the LGBT acceptance movement. During the June 2017 gay pride march in Washington, D.C., a group of protesters chained themselves together and blocked the path of the parade. They were made up of members of the LGBT community who were "black, brown, queer, trans, gender nonconforming, bisexual, indigenous, two-spirit, formerly incarcerated, and disabled, and white allies."[3] They circulated a list of intersectional demands: an end to police involvement in the D.C. pride march, denunciation of corporate sponsors Wells Fargo and Lockheed Martin, and assurances that "trans women of color play a central role in decision-making processes." Gay people who languish under just one form of oppression are increasingly seen as relatively privileged and are thus in some danger of losing control of the LGBT movement to the multi-marginalized.

Or consider what happened to Katie Herzog, a writer for the Seattle newspaper *The Stranger*. Herzog is a progressive member of the left. She's no social conservative—she's a lesbian, in fact. In the summer of 2017, she wrote an article titled "The Detransitioners," about people who thought they were transgender but later changed their minds (more on detransitioning in a bit). Herzog was not claiming that transgender people are wrong or delusional—she very carefully pointed out that trans people wanting to revert to their previous sex is a rare occurrence, though it does happen. But for daring to question the idea that transitioning is always and automatically the right answer for all people who aren't feeling comfortable in their own skin, Herzog was subjected to a torrent of harassment.

"It was a total shit show," Herzog told me in an interview. "There were flyers up in my neighborhood, in coffee shops, calling me transphobic."

Activists burned stacks of the issue of *The Stranger* that had the piece in it, according to Herzog. She was asked to attend a "powwow with self-appointed members of the trans community."

"What started out as an awkward but collegial meeting quickly turned into fifteen trans women yelling at me and snapping and being incredibly hostile," she said. "People in the community wanted me to apologize, and they wanted the paper to invalidate the piece."

Again, I bring up these incidents not to suggest that trans people are particularly crazy—they aren't—but to point out the damage done by extremists.

Some of my criticisms even resonated with Parker Molloy, a trans woman and well-known writer on trans issues who is generally in good standing with the activist community. When I asked to interview her for this book, she sent me a two-thousand-word response decrying the lack of nuance in the things I had written about the trans community dating as far back as 2014. (I have no doubt that she will find plenty to disagree with here as well, though I learned a lot from speaking with her.)

"Most trans people aren't the militant caricatures you see on Tumblr or Twitter," she told me. "Most of them understand that there are nuances to these issues. It's just a lot of people, unfortunately, they're screaming so loudly that I think it distorts the perception of trans people entirely. They seem completely unwilling to listen to reason, which is not true of the trans population as a whole."

Scions of Stonewall

Broad awareness of trans issues is a relatively recent phenomenon, but trans people have always existed. They occasionally occupied prominent places in the gay rights movement; the 1969 Stonewall riots, one of the first notable pro-gay demonstrations, involved several trans women. At the time, they called themselves drag queens or transvestites, as the term "transgender" was not yet in use.

The riots were prompted by a police raid of the Stonewall Inn, a popular gay bar in New York City, in which thirteen people were arrested. According to historical accounts, a cop shoved one transvestite, who responded by hitting him with her purse.[4] At least two gender-nonconforming individuals, Marsha Johnson and Sylvia Rivera, were involved in post-Stonewall activism. They cofounded the Street Transvestite Action Revolutionaries, a group that worked primarily on behalf of homeless drag queens.[5] (Johnson died under mysterious circumstances in 1992—her body was found floating in the Hudson River—and Rivera died in 2002.)

"Some people wrongly think that trans people just appeared later, but they were always part of this movement," Molloy told me.

The marriage of gay activism and trans activism was difficult at best. In the 1970s, some gay and lesbian activists worked tirelessly to exclude trans people, for a variety of reasons. Jean O'Leary, a former nun, lesbian, and second-wave feminist, did not approve of men "impersonating women for reasons of entertainment or profit," and gave a speech at a 1973 gay pride gala in Greenwich Village, decrying this practice.[6] She was interrupted by Rivera, who called her a bitch. The singer Bette Midler attempted to smooth things over with a musical number, to no avail.

In truth, feminists have not always shown much interest in trans people. Germaine Greer, an Australian-born second-wave feminist and author of the influential book *The Female Eunuch*, opined in 1997 that a person who had transitioned from male to female should be denied a position at a women's university, on the grounds that the person was not actually a woman. To this day Greer continues to hold the position that trans women are not really women, saying in 2015 that "just because you lop your dick off and then wear a dress doesn't make you a fucking woman."[7] Her position makes her a leading trans-exclusionary radical feminist, or TERF for short. (The cleverest acronym I have ever encountered is the one used to describe radical feminists who are both sex worker exclusionary and trans exclusionary: SWERF and TERF, like the entree.)

Even the forty-four-year-old actress Rose McGowan, an activist in better standing with the feminist community, criticized *Glamour* magazine's decision to name Caitlyn Jenner its 2015 Woman of the Year. "Woman of the year? Not by a long fucking shot," McGowan wrote on Facebook.[8]

Clashes between certain radical feminists and radical trans activists have occasionally produced violence. Tara Wolf, a twenty-six-year-old trans woman, hit a sixty-one-year-old feminist, Maria Maclachlan, during a rally in London's Hyde Park in 2017.[9] Prior to the event, Wolf had written on Facebook that she planned to "fuck up some terfs," because terfs "are no better than fash," that is, fascists. At trial, Maclachlan pointedly refused to use female pronouns when referring to Wolf. The judge ultimately rejected Wolf's argument that she had struck the much older woman in self-defense, and fined the trans activist £150.

This episode exemplifies the tensions between a second-wave feminism that is worried about people who were born men co-opting their movement and a younger feminism that embraces all people who self-identify as women. The new view has largely won that fight, and this victory has influenced how the broader public discusses trans issues. It used to be said that a man undergoing surgery to become a woman was having a "sex change" operation—but this terminology implied that some underlying truth about the person was being altered. Trans people do not believe they are changing; they are becoming who they were always meant to be, and would have been, if not for random chance. (Indeed, one of the cruelest things you can do to trans people is call them by their birth name instead of the name they chose when they decided to transition—a practice known as "dead-naming.") "Sex change operation" gave way to "gender reassignment surgery," but even this terminology left something to be desired, since "reassignment" isn't really different from "change." The current, most politically correct way of referring to the procedure is "gender-*confirmation* surgery"—terminology that clearly tracks with Zillennials' general hunger for affirmation.

TERFism is clearly unpopular with Zillennials. It might be right to call this development an intersectional success story: younger activists rejected older activists' characterization of trans issues as distinct from gay issues, to the benefit of trans people. But the endless growth of the acronym LGBT, which first came into use in the late 1980s, is one side effect of this triumph. It initially stood for "lesbian, gay, bisexual, and transgender." Then a "Q" was added, which stands for "queer" or "questioning," depending on whom you ask. Next came "I" for "intersex"—people who possess the characteristics of more than one sex—and "A" for "asexual" (or for "ally," which could be anyone who supports the movement). And so on.

Complicating matters is the fact that sex and gender are different things, but often conflated: sex is biological, whereas gender is merely a cultural construct built around sex. Zillennials have made the matter even more complicated—for older Americans, if not for themselves—by subscribing to something called gender fluidity. Many young people—as many as a quarter of teenage Californians, according to one study—think of themselves as neither entirely male nor entirely female, and reserve the right to change how they identify over time.[10] Thus Facebook added fifty more options for the what-gender-are-you section of users' profile pages, including "genderqueer," "cisgender," "androgyne," "gender questioning," and "gender nonconforming."

Media companies' efforts to cater to the gender-fluid generation occasionally border on the absurd. The Zillennial news site *Teen Vogue*, for instance, ran a story with the headline "Gigi Hadid and Zayn Malik Are Part of a New Generation Embracing Gender Fluidity."[11] But the pair of teen icons did little more than don some vaguely gender-neutral clothing for a photo shoot.

Many conservatives are extremely hostile to the idea that sex and gender are mutable. The popular conservative author Ben Shapiro is well known for his invectives against the transgender movement, insisting that they are wrong to pretend that sex is alterable. "It's not rude to say that someone who is biologically male is a male," said Shapiro during a noteworthy debate with a trans reporter, Zoey Tur.[12] Shapiro thinks trans people should be permitted to live their lives however they see fit, but he has maintained that transgenderism is a mental disorder, and one that surgery does not always cure.

As a libertarian, I don't share Shapiro's view. There's nothing inherently wrong with wanting to change one's appearance and using modern technology to do so. Many trans people who feel that they were "born in the wrong body" live much happier lives after transitioning. Moreover, trans activism has played an indispensable role in normalizing the trans experience and helping the broader public to accept trans people as, well, people. Positive portrayals of trans characters in movies and television—Jeffrey Tambor in *Transparent* (though he was later #MeToo-ed) and Laverne Cox in *Orange Is the New Black*—were important as well. And of course, earlier films—including Peirce's *Boys Don't Cry*—helped pave the way.

Some of the most radical members of the trans community, though, are somewhat at odds with currently accepted science relating to transitioning. Indeed, the most contentious debate concerning trans issues has nothing to do with pronouns or bath-

rooms (though we'll get to those in a bit) but rather involves something called "desistance."

Desistance Debates

"Gender dysphoria" is the clinical term for the trans experience:
the feeling that one's internal sense of gender does not match one's
biological reality. It was known as "gender associative disorder" or
"gender identity disorder" until 2013, but the trans community
complained that it was wrong to think of the issue as a "disorder"
at all, and the terminology shifted to accommodate them.

For a trans person, the process of transitioning can involve
hormone therapy—estrogen for trans women, androgen for trans
men—and surgery. The process is life-affirming for most trans
people. But a small number of people who transition later change
their mind, no longer identifying as the sex and gender to which
they transitioned. People who undergo therapy and medical procedures to revert to their original sex are said to have "detransitioned."
This was the subject of Herzog's article—she spoke with several
people who had detransitioned about their experience.

No one could credibly claim that the detransitioners represent
a particularly large contingent: Herzog's article notes that just
2.2 percent of people who transitioned later experienced regret,
according to a Swedish study.[13]

A somewhat larger number of people, though, experience
gender dysphoria but never actually transition. Later in life, their
gender dysphoria ends, and they come to recognize their birth
sex as the one to which they feel they belong. For these people,
transitioning would have been a mistake. This is called desistance.
The science here is far from settled, but some mainstream research
suggests that, on the upper end, as many as 80 percent of young
people diagnosed with gender dysphoria—who identify as a gender
other than their birth gender—eventually desist.

"All else being equal, this research suggests that the most likely
outcome for a child with gender dysphoria is that they will grow

up to be cisgender and gay or bisexual," wrote *New York* magazine's Jesse Singal.[14]

Might this figure be substantially off? Certainly. Studies that arrived at it may have included too many subjects who were incorrectly diagnosed as gender dysphoric. Of course, in order to suss out the truly gender dysphoric, fairly invasive psychological questioning is probably necessary, which runs counter to the activists' desires. Young people, increasingly experimenting with gender fluidity and living outside the gender binary, are in some sense contributing to the confusion here—they may seem dysphoric to the casual eye, but they are really just interested in transgressing gender norms, not in changing their underlying sex. But pointing out this tension does not make one a proper intersectional ally.

One of the leading defenders of the 80 percent figure, the psychologist Kenneth Zucker, has been endlessly attacked for it—in fact, zealots in the trans community successfully got his clinic shut down after lodging a series of complaints that he was harming patients.[15] Zucker's Child Youth and Family Gender Identity Clinic in Toronto had taken a somewhat different approach to treating gender-dysphoric kids than the activists would have liked. Instead of practicing gender-affirming techniques—that is, presuming that his young patients were sincerely dysphoric and recommending a series of treatments to prepare them to transition—Zucker preferred to scrutinize his patients and see if it was possible to make them feel comfortable in their current bodies before proceeding down the path to transitioning. The activists claimed that Zucker was traumatizing the young people who entered his clinic—*how dare medical professionals scrutinize their patients*—in a manner akin to gay conversion therapy: the odious, immoral, and completely ineffective practice of trying to turn gay kids straight. Gay people virtually never desist from having same-sex attractions, but the fact is that gender dysphoria is different, and the best research we have suggests that some number of people who feel a desire to transition—possibly a very large number—change their minds.

Desistance has policy implications. If a large number of people diagnosed with gender dysphoria are eventually going to feel perfectly comfortable in their own skin (or at least no less comfortable than the average person), then it's important not to push serious medical intervention onto kids at an early age. Doctors need to be very, very sure the individual in question is actually interested in living as a different sex and not just experimenting with less rigorous gender definitions.

The World Professional Association for Transgender Health does not recommend gender confirmation surgery for anyone under the age of eighteen. But there are other options for gender-dysphoric teens. They can take puberty blockers, which delay the onset of puberty, giving them more time to decide whether they would like to eventually transition. This is ideal in cases where the individual is actually going to transition—it delays or disrupts certain permanent changes that are more difficult to reverse. Between ages fourteen and sixteen, they can begin hormone therapy, resulting in body changes that are semi-permanent. In some cases, teens who take puberty blockers and cross-sex hormones can become infertile. For the truly gender dysphoric, these are trade-offs well worth making—but the consequences underscore the need to be absolutely certain. Thus the relevance of desistance statistics.

Alice Dreger, a former Northwestern University bioethics professor who writes about gender issues, told me we are starting to see more people talk openly about detransitioning and desistance.

"The gatekeeping has become pretty permeable, and the consequence of that is you're seeing people who probably shouldn't have transitioned and are detransitioning," said Dreger. "These are not people who are angry and anti-trans, but they wish that they had had better screening and better care for their mental health issues."

But some transgender activists become irate when anyone takes these concerns seriously. Zack Ford, the LGBTQ editor at *Think-Progress,* has described desistance as a "myth," and frequently inveighs against Singal for daring to write about the issue.[16]

Singal wrote a cover story for the July/August 2018 issue of the

Atlantic about trans kids and desistance, prompting more outrage from the activist community. Molloy accused Singal of waging a one-man crusade against trans people.[17] Publishing him spreads "pseudoscience and bigotry," according to the writer Dawn Ennis. He was denounced by the Human Rights Campaign and GLAAD. *Jezebel*'s Harron Walker structured an entire article around the question "What's Jesse Singal's fucking deal?"[18] Walker seemed particularly infuriated that Singal would continue to write about trans issues even though some trans people had asked him to stop.

In covering trans issues, Singal in particular has several things working against him: namely, that he is a cis white man. He is not a member of the marginalized community about which he is writing, and thus he is not supposed to disagree with any of its leading members, according to the dictates of intersectionality.

Listening to what marginalized people have to say about their oppression is important, of course. But they should not be beyond reproach, Herzog told me. "Part of the left right now, wanting to always be on the right side of history, especially in light of everything that's happening with the Trump administration, is this knee-jerk reaction for allies to automatically just believe the trans people who are yelling the loudest, which I don't think does a service to anybody," said Herzog. "I understand why people do it, but still, just because a trans person has this perspective, it doesn't mean that it's necessarily correct."

Dreger, too, has gotten her fair share of criticism. Like Herzog and Singal, Dreger is no conservative. In fact, she turned down a fellowship at the Foundation for Individual Rights in Education because she was concerned that the donors were too right-wing. She has made invaluable contributions to the public understanding of intersex people.

Dreger has also written about controversies relating to transgenderism—in articles, and in her 2015 book, *Galileo's Middle Finger*. The book suggests that progressives have often fought as energetically as conservatives when encountering scientific conclusions that clashed with their beliefs. One prominent example highlighted in the book was the trans activist response to the work of psychologist J. Michael Bailey, whom Dreger has defended.

The controversy is complicated, but the gist is this: Bailey had posited that some very effeminate gay men transition to women because this makes it easier for them to pursue sexual relationships with other men, and some other male-to-female transitions arise out of a sexual desire to have a female body, something called autogynephilia. These motivations wouldn't make the trans women any less female, but some trans activists felt that such reasons would constitute a betrayal of the trans identity.

"The reason the trans activists first came after me was because they were trying to basically silence any discussion of autogynephilia," Dreger told me. "They came after me in a way that played into the standard progressive narrative, which is anybody who questions or raises anything uncomfortable about trans identity is an enemy of trans people."

Activists lashed out at Dreger with extreme malice. Some have even tried to get her events canceled by calling in threats of violence. "Some trans activists, not all, it's a very small number, will call my hosts and will make threats," said Dreger. "I've literally, in many cases, had to have armed guards at my talks. And I just find that ridiculous. Nothing has ever come of it, but it's concerning."

When Lambda Literary nominated *Galileo's Middle Finger* for a 2016 Lammy Award in the category of LGBT nonfiction, trans activists launched a campaign to have the nomination retracted.[19] Their efforts were successful.

The feminist blog *Everyday Feminism* once asked Dreger if it could reprint an article she had written that had nothing to do with trans issues: "What If We Admitted to Children That Sex Is Primarily About Pleasure?"[20] Dreger granted permission, and the article went up at the *Everyday Feminism* site. Some time later, Dreger discovered that the site's editors had tossed her piece down the veritable memory hole.

"What happened was that we decided to pull the article from circulation shortly after it went up," the editors admitted. "We weren't aware of some of the articles you've published on trans issues and after a reader brought it to our attention we looked into them. We then realized that while we very much valued the information in the article on teaching children that sex is about pleasure, the views expressed in several of your other articles directly conflicts with the work we're trying to do in *Everyday Feminism*."

"I've seen it over and over again where people are afraid to align with me, be seen with me," Dreger told me. "They do manage to terrify people into silence."

It bears repeating: this is not a criticism of the entire trans community, nor a denial of the dignity of trans people. None of the individuals cited here—Dreger, Singal, Herzog—are social conservatives: they all think trans people should be able to transition, and that this is a good choice for a whole lot of people. (And I agree with them.) The fact that they are radioactive in trans activist circles is revealing.

Bathroom Breaks

The desistance debate is inside baseball; readers who aren't particularly well versed in trans issues have probably never heard of it. I'd be remiss if I didn't spend some time on the more concrete policy issues that most trans people—and not just the activists—would like to see addressed.

In 2018, for instance, the Trump administration made good on a year-old promise to ban trans people from serving in the U.S. military. "Transgender persons with a history or diagnosis of gender dysphoria—individuals who the policies state may require substantial medical treatment, including medications and surgery—are disqualified from military service except under certain limited circumstances," according to a White House memo. The new approach called to mind the toxic "don't ask, don't tell" policy implemented during the Clinton administration, which barred gay individuals from serving openly in the military. Its repeal in

2011 was a major victory for supporters of LGBT equality, and the idea that this progress could suddenly be reversed for trans service members came as something of a shock.

Candidate Trump, after all, never seemed like a true believer in the cause of social conservatism. In fact, in his speech at the Republican National Convention in 2016, he promised to "do everything in my power to protect our LGBTQ citizens from the violence and oppression" of radical Islam. Advance copies of the planned remarks omitted the "Q" in LGBTQ, but Trump included it when the time came.[21]

President Trump, however, has discovered that evangelical voters are his most reliable supporters, and playing to this base is just good politics. Liberty University president Jerry Falwell Jr. described Trump as a "dream president," and Faith and Freedom Coalition president Ralph Reed told the New York Times that Trump had kept every one of his promises.[22] "God must have quite a sense of humor to have brought evangelicals and Donald Trump together," he said.[23] Members of the LGBT community—trans people most of all—are not laughing.

Trans people also feel threatened by government action at the state level. The Human Rights Campaign claimed that at least 129 bills that would have curtailed the rights of trans people were introduced in state legislatures during 2017.[24] Many of these bills, though, were fundamentally different from the ban on trans military members in that they did not actually mandate discrimination—they merely permitted private entities to decline to serve trans people. As most readers are no doubt aware, whether or not a private business such as a bakery can refuse to make a cake for a gay wedding on a First Amendment basis is among the most contentious modern legal questions.

Some anti-trans bills in the states go further than merely allowing private entities to engage in discrimination in accordance with their religious beliefs. A North Carolina law, in effect between 2016 and 2017, mandated that government buildings must require all people to use the public restroom that corresponds with the sex listed on their birth certificate, a problem for trans people who have not been able to get their status formally changed. The law's defenders claimed it was about safety, but there's no evidence that forcing trans women to use the men's room or trans men to use the women's room would do anything other than embarrass trans people.

"I feel like I, as a human being, should have that right to at least not have to basically announce, 'Hello, people of this restaurant, these are the genitals I was born with,'" Molloy told me.

Teen Vogue, the go-to site for progressive Zillennials, has called on states to mandate the use of gender-neutral bathrooms in order to "help remove the gender binary from everyday life."[25] Some public restrooms now feature a single room with a communal sink area and highly compartmentalized stalls that are much more private and secluded than in typical bathrooms. This seems like a promising development, regardless of whether erasing all gender distinctions is a worthwhile government pursuit.

The truly thorny public accommodation issue isn't bathrooms but school locker rooms, where students often have to change clothing in front of each other. There's an obvious conflict here: a trans person who identifies as a girl but still has a boy's body may feel uncomfortable using the boys' locker room, while other girls might feel uncomfortable sharing a locker room with the trans girl. Some conservatives have even suggested that mischief-making boys might announce that they identify as girls in order to gain access to the girls' locker room.

In 2016, the Obama administration's Justice and Education Departments issued guidance to schools instructing them that they were required under federal law to "treat students consistent with their gender identity even if their education records or identification documents indicate a different sex."[26] The law that obligated such action on the part of schools—at least in the minds of Obama-era bureaucrats—was Title IX, the gender equality statute discussed exhaustively in Chapter Four. Interestingly enough, the feds stopped short of recommending similarly egalitarian measures for school athletics. Title IX permits schools to maintain sex-segregated sports teams "when selection for such teams is based upon competitive skill or when the activity involved is a contact sport." I'm not sure how any reasonable person could have wrung such elaborate distinctions out of a one-sentence statute passed in 1972, but then again I am not the assistant secretary for civil rights. In any case, the Trump administration formally rescinded this guidance in 2017. To truly protect trans kids, activists and allies must lobby legislatures to pass laws that make these matters explicit.

Pronoun Problems

And then there are pronouns.

Many trans women—individuals who were born in male bodies but think of themselves as female—would like to be identified with feminine pronouns: "she," "her," "hers." Post-transition, this isn't quite so controversial: many trans women are indistinguishable from cis women, anyway. But trans individuals who still possess the sex characteristics of the gender with which they no longer associate may aspire to be identified using other pronouns, and this irks some people, many of them conservatives, who think language itself is being erased.

"I'm not in the mood for countenancing lies about what men and women are, specifically when I think that there is a goal of redefining a key term for the entire society," Ben Shapiro said in response to a question from a University of Connecticut student in January 2018. "A lie is detrimental to society."[27] I would posit that this isn't a particularly sympathetic position, and that affording people basic dignity would generally mean referring to trans women as women.

But there are somewhat trickier cases. Many trans people do not identify with either masculine or feminine pronouns and would prefer the generic pronoun "they." But "they" is a plural pronoun— it refers to more than one person. And while "they" is sometimes inserted into dialogue when "he or she" would be clunky, it can create confusion—at least in written language—when trying to single out an individual person in a conversation that contains multiple people. Abuse of "they" provides somewhat better evidence that rules of language are being eroded, and not for the better: a man can become a woman (though again, the activists would say that the person in question was *always* a woman), but a single person cannot become multiple people.

A potential solution to this problem is the invented gender-neutral singular pronouns, which are preferred by some members of the trans community—particularly on college campuses. The most common ones seem to be "ze" and "xe." For instance: "I saw Ashley at the protest yesterday. Xe was carrying a sign. Xer sign read, 'Impeach Trump.'"

There are others. The University of Wisconsin–Milwaukee's LGBT Resource Center lists "fae/faer/faers," "ey/em/eirs," "per/per/pers," "ve/ver/vis," "xe/xem/xyrs," and "ze/hir/hirs."[28] These haven't exactly caught fire, and they sound awkward to many people. Conservatives have had a field day parodying them. When the University of Michigan gave students the option of logging in to the web portal and choosing the pronoun that would accompany their headshot and be sent to teachers, conservative student Grant Strobl selected "His Majesty." He later clarified that he wasn't opposed to making reasonable accommodations for students outside the gender binary, but he didn't think it made sense to institutionalize such a policy.[29]

The most infamous stand against mandatory trans pronouns, of course, was made by University of Toronto psychologist Jordan Peterson. Peterson has become one of the best-known public intellectuals in recent years: his books, podcast appearances, and videos cater to a large audience of (predominantly, though not exclusively) young males who share his skepticism of political correctness. In 2016, Peterson claimed that a proposed revision to Canada's Human Rights Act would imperil his free speech rights. The bill, C-16, added gender identity and expression to a list of protected categories; Peterson said this would make it a crime to misgender a trans person or refuse that person's choice of pronouns. Peterson expressed varying degrees of willingness to use trans people's preferred pronouns but objected to the newer, activist terminology—"ze"/"xe" and the like—because these represented a postmodern neo-Marxist assault on the English language, in his view.

Peterson was never actually accused of misgendering a specific student—and told a young trans woman who wished to be called "she" that he would do so—but thought his commitment to free speech obligated him to denounce C-16, which became law the following year.[30]

Critics in the activist community accused Peterson of encouraging violence against trans people. Nicholas Matte, a lecturer in trans studies at the University of Toronto, alleged that Peterson was abusing students.[31] Matte also asserted that pronouns themselves were "part of a cisnormative culture"—that is, a culture in which the cis identity is wrongly seen as normal.

At Wilfrid Laurier University in Ontario, a teaching assistant named Lindsay Shepherd showed a clip from a YouTube video of Peterson discussing his perspective on the pronoun issue. In response, Shepherd was called before the university administration and warned about legitimizing perspectives that would make some students uncomfortable. Permitting a debate about whether to use gender-neutral pronouns had the effect of marginalizing the trans community and contributing to trans erasure—the systematic removal of trans people and the trans experience from public life.[32]

"These debates, regardless of how 'neutrally' they are presented, constitute a form of epistemic violence that dehumanizes trans people by denying the validity of trans experience," wrote Wilfrid's Rainbow Centre on its Facebook page. "We cannot allow for this profound violence to be continued."[33]

Jay Rideout, who identifies as a trans nonbinary queer person, claimed that allowing a debate about pronouns would silence trans students and constitute an endorsement of violence against them. "We need to acknowledge that debates that invalidate the existence of trans and non-binary people or dehumanize us based on gender are both a form of transphobia and gendered violence," wrote Rideout in an op-ed.

It's certainly true that members of the trans community experience a disproportionate share of violence. Trans people, especially trans women of color, are more likely to be killed than members of the general population.[34] The rate of attempted suicide among trans people is a whopping 41 percent, compared to just 5 percent among the general population, according to one study.[35] And of course there's at least some connection between trans people being treated disrespectfully and trans people dying or attempting suicide. But many in the activist community see offensive language itself as a form of violence, having accepted the postmodern arguments detailed in Chapter Two. Words can break bones just as easily as sticks and stones do.

Rebecca Tuvel, an assistant professor of philosophy at Rhodes College, found this out the hard way after penning a defense of Rachel Dolezal, the racial justice activist and African studies instructor who drew universal condemnation for identifying as black even though she was born white. In her "Defense of Transracialism," published in the feminist journal *Hypatia*, Tuvel argued that Dolezal's actions were much less ridiculous than they seemed; if we accept, as many on the left do, that people can identify as female even though they were born male, why is it unthinkable for people to identify as black when they were born white? How can the left embrace transgender people without even considering the possibility that there could be transracial people? (Race, after all, is more obviously socially constructed than gender. While our conception of gender is at least partly based on biological differences between the sexes, the same is not obviously true for race.)[36]

If intersectionality ever absorbs transracial individuals as a properly recognized marginal category, perhaps the treatments of Dolezal and Tuvel will be revisited. For now, Dolezal is a pariah, and Tuvel stands accused of "enacting violence and perpetrating harm" against the transgender community.[37]

Kelly Oliver, a professor of philosophy at Vanderbilt University who defended Tuvel, was similarly accused of violence. "Some said that Tuvel's article harmed them, and I was doing violence to them, even triggering PTSD, just by calling for an open discussion of, and debate over, the arguments in the article," wrote Oliver.[38]

Tuvel had compared Dolezal's situation to that of Caitlyn Jenner, and had discussed Bruce's transition to Caitlyn. In doing so, she called attention to the fact that Caitlyn used to be known—to the entire world—as Bruce. Nora Berenstain, a philosophy professor at the University of Tennessee, accused Tuvel of the forbidden act of dead-naming a trans person. But of course, it isn't wrong to acknowledge the basic fact that Caitlyn used to be called Bruce: everybody knows that, and Jenner is open about it.

Even so, several of *Hypatia*'s associate editors bowed to pressure and issued an unauthorized apology on behalf of the journal. "Clearly, the article should not have been published," they wrote.

Tuvel eventually apologized for using Caitlyn's birth name while remaining apoplectic that the trans community had reacted so unreasonably. "There are theoretical and philosophical questions that I raise that merit our reflection," she wrote. "I deeply worry about the claim that the project itself is harmful to trans people and people of color."[39]

An issue here is that intersectionality provides no basis for adjudicating claims of marginalization that might be in tension with one another. We know that marginalization stacks, and thus a disabled trans person of color is more marginalized than a disabled cis person of color (three matrixes of oppression versus two). But we cannot weigh one kind against another. The originators of intersectionality, of course, would not have foreseen this difficulty, because they concerned themselves primarily with sexism and racism. They had not considered the confusion that would result if their theory was extended to every possible grievance under the sun.

Molloy told me that she took issue with certain people equating wrongful pronoun usage and violence. "I think there are real issues with people saying words are violence, because violence is violence," she said. "That's something I see a lot: misgendering a trans person is violent, someone will say. I think it's more accurate to say that misgendering a trans person is an asshole move that can put them in danger of violence."

Stonewall Must Fall

In 2015, Colorado College's Film and Media Studies Department attempted to screen the movie *Stonewall,* and invited a producer to participate in a discussion with students. The film, a coming-of-age story about a gay teenager set during the Stonewall riots in 1969, had been critically panned and accused of whitewashing the actual history of late-1960s gay liberation. If students had merely complained about the film, they would have been in good company.

But Colorado College activists claimed that the film was not merely awful. To the extent that it had failed to properly credit trans people for the role they played in gay liberation, they said, *Stonewall* had either committed or encouraged violence against them.

"The film is discursively violent," a group of student activists affiliated with the campus's LGBTQIA+ chapter wrote in an open letter.[40] The students formed a new group, RAID (Radicals Against Institutional Damage), for the explicit purpose of boycotting the film and preventing it from being shown on campus.

A professor who supported screening the film told the student newspaper, the *Catalyst,* that even if the film was bad or if it was unfair to trans people, it was still worthwhile to have a discussion about it. The activists did not agree.

"Critical discussion is simply a way of engaging in respectability politics," Amelia Eskani, a first-year student, countered. "I think Colorado College should cancel the screening because the safety and well-being of queer and trans students surpasses the importance of a critical discussion."

Keep in mind that within the context of this debate, the thing supposedly undermining the safety and well-being of queer and trans students was a flawed but inarguably pro-gay historical documentary. One can imagine what the response from activists would have been had the film department attempted to show a movie with a socially conservative agenda.

It's true, of course, that trans people played an important role in Stonewall, but it would be totally ahistorical to negate the role of cis gay people entirely. And yet that's exactly what a subset of activists demand. A left-leaning political writer told an online magazine serving the gay community that he is often shouted down on social media by intersectionality-crazed activists who hate him for his "white privilege."[41] "People literally say that gay white men have done nothing for the movement for the last fifty years," he said. "They're not trying to make the movement intersectional; they're trying to erase other participants who came before them."

This man spoke to the magazine on condition of anonymity, and it's easy to see why. The oppressed are the experts on their own struggle; for others to criticize their tactics—or acknowledge their uncompromising nature—is highly problematic. When the *Guardian* asked RuPaul, the world's best-known drag queen and host of the queer-positive hit show *RuPaul's Drag Race,* about the "militant earnestness of the trans movement," *Vox*'s Caroline Framke suggested that there was something wrong with simply posing this question (Framke's comment: "Yikes").[42]

RuPaul, of course, has done more than most to affirm the dignity of gender-nonconforming people. His show—like drag shows more broadly—involves men dressing up in campy, over-the-top feminine outfits. The show has won four Emmys, and also a GLAAD Media Award for expanding "the mainstream understanding" of the LGBT community.[43] Zillennial news site *Mic* hailed him as an icon in the gay community.[44]

But in 2018, RuPaul committed a sin of intersectionality: he told the *Guardian* that he probably would not let a trans woman participate in his show post-transition. His reasoning was that drag queens are men who dress up in stereotypically feminine garb, and it's not quite the same thing when women do it.

"You can identify as a woman and say you're transitioning, but it changes once you start changing your body," said RuPaul. "It takes on a different thing; it changes the whole concept of what we're doing." RuPaul further suggested that drag "loses its sense of danger and its sense of irony once it's not men doing it."

For this, he was widely denounced by the left. Framke wrote that he had dismissed "trans women, trans men, cis women, and nonbinary people [who] have contributed to the complex, beautifully weird world of drag."

But RuPaul had made his position perfectly clear in an earlier interview with *Vulture*. "We [drag queens] mock identity," he said. "They [trans people] take identity very seriously. So it's the complete opposite ends of the scale."[45]

I can't think of a better way to encapsulate the differences between pre-intersectional and post-intersectional activism, as well as the divide between the older gay equality movement and the newer Zillennial LGBTQIA+ activism, for which identity is the prime source of meaning.

SIX

BERNIE WOULDA WON

THE DEMOCRATIC SOCIALISTS OF AMERICA

On June 26, 2018, the mainstream media was treated to a genuine surprise: a candidate they had never heard of—twenty-eight-year-old Alexandria Ocasio-Cortez—had defeated incumbent Joe Crowley in the Democratic primary for New York's Fourteenth Congressional District. This virtually unknown progressive young woman had taken on the fourth-most-powerful House Democrat—a living symbol of the party's centrist, pro–Wall Street, pro-Israel leadership—and won.

Ocasio-Cortez had run on a staunchly left-of-center platform, which included Medicare for All, essentially a single-payer health care system; free college tuition and the forgiveness of current student loan debt (Ocasio-Cortez, who was working as a bartender as recently as a year before her victory, has loan debt herself); the abolition of U.S. Immigration and Customs Enforcement; a federal jobs guarantee (which is bonkers); and a "New Green Deal" that would invest trillions of dollars in renewable energy.[1] It's a fairly radical platform—one that nobody, least of all Ocasio-Cortez, has any idea how to pay for—that seemed unlikely to attract moderate voters. But attracting moderate voters is *not* a goal for the Democratic Socialists of America, the contingent of the left with which Ocasio-Cortez identifies.

"The way that progressives win on an unapologetic message is by expanding the electorate," she said, outlining her campaign strategy to *Democracy Now!*'s Amy Goodman. "It's not by rushing to the center. It's not by . . . spending all of our energy winning over those who have other opinions."[2]

The Democratic Socialists of America has existed since 1982, when several socialist groups merged to form one supergroup, but only recently have its ranks grown tremendously. Before the election of Donald Trump to the presidency, membership in the DSA—which claims the red rose of socialism as its icon and Twitter symbol—was believed to be about eight thousand. Thanks in part to the popularity of socialism-sympathetic Democratic presidential candidate Bernie Sanders, DSA membership is surging. As of August 2018, the organization claims nearly fifty thousand members and more than 180 local chapters. And the group increasingly consists of young people. In 2013, the median age of a DSA member was sixty-eight. Today, it's thirty-three.

"I personally believe that socialism benefits more people than capitalism," Alex Pellitteri, the eighteen-year-old cochair of the Young Democratic Socialists in New York City, told me. Characteristic of the activists of his generation is his excitement about the growing strength of his movement. "If we can talk to the right people about socialism and make them truly understand both socialism and capitalism, I think that's when you win people over."

Given the sudden demographic shift taking place among anti-capitalist activists, disagreements between the increasingly outnumbered, more doctrinaire Marxists and younger, intersectional socialists are inevitable. One that caught my attention was the experience of an ex-member, a lecturer at UMass Boston named Gary Zabel, who rejoined the group's Boston chapter in March 2016. Upon rejoining, he found that most new members were recent college graduates—people with more privilege than the blue-collar laborers who have made up the backbone of socialist movements. Zabel frequently found himself in conflict with this younger crowd, whom he called "safe space socialists."[3]

"In my nine months as a member of the new Boston DSA, I was unable to discover the names of more than 5 of the 15 members on the group's steering committee," he wrote. "When I pointed out that this was a violation of basic democratic norms, several people told me that the names were missing from the Local's website because of fear of 'doxing,' i.e., online publication of personal data. When I replied that perhaps people who are afraid of making their names public should not be in the leadership of the Local, the response was outrage. Apparently my suggestion would make it impossible for the 'vulnerable'—women, trans people, and people of color were mentioned—to hold leadership positions."

Modern democratic socialists, of course, are ultimately just as beholden to intersectionality as other contingents of the left—though they are more likely to start fights with other factions, out of a belief that socialism is *the* central component of leftism—and thus the needs of the twice- and thrice-marginalized must often take precedence. (Recall from Chapter One the fury of the DSA's Disability Working Group when it learned that the forthcoming Medicare for All campaign did not prominently feature disabled people.) Emotional safety is taken as seriously as physical safety; when Ocasio-Cortez was criticized in August 2018 for banning the press from one of her town hall events, she explained that this had been done so that residents of her district would "feel safe discussing sensitive issues in a threatening political time."[4] Mainstream media is considered mainstream for a reason: its reporters are generally moderate liberals. And moderate people are not viewed as friends.

"One of our main enemies is the center," Bhaskar Sunkara, a twenty-nine-year-old former DSA vice chair and founder of *Jacobin*, a much-lauded socialist magazine, told *The Nation*.[5]

At a November 2017 meeting of the Boston chapter, members voted to approve a code of conduct for the group. The code stated,

"We are a socialist organization, so we expect members to be socialists or leftists interested in learning more about socialism." That seems reasonable. Less reasonable was what came next: "We will take seriously actions grounded in white supremacy and heteropatriarchy, such as Blue Lives Matter and Pro-Life politics. This especially applies to active leaders in Boston DSA."

Abortion is an issue that proves divisive for many political movements, and socialism is no different. The DSA supports what it describes as "reproductive justice" without exception. But the national group also defended Sanders when some on the left attacked him for campaigning on behalf of Heath Mello, a Democratic candidate for mayor of Omaha, Nebraska.[6] Mello was a progressive on the issue closest to Sanders's and socialists' hearts—economic inequality—but a foe of abortion. To win in a socially conservative place such as Nebraska, however, Sanders wisely calculated that some concessions would be necessary.

In a similar vein, Zabel wondered if "the 60 percent of Latino immigrants who oppose abortion" would be welcome at meetings of the Boston chapter "as long as they don't bomb any clinics." The language of the code of conduct presupposed that prospective members would have to agree with the most extreme version of the pro-choice agenda in order to join the socialist movement.

This contention came in for some criticism online. "The brain genius social media interns in Boston DSA expect to organize the working class in their city by banning anyone who criticizes their late term abortion support," one Seattle-area DSAer wrote on Twitter.[7] He later wrote that he thought abortion should be permissible but not celebrated as a good thing in and of itself.

Furious denunciation followed. A Twitter user who identifies as a member of DSA Boston's steering committee tore into the above comments, and even admitted to banning someone she described as a "pro-life Zionist" from the Boston DSA. Whether this person was Zabel I can't say; he did not respond to a request for comment. But it would seem he was right to be suspicious of the Zillennials taking over the group. Another tweeted, in response to the controversy, "ABORTION ON DEMAND WITHOUT APOLOGY IS THE ONLY CORRECT SOCIALIST POSITION."

Anti-Capitalists

To understand democratic socialism, it's helpful to know something about socialism—and its popularity on college campuses with regard to the influence of the first sociologist, Karl Marx, on humanities and liberal arts. Socialism, of course, is an economic system characterized by public ownership of the means of production. Socialism comes in many flavors but tends to involve a government that is empowered to confiscate private property and run the factories for the ostensible good of the collective citizenry. Socialism is the opposite of capitalism, the economic system of most modern successful Western economies, which involves private property, trade, and autonomous individuals liberated from the heavy hand of government. Socialists think capitalism is exploitative and results in unacceptable inequalities; supporters of capitalism counter that their system tends to produce much greater prosperity overall, even if the wealth is not evenly divided.

Over the previous five chapters, we have studied the tree of Zillennial progressivism and its many branches: racial oppression, violence against women, the erasure of trans identities, and so on. Nurtured by intersectionality, these branches have grown strong. But the root of the tree is anti-capitalism. Indeed, for the older and more doctrinaire Marxist thinkers, the branches can seem like distractions.

As we discussed briefly in Chapter Two, Marxism refers to the theories of mid-nineteenth-century thinker Karl Marx, who believed that capitalism was only the most recent incarnation of a historical struggle between different classes. "The history of all hitherto existing society is the history of class struggles," wrote Marx in *The Communist Manifesto* in 1848. This struggle was going to sort itself out—in favor of a universal workers' utopia—just as soon as capitalism was properly destroyed.

To really understand Marx, it's necessary to go even further back. Marx drew inspiration from Georg Wilhelm Friedrich Hegel, a German philosopher who lived during the late eighteenth and early nineteenth centuries. Hegel believed in something he called the *Weltgeist*, which is German for "world-spirit." The world-spirit was constantly trying to better itself, to eliminate imperfections from its essence, and human history was the story of the world-spirit progressing toward the ideal.

Scott Alexander, the pseudonymous proprietor of the essential history blog *Slate Star Codex*, mockingly described Hegel's view as naively utopian: "As it overcomes its various confusions and false dichotomies, it advances into forms that more completely incarnate the World-Spirit and then moves onto the next problem. Finally, it ends with the World-Spirit completely incarnated—possibly in the form of early 19th century Prussia—and everything is great forever."[8]

Marx enthusiastically appropriated Hegel's idea. Communism, in Marx's view, was the perfect social system, in which everything would be awesome for everyone. It was also inevitable—the world-spirit took its time, but we would get there eventually. And it was final—once humankind had achieved a fully equal, classless, communist society, there would be nothing left to fix.

Capitalism was the next-to-last step in the grand historical march toward communist utopia, according to Marxist thinking. It was an important historical development, mainly because history needed to get through capitalism to progress to communism. Capitalism would sow the seeds of its own destruction as rapacious bourgeois capitalists waged war on each other in pursuit of greater profits, reducing rivals to destitution. The pace of this destruction would accelerate, and the entire capitalist system would eventually collapse on itself. A classless society would rise in its wake, enduring in perpetuity.

Marx studiously avoided the matter of how this utopian society would function, organize itself, or be governed. He was disinterested in such practical questions as who would decide how much food each person gets. It was just going to happen: the capitalism system would collapse, the workers would overthrow whatever members of the bourgeoisie remained, and then there would be no more class-based antagonism—everyone would now belong to the same class. Since class-based antagonism is the root cause of all human strife, the establishment of a class-based society would bring about utopia. World-spirit completely incarnate.

In practice, Marx's magical thinking has not worked out well, either because the theory is bunk or because human beings aren't yet capable of carrying it out. In the century and a half since Marx's death, socialist revolutions guided by Marxist ideals have failed to abolish class; instead they always end up empowering a new ruling class consisting of the revolutionaries who seized power (known as the vanguard). In nearly all cases of actually occurring communism, this new vanguard proved to be at least as brutal and repressive as whatever had held power before it. See Stalin's Russia, Mao's China, Pol Pot's Cambodia, and countless others for historical examples of this.

An important feature—and not incidental to the repression that occurs in its name—is that Marxism does not recognize individual rights, such as freedom of speech, freedom of conscience, or the right to vote. Whatever rights are being enjoyed by the oppressors—the bourgeois capitalists—should be trampled underfoot. Restrictions on political rights and the seizure of private property can always be justified on orthodox Marxist grounds, since the world-spirit is just working its way toward a classless society.

It's important to recognize how different Marxist socialism is from liberalism. Liberalism comes in many flavors: *New Deal liberals* support social and political freedom, but think the government has a strong role to play in smoothing out the kinks in the economy (kinks like the Great Depression of the 1930s); *classical liberals,* also called libertarians, consider New Deal liberalism a departure from true liberalism and think the government should generally respect people's social and political freedoms, as well as their economic freedoms; *neoliberals,* also called *market liberals,* fall somewhere in between—like New Deal liberals, they want the government to intervene in economic matters when necessary, but like classical liberals, they recognize that market forces can work when government fails. But all kinds of liberals are generally at odds with leftism, and the dislike is mutual. Conservatives pillory liberals for not being conservatives, but the left thinks liberals are too conservative. Liberalism, you will remember from Chapter Three, is synonymous with white supremacy for a certain kind of far-left radical.

The Marxist left, of course, has almost no real political power. Even Sanders, the most prominent socialist-sympathetic politician, is something of a faux Marxist. When asked to describe his ideal government, he has pointed to countries like Denmark, which provide a generous social safety net to citizens while maintaining fundamentally capitalist, market economies—a prime example of neoliberalism rather than socialism.

But there is one sector of American society where Marxism's influence has continued to grow, and its adherents have seized some tangible power: the university. For nearly a hundred years, academia has kept Marxism alive and thriving.

In the 1930s, a group of European Marxist thinkers, Herbert Marcuse among them, developed something they called "critical theory." Critical theory was heavily inspired by the work of Antonio Gramsci, an Italian sociologist and Communist Party leader. (Gramsci was arrested by Benito Mussolini's fascists and died in prison in 1937.) While Marx had held that the proletarian revolution was inevitable, by the early twentieth century his acolytes had grown despondent waiting for their version of the rapture. Gramsci was chief among the Marxists who came up with an explanation: the bourgeoisie did not just hold economic power—they also held cultural power, and they used this power to shore up capitalism. According to Gramsci, the workers shared the same cultural values as the capitalists and would never rise up against them until there was a broad cultural shift throughout society. It was not enough for the abolition of class to be in the economic interests of

Marx-friendly sociologists have worked tirelessly to keep critical theory relevant to the activist left, and significant intellectual efforts were made to reconcile the class-based model of oppression with the other kinds of oppression more immediate and familiar to intersectional young people. For instance, George Ciccariello-Maher, the former Drexel University professor mentioned in Chapter Two, told me in an interview that the history of white supremacy in America—slavery, Jim Crow, and so on—easily fits into a Marxist worldview.

"White supremacy structured on the basis of slavery has been hugely important to maintaining the power structure, and that is in many ways a Marxist understanding, in the sense that race and slavery were used to divide the poor into white and blacks so that they would not unify," Ciccariello-Maher told me. "This is the underlying theme of what I think is the essential text or understanding of U.S. history, which is W. E. B. Du Bois's *Black Reconstruction,* about the aftermath of the Civil War."

Ciccariello-Maher was referencing Du Bois, a black sociologist who wrote during the early and mid-twentieth century. Thus racism, a monumental source of oppression throughout the United States' history, could be cast in Marxist terms as well. And historically, that's exactly what happened. As I mentioned in Chapter Two, the Black Panthers—a radical leftist identity group active in the 1960s and '70s that favored racial separation—was explicitly Marxist in its outlook.

Recall that previously I said young activists frequently share famous quotes from activists of yore on social media. I once saw a young racial justice activist at Reed College post a picture of Stokely Carmichael and an accompanying quotation on her Facebook wall. Carmichael was a civil rights activist and eventually the leader of the Black Panthers. Here is the quote: "If a white man wants to lynch me, that's his problem. If he's got the power to lynch me, that's my problem. Racism is not a question of attitude; it's a question of power. Racism gets its power from capitalism. Thus, if you're anti-racist, whether you know it or not, you must be anti-

the oppressed; the oppressed had to first realize their ⟨
was illegitimate and capitalism was wrong and backwar⟨

And so the new Marxists invented critical theory. ⟨
name, critical theory isn't a theory at all—it's a metho⟨
approach, or a lens for evaluating social phenomena. The
to offer a critique of society as it was organized, rather tha⟨
explanation for how it had come to be so. Critical theoris
to expose the root conflict—class struggle—at the heart ⟨
social interactions, and denounce it under the guise of s⟨
ence. The purpose of critical theory was to promote *social*
economic equality based on the overthrow of the ruling ⟨
class—by preaching the wrongness of capitalism and the r⟨
of Marxism and socialism.

In subsequent decades, critical theory spread like ⟨
through the academy, hitting the liberal arts, social scienc
humanities the hardest. Most people know that professors ar
left-leaning than the average American; what they might not ⟨
is that many professors teach from an explicitly Marxist persp⟨
or at the very least apply critical theory to the subjects they ⟨

Critical theory programs are now offered at a host of univer
Ph.D. students at the University of California at Berkeley can
a certificate in critical theory while applying those insights to
main concentration.[9] University of Arizona graduate student⟨
minor in "social, cultural, and critical theory."[10] Northwe⟨
University hosts a critical theory project that involves acade⟨
from all over the globe.[11] There's a critical theory program wit⟨
the School of Humanities at the University of California at Irv⟨
and also one within the Department of Comparative Literatur⟨
the State University of New York–Buffalo.[12] Literature, histo
and political science are often taught through the lens of criti⟨
theory. Since the 1980s, fields that focus on a specific grou⟨
marginalization—women's studies, queer studies, African Ame⟨
can studies—have proliferated, and these frequently involve a Mar⟨
ist perspective. Critical theory's application to race even has its ow⟨
name, critical race theory.

capitalist. The power for racism, the power for sexism, comes from capitalism, not an attitude."

Capitalism, not racism or sexism or any other ism, is the ideology that powers evil. This is the sentiment of an important activist who in 2017 is revered, remembered, and even retweeted.

Some data to back up my assertion that Marxism endures: According to the Open Syllabus Project, a database that tracks information from publicly available syllabi, *The Communist Manifesto* is one of the most frequently assigned economic texts on college campuses, beating out Adam Smith's *The Wealth of Nations* and Paul Krugman's *Economics*.[13] That wouldn't necessarily be a bad thing—students should learn why Marxist ideas are economically unsound, impractical, and out of date. But Phil Magness, a historian and adjunct professor of public policy at George Mason University, dug into the Open Syllabus Project's data and found something revealing: *The Communist Manifesto* wasn't being assigned as an economics text. Most of the data points—more than 97 percent, by Magness's calculation—came from syllabi being used "in fields that venture far astray from economics, with the highest concentrations coming from the humanities."[14]

In a 2007 survey, just 3 percent of college professors self-identified as Marxists. But that number rose to 5 percent when only humanities professors were counted (another 19 percent described themselves as radicals). In social science, it was worse: a whopping 18 percent of social science professors described themselves as Marxists. Bryan Caplan, a professor of economics at George Mason University, lamented that this was akin to finding out 18 percent of biologists described themselves as creationists.[15]

Within the field of social science, the most Marxist-sympathetic concentration was, unsurprisingly, sociology: a quarter of surveyed sociologists described themselves as Marxists.[16]

Caplan suspects that the number of self-avowed Marxists in academia has dipped since 2007. But the ideological position of the average academic has continued to drift left in recent years. Some professors might deny being outright Marxists but instead teach an extremely Marx-friendly worldview, like critical theory. There are many ways for academics who are essentially Marxists to define themselves other than Marxist.

It would be silly to think that illiberal Zillennial activism is solely or even predominantly the result of classroom indoctrination. As I've written previously, my conversations with activists suggest that activist students are more likely to radicalize each other, and that many activists were radicalized before they even entered college. But Marxist academics provide a culture, a vocabulary, and an intellectual defense of activist tactics—a base of support the most well-read and well-studied young radicals can summon when needed. Zillennial activists are speaking the language of Marx and Marcuse, whether they realize it or not. For instance, when I interviewed Haik, a student at the University of California, Santa Cruz, about his disruption of a College Republicans meeting, he disagreed with me that it was about the College Republicans' free speech. "It's not about free speech, it's about the institutional power," he told me.

Haik, who used the word "comrade"—the term of endearment favored by Marxists—to describe his friends and fellow travelers, hoped to disrupt the institutional power being wielded by conservatives who support "economic policies that subjugate people across the lines of race, class, gender sexuality, etc." Peel away the layers of intersectionality, and anti-capitalism, grounded in Marxist theory, is what remains.

Socialism, but Democratic

Today's anti-capitalist activists differ from their immediate predecessors in two important ways: they are intersectional and they are democratic. They are intersectional because they are sensitive to forms of oppression that doctrinaire Marxists would have considered distractions from the real issue, class struggle. They are democratic in order to distance themselves from the horrible repression that occurred under authoritarian socialist regimes in Latin America, Europe, Africa, and Asia.

The DSA is not a political party and does not run candidates of its own. It endorses candidates from other parties—most notably the Democratic Party and the Green Party—in cases where those candidates' goals align with DSA goals. Compared with the haphazard activism discussed in previous chapters, the DSA is remarkably organized. The DSA has elected leaders, chapters, and working groups that focus on specific issues.

The founder of the DSA, the socialist writer and political scientist Michael Harrington, was staunchly anti-communist. He believed the failures of communist countries proved that socialism needed to be fully democratic to work. In fact, during the drafting of the Port Huron Statement in 1962—the political manifesto produced by the leftist group Students for a Democratic Society—Harrington argued that the statement did not denounce the Soviet Union in strong enough terms.[17] Twenty years later, after breaking with the Socialist Party, Harrington merged with the New American Movement, the vanguard of the New Left, to start the DSA.

Unlike so many of today's leftists who view liberals as essentially in league with fascists, Harrington was committed to working with the liberals and winning them over. "I share an immediate program with liberals in this country because the best liberalism leads toward socialism," he once said.[18]

In practice, democratic socialists do not always do a very good job describing what their beliefs are, or how they differ from socialism. On MSNBC, Ocasio-Cortez defined democratic socialism as "democratic participation in our economic dignity" and "the basic elements that are required for an economic and socially dignified life in the United States," a vague description that prompted mild criticism from left-of-center news anchor Chris Hayes.

Pellitteri defined democratic socialism as a system that gives ultimate power back to the people. "It's just practical for the workers to own the means of production," he told me. "And for the workers to be able to control the profits that they make as a result of their labor. That is one of the few ways that a worker can truly have power in society."

"Workers controlling the means of production" is the textbook definition of plain old socialism. Democratic socialism, then, does not seem to differ all that much from socialism in terms of goals; rather, it differs regarding the means of achieving them. It also differs in terms of its intersectional emphasis. Members of the DSA frequently talk about the full range of oppressions visited on marginalized people because of exploitative capitalism.

"The idea is that you cannot be free unless everybody is free," Pellitteri told me, "[that] we cannot have peace unless everyone has peace, is very present in DSA. We try to change the entire system that affects everyone as opposed to changing separate parts of that system which might affect individual people." Consequently, the DSA directs its energies to combating not just economic inequality but also criminal justice inequities, environmental problems, and other issues.

Immigration has occasionally emerged as a divisive issue. When *Vox*, a left-of-center news site that often takes a neoliberal perspective on economic issues, asked candidate Sanders about adopting a more globalist perspective on inequality, Sanders vehemently denounced the idea of open-borders immigration, calling it a right-wing Koch brothers proposal that "essentially says there is no United States."[19] The Koch brothers (disclaimer: David Koch sits on the board of the Reason Foundation, which publishes the magazine I write for) are to Sanders's left on immigration—as an older socialist, Sanders believes immigrants take jobs from blue-collar workers and undermine the bargaining position of organized labor.

But younger socialists are less tied to the idea of organized labor as the backbone of their revolution, in part because blue-collar workers tend to be more socially conservative and thus at odds with intersectional requirements. It is thus no surprise that Trump successfully courted the labor vote, winning upset victories in rust belt states such as Michigan and Pennsylvania.

"While I still like [Sanders], I still admire him, I'm definitely more to the left of him," said Pellitteri.

In the era of Trumpian attacks on the dignity of immigrants, "Abolish ICE"—as in U.S. Immigration and Customs Enforcement—has become an important slogan for younger democratic socialists, including Ocasio-Cortez, who ran on this issue explicitly. The person most directly responsible for the widespread adoption of this message by DSA types is Sean McElwee, a twenty-five-year-old activist and researcher, who first tweeted the phrase "Abolish ICE" in February 2017. He eventually changed his name on Twitter to "Abolish ICE" as well. Fortuitously for the movement to abolish ICE, immigration issues captured the public's attention in the year that followed. The media began paying a lot of attention to the Trump administration's practice of detaining and separating immigrant families caught crossing the border illegally, a policy that was begun under the Obama administration but accelerated by Trump. The federal government's mistreatment of very young children has made ICE deservedly unpopular. (As a libertarian who favors smaller government, I would shed no tears if ICE was abolished.)

McElwee maintains spreadsheets tracking how well each of his tweets about abolishing ICE performed on the social media site, and has reached out to Democratic staffers to garner support for the movement.

"[Now] there are normie motherfucking progressives that want to abolish ICE," McElwee told *BuzzFeed*, in language characteristic of DSA radicals—note the disparagement of "normie," as in normal, mainstream liberals.[20]

Characteristic of the infighting that often plagues lefty social movements, some on the left are offended by any attempt to make some kind of common cause with "normies." Brendan James, a former producer and cohost of the popular socialist podcast *Chapo*

Trap House, criticized McElwee as "a college-educated white man showing up at the 11th hour, tweeting, and taking credit for other people's work."

"This is about a political moment," James told *BuzzFeed,* "and if you're on the left, you want to watch out for careerists and climbers, because their work usually helps dilute radical ideas and prime them for establishment Democrats." And nothing could be worse than that.

It's undeniable that democratic socialism, as exemplified by the DSA, is enjoying something of a moment. Zillennials have only distant memories of the Cold War and thus do not view socialism as some kind of existential military threat to the United States. While their predecessors on the New Left were in some cases sympathetic to the Soviets, Zillennial socialists are ready to let the past die—and, ideally, capitalism along with it.

Much has been made of polls that suggest millennials have a more favorable view of socialism than capitalism.[21] Of course, if socialism is defined in Ocasio-Cortez's terms as simply "economic dignity," then it's easy to see why it's so popular. A lot of young people want economic dignity; this does not mean they necessarily believe government should nationalize industries, confiscate the means of production, and deport the bourgeoisie to Siberia. And conservative pundits and politicians did tremendous work during the Obama years to distort the definition of socialism; in arguing that everything Obama did was insidiously socialist, they have only themselves to blame for the fact that young people associate standard Democratic economic policies with socialism.

Fragile Finances

If young people are skeptical of capitalism and increasingly taken with utopian-sounding solutions that involve collective, democratic action to reduce income inequality, it probably also has something to do with their relatively fragile financial circumstances. The selfie generation's second wave finished college during the aftermath of the 2007 financial crisis, and the picture isn't a pretty one. The cost of obtaining a degree—a piece of paper essentially treated as a minimum requirement for surviving in the modern world—has skyrocketed over the last twenty years, and yet jobs and financial security for graduates are more elusive than ever.

"The average college student takes out tens of thousands of dollars in loans from the government to go to school—tenacious debt it will likely take a decade or more to pay off, and on which default isn't a practical option," wrote Malcolm Harris, a leftist writer and fellow twenty-nine-year-old, in his 2017 book on our generation's dire economic straits, *Kids These Days: Human Capital and the Making of Millennials.* "But with higher rates of enrollment, it's not enough to just attend college, especially given the costs; a degree has become a prerequisite, not a golden ticket. Meanwhile, the university has turned into a veritable industrial complex, complete with ever-expanding real estate holdings, hospitals, corporate partnerships, and sports teams that are professional in every sense of the word—except that the players work for free."

Harris writes from a leftist perspective, which means he tends to blame the deficiencies of modern life on the capitalist system. Whether the Great Recession was caused by an absence of government intervention into the economy or an abundance of it is a topic that would take an entire book to address. But explicit government policy seems the most likely culprit in the specific case of higher education's cost disease, at the very least.

In fact, the government subsidizes student loans, offering low interest rates to students who must borrow to attend college. Since the government pays the upfront cost on behalf of the student, universities have every incentive to jack up the price: Uncle Sam can pay it, and students aren't expected to square their debts until some distant point in the postgraduate future. The government always collects in the end: student loan debt, unlike other kinds of debt, cannot be discharged through the bankruptcy process. Some debtors *can* have their loans forgiven under the Education Department's Public Service Loan Forgiveness Program, but this requires graduates to work for the government or a nonprofit such as the Peace Corps while continuing to make monthly loan repayments for at least ten straight years.[22]

"Students are absolutely fucked right now," George Ciccariello-Maher, the former Drexel University professor, told me. "Millennials are coming out of college with huge amounts of debt, with no access to real jobs . . . the baby boomers who are mocking millennials had absolute access to jobs and buying homes and all of these privileges that students today are not going to have."

Considerable evidence suggests that federal efforts to make college more affordable have backfired in the long term. Graduates now hold nearly $1.5 trillion in collective student loan debt. The average graduate of the class of 2016 owes $37,000. A July 2015 study by the Federal Reserve Bank of New York found "that institutions more exposed to changes in the subsidized federal loan program increased their tuition disproportionately around these policy changes, with a sizable pass-through effect on tuition of about 65 percent."[23] A paper from the National Bureau of Economic Research's Economics of Education Program found an even more pronounced correlation between subsidized loans and tuition rates. Between 1987 and 2010, "expanded student loan borrowing limits [were] the largest driving force for the increase in tuition," according to the authors' findings.[24] These studies would appear to confirm suspicions first raised by William Bennett, secretary of education during the latter years of the Reagan administration, that "increases in financial aid in recent years have enabled colleges and universities blithely to raise their tuitions." This idea, dubbed the "Bennett hypothesis," grows more plausible with each passing year.

It would be one thing if students were taking on more and more debt in pursuit of guaranteed, high-paying jobs. But employment prospects for recent graduates are less certain than ever, and even those who do find jobs aren't necessarily in great shape. Underemployment—the condition of working a job for which the employee is overqualified—is a huge problem for millennial job-seekers. The Federal Reserve Bank of New York puts the underemployment rate for recent graduates at 43.7 percent. While that's only 5 percent higher than it was at the turn of the century, it's actually much worse considering that graduates paid a *lot* more for their education in 2017 than they did in 2000. Ohio University economist Richard Vedder noted that underemployed graduates "sometimes resort to taking jobs as Uber drivers or baristas," and added, "With some inexpensive vocational training, they could easily get jobs that pay much better."[25]

What students study matters a great deal, of course. According to Vedder, electrical engineering majors earn twice as much as psychology majors. And that's just one example. A recent graduate who majored in business was expected to be making $48,000 on average just after college, while a graduate who majored in social work or the arts could only expect a starting income of $31,000, according to research conducted at Georgetown University in 2015.[26] (The data cover the 2009–12 Great Recession period; job prospects for everybody have recovered somewhat since then.) Graduate school discrepancies were in some ways even starker: a worker with a liberal arts graduate degree was making $52,000, whereas a mathematics graduate degree holder was making $79,000.

Millennials who studied math, engineering, or computer science were more likely to get jobs, and high-paying ones at that. On the other hand, millennials who studied humanities, psychology, or art were hardly better off than people who had skipped college altogether and instead gotten a job right after high school. In fact, they were arguably *worse* off, since they had mountains of debt with which to contend; the people with only a high school diploma avoided this fate. Social science majors had higher unemployment rates than experienced high school graduates.

You will have probably noticed that the majors with the most soul-crushingly bad financial prospects are the ones that activists tend to pursue, like sociology, the humanities, art, psychology, and the explicitly identity-based subjects such as gender studies, African American studies, Asian American studies, queer theory, et cetera.

It's no wonder so many of these students are stressed out, feeling a little fragile, or triggered by what critics would call "real life." Real life is about to hit them where it really hurts: their wallets.

Maybe that's why so many young people—and not just the card-carrying activist types—were excited about Sanders's proposed revisions to federal education policy: make college free, allow student loan debtors to refinance, and reduce the government's ability to profit off its loan program. Activists have gone further: debt forgiveness en masse was a major goal of the 2011 Occupy Wall Street movement, which arose in response to the economic crisis. Not content to wait for reform, some activists pledged to cease making repayments on their loans entirely. The Occupy Wall Street movement fizzled, but young activists remain dedicated to overthrowing a financial system that led to their impoverishment while the rich got richer. From their point of view, that's capitalism.

Late Capitalism and Weird Twitter

Social media is an essential component of Zillennial activism of all kinds—arguably, *the* essential component, since most organizing and information gathering are done on Twitter and Facebook.

"Facebook is a big thing," Haik told me. "I feel like a lot of organizing started over Facebook."

"I get a lot of my information by following a lot of different sources on Twitter and then reading from there," Jacqueline, the Evergreen College activist, told me. "I know that's a really millennial answer."

And if you're looking for explicitly Marxist, socialist, communist, and anti-capitalist activism, Twitter is the place to look. A thriving community of incredibly crude and militantly extreme anti-capitalists exists on the social media site. You may know them by the red roses (or in some cases hammers and sickles) in their handles.

"I'm a trans woman," wrote one such Twitter user, who describes herself as a queer anti-imperialist proletarian feminist and Maoist. "I #ResistCapitalism because private property and capital are the basis of my exploitation and my oppression."[27]

Marxist Twitter users affectionately tweet images of Argentine revolutionary Che Guevara accompanied by one of his quotes, "True revolutionaries are guided by feelings of love."[28] (Guevara, a particularly murderous member of Fidel Castro's inner circle, also once said that people must possess "a relentless hatred of the enemy, impelling us over and beyond the natural limitations that man is heir to and transforming him into an effective, violent, selective and cold killing machine.")[29] One such Twitter user, Lamont Lilly, an activist affiliated with the Workers World Party, linked to a speech he gave encouraging Black Lives Matter to be more explicitly Marxist.[30]

Members of this community, branded "weird Twitter" by media reporters who follow it, often tweet statements that seem semi-satirical, like "#fullcommunism" or "All I want for Christmas is white genocide" (that one was Ciccariello-Maher himself, actually).[31] The lingo can be difficult to follow. "Brocialists," a portmanteau of "bro" and "socialists," refers to leftist guys who are stereotypically masculine and interested in guy stuff—sports, working out, girls, and so on—but also think the workers should seize the means of production. "Tankies" are leftists who defend Stalin and Mao. In regular parlance, "corn cob" is a derogatory term for a gay man. But on weird Twitter, to get "corn-cobbed" is to lose an argument so badly you that you "slowly shrink and transform into a corn cob."[32] (You just had to be there for that one.)

Frost, the leftist writer and participant in the *Chapo Trap House* podcast who was involved in the dispute with the DSA's Disability Working Group, coined the term "dirtbag left" to describe this movement—a movement that isn't interested in civility or politeness toward its critics. For the dirtbag left, we are living through a time period known to earlier Marxists as late capitalism: the end stage of capitalism, which occurs just before the glorious communist revolution. Zillennial lefties see every excess of modern consumerist culture as evidence of late capitalism: like a pair of jeans smeared with fake mud selling for $425 at Nordstrom, or a basic economy section of an airplane that boards after absolutely everybody else—even the pets.[33] "Now, [late capitalism] is everywhere, in thousands of social-media posts and listicles aimed at Millennials and news stories about modern malaise," wrote the *Atlantic*'s Annie Lowery in a 2017 article.[34] For leftists who see evidence of late capitalism all around them, it's like being convinced the rapture is just around the corner.

Unsurprisingly, the dirtbag left reserves many of their harshest criticisms for neoliberalism, a kind of centrist, market-friendly liberalism that thinks capitalism should be regulated, not destroyed. In embracing market forces (albeit more selectively than classical liberals or libertarians), neoliberals haven't just sold out their own kind—they have sold their very souls. (Think Judas Iscariot rather than Benedict Arnold.) The dirtbag left is not a cohort that particularly cares for Hillary or Bill Clinton; Clintonian triangulation is often held up as the apotheosis of neoliberalism. In fact, leftists feel almost vindicated by Hillary's defeat. Bernie bros think Hillary cheated their man out of the Democratic Party's 2016 presidential nomination, ultimately snatching defeat from the jaws of victory, since they believe Sanders would have ultimately defeated Trump where Hillary could not. (Thus the title of this chapter; I admit it seems perfectly plausible to me that Sanders would have indeed beaten Trump.)

International leaders such as French president Emmanuel Macron and Canadian prime minister Justin Trudeau are despised by many lefties as well, despite Trudeau's popularity with feminists. "Stop pretending these global leaders are woke baes!" demanded a writer for *Vice*.[35] ("Bae" is slang for "important friend," beloved by the Zillennials who eagerly appropriated it from black culture.)

The Democratic Party is at best a hugely flawed vehicle for promoting good policy, according to many leftists. But there's hope it can gradually be pushed in a more hard-left direction: thus the efforts of the DSA.

Bill Ayers, the education theorist and radical activist known for his involvement in the Weather Underground during the 1960s and '70s, told me that before Trump won the election, he had already planned to travel to Washington, D.C., for the inauguration—in order to protest Hillary Clinton, the presumed next president of the United States.

"I was going to Washington to be part of a peace demonstration against Hillary Clinton," Ayers told me in an interview. "She would have had her neoliberal, pro–Wall Street, pro-war agenda, and we would have been protesting peacefully, happily over in our corner with our picket signs."

In addition to ending global capitalism, the anti-capitalists have a lengthy policy wish list. They want institutions of higher education to divest their endowments of holdings in companies that run private prisons (privatization and prisons both being bad things) and Israeli companies (leftists stand uniformly with Palestinians against Israel). They want a higher minimum wage and, as previously discussed, student loan debt forgiveness. They want single-payer health care, subsidized birth control, and more welfare spending. And they want to pay for it by implementing a more progressive tax system under which the wealthy shell out more money.

Trump is an enemy of the people, and an enemy of leftists, too. But anti-capitalists are not especially obsessed with attacking Trump—probably because Trump isn't actually a very doctrinaire Republican when it comes to economic freedom. As discussed previously, there is even a sense in which Trump and the hard-core Marxists are competing for the same voters: blue-collar workers who are concerned about diminishing organized labor protections, jobs disappearing overseas, and being on the losing side of international competition. Leftists think Trump is an insincere friend to the common man, but at least the president purports to hate globalism and free trade as much as they do. The plain old Republican economic agenda—tax cuts, deregulation, and so on—is far more loathsome.

Even so, Trump's 2016 victory didn't represent as much of a

departure from typical Republicanism as many on the left were hoping. Laila, the twenty-six-year-old Muslim activist, told me she was very worried about the new administration getting rid of mandatory birth control coverage—something that did indeed come to pass in October 2017.[36] (Employers with a faith-based objection to offering birth control may now receive a waiver.)

"Women's birth control might be taken away," Laila told me. "Once that becomes a topic that is widely known, shit's going to hit the fan when it comes to the women in the U.S. Because you can't give people a taste of what they could have, and what they're having, and then suddenly say, 'Hey, actually, blah, blah, blah, budget, blah, blah, blah, blah, blah, blah, money,' or whatever, and then try and roll it back."

If there's one issue where leftists are definitively, positively closer to die-hard Trump supporters, it's Russia. Leftist writers and activists frequently lampoon the mainstream and liberal media's obsession with the idea that the Trump campaign colluded with Russia, thus making him president. It may be that Marxists have good memories; the last time powerful American institutions were talking seriously about the problem of Russian meddling in U.S. democracy was the Red Scare of the 1940s and '50s, which targeted alleged communist sympathizers and leftists. Leftists are also friendlier to Russia in general than many more moderate liberals and neoliberals. For neoliberals, Russia is an oppressive enemy. But for leftists, there is no greater force for geopolitical evil than the United States—a warmongering, imperialist, Israel-backing, capitalist-promoting Great Satan. As the activists at the Inauguration Day protests proclaimed (via their signs), "Trump is the symptom, capitalism is the disease, socialism is the cure."

It's easy to see how the left's anti-capitalism could continuously reaffirm itself. Marxism and its variants teach that capitalism is inherently exploitative and speeds up the pace of life as it grinds everyone into dust. As capitalism advances into late capitalism, the absurdities of the free market system become more pronounced while competition forces everybody to battle each other into an early grave. Eventually, everyone simply collapses into a pit of student loan debt, depression, and joblessness.

"If I were a millennial I would be rioting in the streets," Brianna Wu, a Gen Xer running for Congress from Massachusetts, told me in an interview. "You guys are more screwed over than any generation in modern American history." Wu, a videogame developer who became the target of GamerGate harassment because of her outspoken feminism, was running as a Democrat, but she thinks the party has failed miserably to promote the economic interests of millennials: "The Democratic Party is completely blowing it. . . . We have got to be a party that stands up for civil rights, a party that stands up for income equality, a party that stands up to the abuses of Wall Street."

It remains to be seen whether democratic socialists and other radical political candidates can succeed in pulling the Democratic Party to the left and then actually win elections. More mainstream Democrats must contend with a difficult contradiction: the energy and enthusiasm are on the side of the stridently far-left Zillennials, but activists representing this contingent despise moderates, centrists, and neoliberal "shills." It's possible that any attempt to court this group will fail, since their revolutionary vanguard— weird Twitter, *Chapo Trap House,* select members of the DSA— might rather lose to Trump than campaign for a member of the Clinton family.

Even well-to-the-left Democratic candidate Cynthia Nixon— formerly of *Sex and the City* fame, more recently a candidate for governor of New York—experienced some difficulty securing socialist support, despite the fact that she was running against the despised moderate Democrat Andrew Cuomo. New York DSA members took a straw poll in July 2018: a third of the gathered group wanted to endorse Nixon, another third was unsure, and the final third thought she was unacceptable. According to one member, "We don't just grant endorsements to progressives who beg us for one. We endorse people who can advance the anti-capitalist struggle."[37]

SEVEN

THE OTHERS

GREENS, GUNS, AND MORE

The coalition of progressive intersectionality is vast, and it includes many more groups than this book has room to discuss in great depth. In this chapter, I will provide quick snapshots of a few aspects of Zillennial activism that have not been covered yet, beginning with the greens.

Eco-Mysticism

It was a hot spring day in Washington, D.C., and I found myself on the National Mall, conversing with four people who were each operating a giant puppet from the inside. The puppets had masks and robes fitting a distinct color and theme. There was a red fire puppet, a blue water puppet, a white wind puppet, and a green nature puppet.

"We're the Element Puppets," the woman underneath the wind puppet's robes told me. "From Louisville, Kentucky."

The puppeteers, and hundreds of other people, had come to D.C. on June 23, 2018, for a mass rally hosted by the Poor People's Campaign: A National Call for Moral Revival, which was founded in December of the previous year. The Poor People's Campaign had attracted numerous sponsors, including various interfaith groups, unions, and even Ben and Jerry's. The actor Danny Glover made an appearance, as did the Reverend Jesse Jackson.

As always, it was an intersectional event. Speakers began their remarks by listing the oppressions relevant to their own lives: one noted that she was trans, struggling with mental health issues, and economically disadvantaged, for instance. Later, another speaker claimed to "exist at the intersection" of womanhood, blackness, and queerness. In the crowd, a representative protester carried a sign that demanded, "Stand against anti-Muslim bigotry + healthcare for all," as if these were related things.

The event began with a religious ceremonial performance by representatives of the San Carlos Apache Nation, who sang and played the drums. "Please join us in this religious ceremony," said their leader, a Native American man. "Explode that evil away so the people can live."

The rally's master of ceremonies was the Reverend William Barber II, a middle-aged Protestant minister with a booming voice and a grand presence. He was a high priest of intersectionality, frequently urging the protesters to see how various kinds of oppression were related—and to raise their fists in the air for solidarity.

"I care about racism," said the minister, who is black, "but you can't end racism without ending the military economy . . . we're going to shut it down for love and for justice."

Eventually, a teenage girl took to the podium to read her spoken-word piece, titled "I'm Tired of Poems About Oppression." I missed the girl's name; Barber had instructed everyone in the crowd to hold hands with the person standing next to them, and before I could seclude myself, a brown-haired hippie named Dmitri had taken my hand. He soon realized I was trying to take notes, and kindly let go—instead opting to place his hand on my back as I wrote. I had missed the first part of the poem, and tuned in just as the poet was saying, "I'm tired of white feminism, and white women who voted for Trump. . . . I'm tired of feminism that isn't intersectional."

The rally stressed four core issues, the wages of an exploitative, capitalistic country: racism, poverty, the military economy, and ecological devastation. It had a workmanlike quality to it; once one set of speakers finished, the emcees summoned the next set to the stage. "Next it's our ecological devastation speakers," said one of Barber's cohosts. "Ecological devastation speakers, please come up." The ecological devastation speakers were introduced by a Jewish religious leader, further emphasizing the quasi-religious nature of the environmental activists.

"The whole earth belongs to God," insisted the rabbi. "Not to corporations."

Unlike many of the other strains of progressive activism profiled for this book, the environmental movement hasn't changed all that much. Activists have experienced undeniable successes: the main environmentalist cause—addressing climate change—is now a mainstream one, embraced by nearly everyone in the Democratic coalition, and even some on the Republican side. The election of Donald Trump to the presidency was a significant setback, of course; he promptly withdrew the United States from the Paris Agreement, a pact with other nations to voluntarily reduce carbon emissions. At the same time, carbon tax proposals continue to generate increasing interest from folks on both sides of the aisle.[1]

The modern environmental movement can trace its origin to *Silent Spring*, the 1962 book by conservationist Rachel Carson that argued pesticides were destroying the environment. Thanks in no small part to Carson, public pressure mounted against manufacturers of the insecticide DDT, and the U.S. government eventually banned its use. (Critics contend that DDT was a highly effective tool for preventing malaria—it killed mosquitoes—and that abandoning it increased deaths in the developing world.) In 1970, President Richard Nixon signed a bill authorizing the creation of the Environmental Protection Agency, in part due to the demands of environmental activists.

In the decades since, environmentalists have achieved significant victories. Air pollution has decreased in most corners of the world, the rainforests are growing back, and U.S. reliance on coal is decreasing.[2] According to my colleague Ronald Bailey, "Global tree canopy cover increased by 2.24 million square kilometers (865,000 square miles) between 1982 and 2016."[3]

Activists, though, have often come across as pessimistic—at times apocalyptic. In the 1970s, they were persuaded by the biologist Paul Ehrlich that humankind would soon exhaust the planet's resources, and millions would starve. Nothing of the sort happened, of course: technological innovation saw to that. Thanks to people like Norman Borlaug, the criminally underappreciated father of the Green Revolution, better crop yields made it possible to feed the world's growing population while consuming less farmland and other resources.

Today, the environmentalist left is often sidetracked by intersectional considerations. "A particularly pernicious form of denialism is the conceit within the political left that we must cure longstanding social ills such as inequality, corporate greed, racism, and political corruption along the way to dealing with climate change," wrote professors Joshua Goldstein and Steven Pinker in the *Boston Globe*.[4]

Indeed, the progressive left's anti-capitalism intersects with its environmentalism. Monsanto, a massive agricultural company, has often been scapegoated on both fronts. Activists have claimed that Monsanto's genetically engineered crops are unsafe, and they demand regulation to warn people of the danger. Scientific consensus, however, holds that genetically modified crops are perfectly safe for consumption.

On campus, environmentalism is often taught from an explicitly anti-capitalist perspective. Since anti-capitalism is the underlying leftist cause, it overlaps significantly with a number of movements that don't presently have distinct, obvious, flashy subcultures. For instance, there are pro-environment leftists who want institutions to divest from companies that produce fossil fuels. And environmental studies classes are sometimes taught from a Marxist perspective: a 2016 workshop at Michigan State University educated students about the possibility of a green *and* red (in the communist sense) future.

"Given the worsening poverty and environmental crises characteristic of contemporary global capitalism, questions about sustainable human development are surely becoming absolutely central for all 21st century socialist thinkers," the event's website stated. "Marxist philosophy offers a substantial theory of the social-economic form that determines our capitalist world and opens up the possibility of envisioning a post-capitalist future."[5]

Modern environmentalists are often anti-globalist as well, since they believe corporations exploit resources in the third world, where regulation is less stringent. On this front, they are strange bedfellows with the Trumpian right, which is also anti-globalist, albeit for completely different reasons.

The most notable recent environmental justice flare-up was the Dakota Access Pipeline protests of 2016 and 2017, which pitted the federal government against Native American activists who were concerned the new pipeline would harm the environment. Both Sanders and Obama met with activists at the Standing Rock Indian Reservation to hear their demands, and solidarity marches were held all over the country. Shortly after taking office, Trump moved ahead with the pipeline project, and the National Guard evicted all protesters who still remained on-site.

Aside from Standing Rock, explicitly environmental activism seems to have taken something of a backseat these days. Even the Poor People's Campaign had to ground its environmentalism in anti-capitalist rhetoric and kooky spirituality to attract a crowd. If I had to guess, I'd say that the environmentalist cause doesn't mesh particularly well with identity-based intersectionality. That's because the victims of environmental calamity are, well, everyone. Aside from very narrow issues where specific groups are harmed— like the indigenous people of Standing Rock—environmentalism is largely about saving the entire world. It's too "all lives matter" for 2019.

In the first few weeks of 2019, environmental issues made a

brief return to the forefront of American politics with Rep. Ocasio-Cortez's introduction of the Green New Deal, a resolution to combat climate change. As is typical of intersectionality-influenced activism, the GND significantly overreached, including demands wholly unrelated to the environment, such as affordable housing and education for all, paid family leave time for workers, and "economic security for all those who are unable or unwilling to work." This provision appeared on a fact sheet accompanying the GND, drawing so much criticism that Ocasio-Cortez's staffers eventually claimed it was erroneous and released by mistake. The left might consider that many people would like the government to do more to help the poor, the working class, and the environment, but draw the line at bailing out all those who obstinately refuse to take care of themselves.

Deafening Silence

Though leftists are stridently anti-war, there is currently no tangible anti-war movement to speak of in the United States. Leftist activists routinely march in opposition to Trump, sexual harassment, income inequality, and even climate change. But the continued U.S. military involvement in the Middle East no longer merits much more than a shrug, organizationally speaking.

Anti-war advocacy was one of the main causes of late-1960s activism, of course. But even as recently as the 2000s, opposition to war was of central importance to young activists—and not just for leftists but for liberals and libertarians as well. During my years as an undergraduate at the University of Michigan (2006–10), campus anti-war demonstrations were common. The two most widely admired politicians—the ones who generated the most excitement and the largest crowds—were the most stridently anti-war major candidates on both the left *and* the right: Barack Obama and Republican congressman Ron Paul. It might surprise readers that Paul, a conservative libertarian with right-of-center social views, could draw a crowd of two thousand cheering left-leaning college students at the University of Michigan, but in 2007, he did just that.[6] (I was there in the audience.) Paul wanted U.S. forces to withdraw from Iraq and Afghanistan, and students loved him for it, despite his other policy views, which were libertarian or conservative. I remember talking with a colleague at the *Michigan Daily*, an extremely left-of-center female student of color. She told me Barack Obama was her first choice to be the next president. Her second choice was Ron Paul.

But after Obama was elected president, the noise faded. Less than a year into his first term, President Obama was awarded a staggeringly premature Nobel Peace Prize; Nobel Committee members hoped that he would interpret the award as a mandate to pursue global peace initiatives. The wars in Iraq and Afghanistan dragged on anyway, and the U.S. government involved itself in additional military conflicts in the Middle East during Obama's two terms: in Libya, Syria, Yemen, and elsewhere.

The wars didn't end, but attendance at anti-war rallies plummeted in the years after Obama's election. While many of the most hard-core activists remained interested in anti-war activity, partisan Democrats fled the movement, falsely content that their mission was accomplished.

"The antiwar movement demobilized as Democrats, who had been motivated to participate by anti-Republican sentiments, withdrew from antiwar protests when the Democratic Party achieved electoral success, if not policy success in ending the wars in Iraq and Afghanistan," argued a team of University of Michigan researchers in a paper that analyzed rally attendance data.[7]

Bill Ayers, a consistent opponent of war, told me that burnout can be a real problem. "I think that we had a moment in 2003 when the anti-war movement threatened to reorganize itself and become a real force," he said. "How we failed to do that, I'm not wise enough to unpack that. But we had a moment in 2003 where the country was against this intervention. The world was against it. And the intervention happened anyway."

It's possible that an increased reliance on drone strikes has made war seem distant and alien, like it's happening on some other planet. It's also possible that we have come to think of U.S. military entanglements in the Middle East as normal and unavoidable. Young people born after 9/11 will soon be old enough to enlist in the armed forces and be sent to Afghanistan to fight in a war that has lasted for their entire lives.

"If we can't find a way to make war a central issue, we are in a world of trouble," said Ayers.

At least for now, this seems like an impossible task. Opposing war was easier when the warmonger was President George Bush, a conventionally hawkish Republican. But after eight years with a defiantly hawkish Democrat in power, the issue is scrambled and confused. For those of us who continue to think U.S. leadership—whether it's Bush, Obama, or Trump—is too eager to deploy military methods in service of regime change in the Middle East, the anti-war movement's absence is keenly felt.

Post-Parkland

"We are tired of gun violence—our school could be next," a trio of girls—ages thirteen, thirteen, and eleven—informed me. "What if it is?"

It was March 2018, and I was at the March for Our Lives rally in Washington, D.C., where an estimated two hundred thousand people—many of them teenagers—had turned out to oppose gun violence in schools. Survivors of the horrific mass shooting at Marjory Stoneman Douglas High School in Parkland, Florida, had organized the event, and the many young people I interviewed were terrified that they would be next.

"I don't feel safe in school," a Maryland high schooler told me.

"Every fire drill, every alarm that goes off, I'm worried," said one of the thirteen-year-olds.

For many of the attendees, the obvious solution was to ban guns. Some wanted to ban all guns; others just wanted to get rid of so-called assault weapons.

"We should stop having guns anywhere at all," a teenage boy told me. "I feel like guns should be outlawed."

But it wasn't just guns: many young people wanted more security guards, police officers, metal detectors, and other school security measures to be put in place. Kids are vulnerable, and school is a dangerous place, their thinking goes. And whenever a mass shooting happens, their worst fears are confirmed.

The anti-gun movement added a number of passionate young activists to its ranks in 2018, following the Parkland tragedy, in which an unhinged former student named Nikolas Cruz shot and killed seventeen students and staff members at the school. Among the survivors, three students—David Hogg, Cameron Kasky, and Emma González—quickly emerged as spokespersons. All three were well-spoken and telegenic. Kasky, a baby-faced seventeen-year-old self-described "theater kid," debated Florida senator Marco Rubio at a CNN town hall event a week after the shooting; the teen effortlessly eviscerated the senator, who tripped over himself trying to explain why he couldn't just stop taking money from a pro-gun lobbyist group, the National Rifle Association.

Hogg, a high school correspondent for the *Sun-Sentinel* newspaper with an interest in video journalism, was particularly well prepared to become the face of teen anti-gun activism. Tall and handsome, he delivers speeches at rallies as if he's been doing it for years. Though neither Hogg nor his allies responded to a request for comment, I did meet him briefly at a party in Washington, D.C., in the spring of 2018. Off camera, he was stoic and a bit out of sorts, though it couldn't have been easy being the only person at the event who wasn't old enough to drink.

González, the daughter of a Cuban immigrant and president of Marjory Stoneman Douglas's gay-straight alliance at the time of the massacre, comes across as the most radical of the group—perhaps by accident. Her chosen hairstyle is a buzz cut, but not because she's trying to make a statement.

"People asked me, 'Are you taking a feminist stand?' No, I wasn't," she told the *Sun-Sentinel*. "It's Florida. Hair is just an extra sweater I'm forced to wear."[8]

Nevertheless, Jorge Duany, a professor of anthropology at Florida International University, told the *Washington Post* that González's "queerness connects her both to a U.S. politics of social justice and to Cuban and Cuban American struggles for queer rights. She is part of a generation that feels freer about claiming identities and loyalties."[9]

That's something we've seen explicitly with young progressive activists: an appeal to overlapping identities, in keeping with the tenets of intersectionality. Even so, post-Parkland anti-gun activism—the youngest movement I've studied for this book—seems reasonably focused on its single issue and has thus far avoided some of the problems that have plagued other Zillennial activists. To their credit, the March for Our Lives organizers have remained laser-focused on chipping away at gun rights, and have expressed a willingness to work with anyone on the left, on the right, or in the center who shares their goals. They do not, for instance, blame everything on capitalism. (Of course, there's still time—Kasky, Hogg, and González have yet to take a course in critical theory.)

While intersectionality has not warped the priorities of the anti-gun movement, the other staple of Zillennial activism—safety culture—is omnipresent. The survivors of mass shootings, of course, have better reason than most to be feeling unsafe, to be extra sensitive to safety concerns, and to ask what reasonable steps could be taken or what new policies implemented to reduce the likelihood of mass shootings.

Mass shootings, though, are not particularly common events. As we discussed in the introduction, overall gun violence has declined precipitously since the early 1990s, and school shootings are no exception. According to James Alan Fox, a professor of criminology at Northeastern University, shootings in schools are no more common than they used to be—indeed, they are less common.[10] Fox's research describes school shootings as "incredibly rare events." The data simply do not support the contention that school shootings have reached epidemic proportions.

This would come as news to the kids at the March for Our Lives rally, who spoke as if the fate of every kid in America would be to perish in a mass shooting until and unless the Second Amendment is repealed. And it wasn't just rally participants—organizers humored this narrative. The March for Our Lives website contends, "Our schools are unsafe. Our children and teachers are dying. . . . Every kid in this country now goes to school wondering if this day might be their last. We live in fear."

This level of fear just isn't validated by the data. Death by accident—car crash, drowning, choking—is significantly more likely than death by mass shooting.[11] Even among gun deaths, tragedies such as Parkland and Newtown are a departure from the norm: most gun deaths are suicides, one-off homicides, or accidents, and they typically involve handguns, which kill far more people each year than assault rifles.[12]

One can still think gun control is an important public policy for combating overall violence—fewer guns would probably mean fewer suicides, for instance.[13] But the bottom line is that mass-casualty school shootings are already so rare, it would be fairly difficult to craft a public policy that would further reduce them.

Why, then, is the culture of fear surrounding mass shootings—and school shootings, specifically—so pervasive? To answer that question, we need to wind the clock back two decades, to April 20, 1999. I would argue that this single day was a huge contributor to the rise of safe-space culture in American schools. It is at least as important as September 11, 2001, in terms of understanding the psychological factors and explicit government policies that undergird Zillennial safety needs.

April 20, 1999, was the day two teenagers, Eric Harris and Dylan Klebold, murdered thirteen of their classmates and teachers—and wounded two dozen others—in what became known as the Columbine massacre. The tragedy, the deadliest high school shooting in history up to that point in time, created mass panic about violence in schools. In response, policymakers codified a new regime of permanent coddling in American education aimed at addressing the root causes of Columbine. Unfortunately, most people vastly misunderstood the *why* of Harris and Klebold, and the policies that kicked into high gear in Columbine's wake—anti-bullying initiatives, zero-tolerance discipline, and school resource officers—reenvisioned school as a place where kids would feel protected from all dangers, physical *and* emotional. If the "safe space" is a symbol of modern American education gone wrong, Columbine and its aftermath played a surprising, subtle role in getting us there.

News coverage in the wake of Columbine fixated on bullying as the easiest explanation for the actions of the killers. A typical news story in the *Washington Post* decried Columbine's "cult of the athlete" and its penchant for turning a blind eye to jocks tormenting social outcasts like Harris and Klebold.[14] "The sports trophies were showcased in the front hall—the artwork, down a back corridor," the *Post* lamented, as if the likelihood of this arrangement producing a mass shooting was obvious in hindsight.

Bullying was bad at Columbine, but there's surprisingly little evidence that the killers were pushed past some breaking point. On the contrary, there's good evidence that Harris, in particular, was a sociopath bent on doing something truly evil, independent of the circumstances at his school.

Writer Dave Cullen's 2009 book, *Columbine,* shattered many of the myths associated with the attack. Harris and Klebold, Cullen writes, were *themselves* bullies—a fact that better reflects the reality of the high school experience, where alliances and enmities between various students shift more frequently than on an episode of *The Real Housewives of Orange County.* Nor did they specifically target their tormentors during the attack: while some of the people they shot were athletes, none of these victims had been known to go after Harris and Klebold. Harris, according to Cullen, was the

real mastermind. (Klebold, a more traditionally troubled kid, probably would not have pulled it off on his own.) Harris was driven
not by revenge or even hatred but by his contempt for those he
deemed inferior, including "people who say that wrestling is real,"
"people who use the same word over and over again," and "Star
Wars fans." "GET A FRIGGIN LIFE YOU BORING GEEEEEEKS!"
he wrote on his website.

"These are not the rantings of an angry young man, picked on
by jocks until he's not going to take it anymore," wrote Cullen in
Slate. "These are the rantings of someone with a messianic-grade
superiority complex, out to punish the entire human race for its
appalling inferiority."[15]

Other popular motivating factors—violent videogames, Mar-
ilyn Manson's music, the "trench coat mafia," and America's
violent gun culture (the preferred explanation of Michael Moore's
documentary film *Bowling for Columbine*)—have been similarly
debunked.

"All these theories had one theme in common: that the perpetrators were actually victims," wrote *New York Times* columnist
David Brooks in 2004. "In retrospect, it's striking how avidly we
clung to this perpetrator-as-victim narrative."[16]

The panic that followed bears a lot of similarities to the panic
over kidnappings and stranger danger (detailed in the introduction)
that helped codify policies discouraging children from being independent. To stop bullying—and the violence that would surely
result from it—schools needed to adopt zero-tolerance policies
aimed at weeding out problematic kids. Bringing a weapon to
school, talking about weapons, playing with objects that weren't
weapons but looked like weapons: all of these were verboten. Such
policies became more and more ridiculous over the years, until in
2013, a seven-year-old boy from Maryland was suspended for
chewing his Pop-Tart into the shape of a gun.[17] More recently, in
March 2017, a five-year-old girl, Caitlin, was suspended for holding
a stick that looked like a gun while playing make-believe during
recess.[18] (She was pretending to be a royal guard.) A spokesperson

for Hoke County Schools defended the decision to suspend Caitlin on the ground that she "posed a threat to other students when she made a shooting motion" with the stick. There was even a fourth-grader from Odessa, Texas, who was suspended for "making a terroristic threat" against another student: the boy claimed his magic ring could make a classmate disappear like Bilbo in *The Lord of the Rings* movies.[19]

Again, school violence was decreasing before Columbine, and continued to decrease after. But media obsession with school shootings captured the public's overactive imagination, and a spate of bad policies followed. Zero-tolerance policies were just the tip of the iceberg. Consider this: Before 1975, there were virtually zero cops in schools. But a nationwide spike in crime—the crime rate rose a whopping 80 percent between 1975 and 1989—changed that. While policymakers confronted real violence in the streets, they came to fixate on schools as places where firmer policing was required. Schools began to hire school resource officers (SROs) to patrol the hallways and take on an increased role in meting out discipline to wayward students. By 1997, about 20 percent of public schools employed some kind of cop.

Beginning in 1999 (the same year, one notes, as the Columbine shootings), the federal government stepped in. The Department of Justice's Office of Community Oriented Policing Services (COPS) started doling out millions of dollars to school districts for the purpose of hiring SROs. Between 1999 and 2006, some three thousand school districts took advantage of $753 million in federal funds, hiring cops left and right. In 2010, that same office initiated the COPS Hiring Program, which gave a whopping $1 billion to local municipalities over the years for the purposes of hiring and retaining police officers. School resource officers were the second-most-common beneficiaries of this funding. The COPS office claims that its grants have made it possible for schools to hire some seven thousand police officers over the last twenty years. It is now the case that 43 percent of public schools, including two-thirds of middle schools and high schools, employ a police officer.

I can think of no better way to convince an entire generation that the world is unsafe and that students are especially vulnerable than to install police officers in every elementary school, expel or arrest anyone who engages in deviant behavior, and incessantly engage in fearmongering about mass shootings.

We expect young people to value freedom, autonomy, and individuality, and we're frustrated that so many college students want administrators to make them feel safe from offensive ideas and hurtful words—to stamp out dissent and punish imperfection. But perhaps we shouldn't be so surprised that young people feel this way: after all, their formative years were spent in educational institutions that have become undeniably more carceral—where people who provoke the authorities, test the boundaries of acceptable behavior, or say or do inappropriate things are weeded out. It's no wonder they recoil in horror at the kind of absolute freedom that can be found (ideally) in college: they have been taught that school is a dangerous place, but the authorities are there to make everybody feel safe and comfortable.

Given the role media and government have played in fostering safe-space culture, it's brutally unfair to blame the kids themselves for craving comfort. If Zillennials suffer from learned helplessness, it's really the previous generation's fault. And yet the Parkland survivors are routinely pilloried by conservative media. Hogg and González have been victims of vicious conspiracies; a fake photo purporting to show González shredding a copy of the Constitution spread like wildfire among right-wing Twitter users. When Hogg complained publicly about being rejected by UCLA, conservatives mocked him relentlessly. He was also "swatted" by an unknown prankster; "swatting" is a new phenomenon that involves filing a false police report claiming there is a dangerous armed person at a specific address. The SWAT team then shows up to the address, prepared for a hostage situation. The odious practice has already cost innocent people their lives. (Neither Hogg nor his family was at home when the SWAT team arrived, thankfully.)

Instead of heading to college in 2018, Hogg decided to take a year off from school to focus on political outreach in the run-up to the midterm elections. March for Our Lives is now primarily concerned with registering young people to vote in hopes of gaining more support for national gun control measures. According to its website, "Now is the time for the youth vote to stand up to the gun lobby when no one else will." In the past, the anti-gun movement has had difficulty keeping its momentum going—the American public loses interest in the issue as the most recent tragedy fades from memory. We have yet to see whether this time will be any different.

Born in the TPUSA

"The left hates the idea that there are other ideas," said Charlie Kirk, the fast-talking twenty-six-year-old founder and president of Turning Point USA (TPUSA), an activist group for conservative students. "There's a reason leftists ostracize others from campus. They don't like to be around people who disagree with them. They are wildly intolerant."

Kirk is tall and dark of hair, and on this day he was dressed in a snappy navy blue suit. He was speaking from the stage at TPUSA's July 2018 High School Leadership Summit in Washington, D.C. The event featured quite a roster: attendees enjoyed speeches from Attorney General Jeff Sessions, House majority whip Steve Scalise, Fox News host Jesse Watters, podcaster Dave Rubin, and dozens of other right-of-center celebs. A few hundred conservative high school students sat in the audience—several wearing red "Make America Great Again" hats. These are kids who profess to love capitalism—there was an "I ♥ Capitalism" banner on the stage— and especially love Trump, even though the two are often in deep conflict. (Just hours before Kirk appeared onstage, Trump had tweeted, "Tariffs are the greatest!")

Young people lean to the left, and so the attendees at the TPUSA event shared the bond of holding beliefs unpopular among their peer group. "How many of you lost friends for posting about politics?" asked Kirk. Virtually every single person in the audience raised a hand.

I spoke with some of the teens in between sessions. Nearly all had been bullied by their classmates for holding conservative views, which was part of the reason they considered the left to be horridly intolerant. Many identified with Kyle Kashuv, a pro-gun Parkland survivor who has become a notable young conservative activist in the last year and who lost friends for coming out as a Second Amendment supporter in the wake of the massacre.

"I had lost like 90 percent of all the friends I've had because of it," Kashuv told me. "It shows that people just don't have the ability to be friends with people who have disagreeing opinions with them."

Kashuv's pro-gun views might have made him a pariah in Parkland, but at TPUSA—where he now serves as director of high school outreach—he's a celebrity. His appearances onstage—he introduced most of the speakers and participated in an "ask me anything" session—frequently drew wild cheers, and everybody wanted to get a picture with him.

One attendee, a fifteen-year-old I'll call Rachel, who struck up a conversation with me while I was searching for an outlet to charge my iPhone, described Kashuv as "looking like a snack." I had no idea what that meant. It's slang for someone who's considered attractive, she explained.

Rachel, echoing other students' comments, told me people at her school turned against her when they found out she was a conservative. The summit was a welcome relief from that, and also a reminder that she wasn't alone.

"I think we just all realized this was a place we could be ourselves, because we are so used to not being ourselves," she told me.

Rachel had made plenty of new friends at the conference, including Sam, an exceedingly chatty sixteen-year-old who hoped to enter the military—just as soon as he finished educating me on every aspect of his conservative worldview. Indeed, this was the norm; while activists at leftist gatherings frequently greet me and other members of the press with skepticism and caution, these right-wing teenagers couldn't wait to confess their unpopular opinions. I later found myself desperately trying to escape a conversation with another attendee who was hell-bent on convincing me that term limits were indefensible on conservative grounds, something I could not have had less interest in debating.

Another teen, Amara, was a bit more reserved than her friends Rachel and Sam. She was also fifteen, and ethnically mixed: part Hispanic, part black, part white. She told me she wanted to be a journalist—before becoming president.

Conservatives are often parodied as disproportionately white and disproportionately male—thus the stereotype of the College Republican frat bro—but the summit included plenty of young women and people of color. I heard one Latino teen from New York City explaining to his friends that some of his relatives were illegal immigrants, and he wondered if he should call ICE on them. Despite her Trumpian immigration views, Rachel told him not to be a snitch.

These were very conservative kids: not just on immigration but on the economy and abortion as well. They were more mixed on gay marriage; when speaker Dave Rubin reminded the audience he was gay and asked if that mattered to them, their loud cheering seemed to confirm that it did not. Many also shared the libertarian perspective that at least some drugs should be legalized. Some were staunchly faith-inclined; others were atheists. When I asked Kashuv whether he was religious, he replied, "Not quite."

One gets the sense from talking with these kids that the most important issue—aside from illegal immigration, perhaps—is political correctness. Fearful that social media mobs would come for them, their sense of victimization was as palpable as that of anyone on the intersectional progressive left. The issue of "shadow banning"—also called "stealth banning" or "ghost banning"—was of paramount importance to them. That's when a social media platform such as Facebook or Twitter takes steps to prevent people from seeing a user's posts and content but does not block or ban the person in ways that would be obvious. For instance, Twitter's search function has been accused of obscuring content from prominent Republicans. (Twitter denied that it was doing this, but its denial—"You are always able to see the tweets from accounts you follow, although you may have to do more work to find them"—actually seemed to confirm the practice.)[20]

The issue has drawn attention from President Trump himself, who tweeted, "Twitter 'SHADOW BANNING' prominent Republicans. Not good. We will look into this discriminatory and illegal practice at once! Many complaints."[21] Twitter, though, is a private company, and the federal government meddling with its internal speech policies would be an obvious First Amendment violation. In any case, Trump is widely loved by these teens: he's the Zillennial conservatives' political icon, as President Ronald Reagan was for the generation of conservatives who came of age during the 1980s.

Of course, many of these kids hold political views that are still in flux. When I asked Kashuv what kind of conservative he was, he admitted that he was still developing his viewpoint. In the meantime, I should consider him "just a big constitutional guy," he said.

Like so many young conservatives of his generation, Kashuv was heavily influenced by Jordan Peterson and Ben Shapiro. The latter has become something of a mentor to Kashuv, giving him tips before television appearances and speaking engagements. The former is more like a life coach.

"I think Peterson is actually resulting in a massive change in our youth today, especially with the male youth," Kashuv told me. "He's giving them hope, and he's telling them how to better their lives, and he's actually influencing thousands of people every day."

TPUSA was founded by Kirk in 2012, when he was eighteen. The organization's mission is to educate students about free markets and conservative principles, and counter the left-wing bias on university campuses. Kirk has rapidly built an impressive organization with a multimillion-dollar budget. The billionaire Foster

Friess, a well-known funder of conservative causes, provided the organization with its initial funding.

TPUSA had a breakout year in 2016. That's when Kirk debuted his "Professor Watchlist," which is exactly what it sounds like: a list of liberal professors across the country who produced some scholarship, or made statements in class, implying a leftist world-view. The idea is to counter in-class bias. A representative entry for a politics professor at Virginia Tech University highlights her view that burning fossil fuels is "a reassertion of white masculine power on an unruly planet that is perceived to be increasingly in need of violent, authoritarian order."[22]

That might be a silly way to frame the renewable energy issue, but does this professor—and hundreds of others like her—really deserve to be named and shamed, absent any real evidence that she is actually biased against conservative students?

Policing professors for dissident leftist views is not exactly in keeping with a commitment to the ethos of free speech, which is one reason the watch list has drawn criticism from more principled advocates for campus free expression. Sarah Ruger, director of free speech initiatives at the Charles Koch Institute—the charitable foundation run by the libertarian Koch brothers—has described such efforts as "McCarthyism 2.0" and "entirely antithetical to who we are."[23]

The conservative Young America's Foundation (YAF), a rival organization that has existed since the 1960s, has likewise criticized TPUSA. In a leaked internal memo, YAF warned that "the long-term damage TPUSA could inflict on conservative students and the Conservative Movement can no longer be ignored."[24] Kirk's defenders slammed the memo as nothing but sour grapes.

Criticism has also come from students formerly affiliated with TPUSA. Kaitlin Bennett, an organizer for TPUSA's Kent State University chapter who resigned in fury during the fall 2017 se-mester, accused Kirk of throwing her under the bus after a stunt gone wrong. The chapter had organized a mock safe space—complete with a grown adult in a diaper—in order to protest the concept, but the diaper-wearing person looked so ridiculous that the tactic backfired. Bennett claimed that Kirk initially congratulated her, saying, "Keep up the triggering, good job," but then turned on her after people began tweeting pictures of diapers at him.[25]

Many on the right believe TPUSA is too obsessed with attacking the left. At the leadership summit, both UN ambassador Nikki Haley and education secretary Betsy DeVos gave speeches imploring the teens to focus on trying to persuade liberals, not just trolling them.

It's good advice; whether the TPUSA network will take it is another matter. During the summit, audience members frequently broke into trollish cheers of "Lock her up!" with reference to former secretary of state Hillary Clinton. When they did so during Sessions's speech about the importance of free speech on campus, the attorney general repeated the line and laughed.

EIGHT

BLEACHED

SOCIAL MEDIA AND THE ALT-RIGHT

The Lincoln Memorial in Washington, D.C., might seem like an awkward place for white nationalists to hold a rally—racists can't really claim President Abraham Lincoln, liberator of slaves, as an alt-right forefather. But maybe that's the point. For the new young far-right white nationalist activists, much of what they do is deliberately ironic: a joke, intended to "own the libs" (i.e., infuriate liberals). But these jokes are a cover for a truly disturbing belief system.

In June 2017, members of the racist alt-right gathered near the Lincoln Memorial to hear speeches from leaders of their movement, including the militantly anti-PC YouTube personality known as Baked Alaska (who, in a previous life, was a videographer for *BuzzFeed* until the over-the-top political correctness of his colleagues drove him into the arms of the alt-right) and forty-year-old alt-right intellectual leader Richard Spencer.[1] Spencer's event took place next to the reflecting pool; leftist protesters organized a counterdemonstration on the steps of the memorial, well within shouting distance. I covered both events, interviewing attendees about their reasons for coming.

I had scarcely set foot in the alt-right rally zone when someone called my name—an old acquaintance from college recognized me, and came over to say hello. Let's call him Daniel.

Daniel looked different than he had the last time I saw him: he had bleached his brown hair blond and wore it long on top, buzzed on the sides. He was also beginning to grow a beard. His attire was equally notable: khaki pants and a T-shirt depicting Donald Trump standing atop a tank, wielding a machine gun, flanked by an American flag and an eagle with a rocket launcher.[2]

I had known Daniel as a friendly, polite, thoughtful kid with moderately conservative or libertarian tendencies. And yet here he was at a Richard Spencer rally. I asked him—not too pointedly—why he had come. He was "just checking it out," he told me.

As we chatted, I learned that Daniel had recently gotten married: to a Muslim woman, in fact. I asked what she thought of Daniel being here. He explained that she was supportive and had even wanted to come herself, but Daniel had talked her out of it—due to an unspoken concern for her safety, I gathered.

Another rally attendee came up to us. I didn't know this young man, but Daniel evidently did. I'll call him Adam. He was wearing a red "Make America Great Again" hat and holding a sign featuring a drawing of a helicopter and the message "Free rides for commies," a reference to the extrajudicial killings of political dissidents that occurred under fascist regimes in South America. The alt-right makes this reference approvingly: it's good to throw their enemies out of helicopters, or at least funny to joke about it.

The strangest moment of this meeting occurred when Adam took note of Daniel's new hair color and said, "You look like a fashy Eminem"—"fashy" not as in "fashionable" but as in "fascist." The remark was clearly intended as a compliment.

What is the alt-right? Simply put, it's a movement of young social-media-savvy white nationalists who think conservatism is a better home for them than liberalism due to the latter's affection for multiculturalism, which they consider anathema. But mainstream conservatism is scarcely better in this regard, and so the radicals needed to supplant the right as it currently exists. Thus the *alt*-right: an alternative to the right that's neither more nor less conservative but something else entirely.

I've cautioned previously that we shouldn't overstate the Zillennial left's size and influence—most people are politically indifferent, and we can't judge an entire generation based on its most extreme members. The same holds true for the weird movement known as the alt-right. The June 25 rally involved at most two hundred people, not all of them devout followers. This is a radical fringe movement with blessedly little power to affect public policy. "While the alt-right is real and visible, there's no reason to believe it's a very vast group or one that will stick around for very long," wrote the journalist Olivia Nuzzi in the *Washington Post*.[3]

The movement itself sees things differently, and cites Trump's victory as proof that its ideas are gaining traction. Trump isn't a member of the alt-right, of course, but he speaks their language more closely than any other major Republican figure. Trump adviser-turned-occasional-rival Steve Bannon is well aware of the alt-right's existence, and under his leadership, the conservative website *Breitbart* intentionally catered to this audience. The alt-right is still very much a fringe movement, to be sure, but it's one that occupies a place of increasing energy on the right.

That's especially true when one considers just young people—the subject of this book. Conservatives constitute a minority of politically interested young people, who are themselves a minority of Zillennials. But among this minority within a minority, the alt-right is ascending. Its members are surprisingly young, well read, and college educated.

As we have seen throughout this book, leftists wield significant influence on some college campuses. The alt-right doesn't have a comparable base of power, but its members have played an important role in infesting social media sites and making them miserably toxic places. Their campaigns of harassment against people they deem inferior—blacks and immigrants, but also Jews and Muslims, women, and Democrats—make them well worthy of study.

As was the case with the extreme anti-capitalist left, readers will be struck by the weirdness of alt-right lingo and habits. The alt-right's mascot is a cartoon frog named Pepe that originally had nothing to do with racism or even politics. Its members would like to live in a fictional country called the Republic of Kekistan, where political correctness would be outlawed. A day in the life of an alt-right-affiliated young man (the movement is overwhelmingly male) might involve waking up, logging on to Twitter, and sending rape threats to feminist writers, genocide jokes to Jewish writers, and trolling criticism to journalists in general. Such acts of provocation and abuse are called "shit-posting" in Internet meme culture. When Twitter retaliates and bans the harassers from its platform— something the social media company has the absolute right to do—alt-right activists complain that overly sensitive liberals are trampling their free speech rights. Many think social media should be considered a public utility rather than a private entity.

It can be hard to believe that there are actual people hidden behind the frog avatars and Holocaust humor. But they're real. While I was at the rally in front of the Lincoln Memorial, I overheard one attendee tell another: "I'm working so many hours now I don't even have time to shit-post."

What began for some as politically incorrect humor morphed into something far, far darker. The alt-right activist Christopher Cantwell—derisively dubbed "the crying Nazi" when video footage surfaced of him shedding tears after being repeatedly peppersprayed during a scuffle with antifa—recalled for me an incident that took place before his conversion to white nationalism, when he was engaged in an argument about feminism on Twitter. Cantwell's opponent, a black man, eventually branded Cantwell a misogynist.

"I just hate those stupid accusations," Cantwell, a bald, bulky thirty-seven-year-old who speaks with a thick New York accent, told me in an interview. "So I say, 'Well, if you think my misogyny is bad, wait until you get ahold of my racism.' And I called him a nigger. I just thought this was funny."

Identitarians

The intellectual precursor to the alt-right was "paleoconservatism," a movement that took shape in the 1980s but can trace its own intellectual development to the conservative noninterventionism of earlier twentieth-century figures such as Senator Robert Taft, who opposed America's entry into World War II. Like traditional conservatives, paleocons stressed the importance of limited government and social conservatism. But they were inclined toward isolationism when it came to issues involving foreign countries: immigration, free trade, and war.

This was not exactly an odd mix of opinions for a strain of conservatism to hold. Republicans in the mold of President William McKinley, the first twentieth-century president, supported tariffs on grounds that they protected American industry from unfair foreign competition. And it was not until recent times that the Republican Party became synonymous with a hawkish foreign policy: World War I, World War II, the Korean War, and the Vietnam War were all joined or escalated under Democratic administrations.

In the 1980s, Ronald Reagan's massive electoral victories elevated the status of conservatism. But by this time a rift was apparent between the paleoconservatism of Pat Buchanan, who served as Reagan's director of communications from 1985 to 1987, and a more hawkish conservatism. This split became much more apparent in subsequent Republican administrations; in the early 2000s, the dominant strain of conservatism became known as "neoconservatism," which advocated robust military intervention abroad in response to the 9/11 terrorist attacks.

Buchanan unsuccessfully sought the Republican presidential nomination in 1992 and 1996, and by 2000 he had bolted for the Reform Party. In 2002, he cofounded the *American Conservative* as a paleoconservative alternative to more hawkish conservative opinion journals such as *National Review* and the *Weekly Standard*.

Today the *American Conservative* remains a well-respected publication. But, as *Vox*'s Dylan Matthews noted, the magazine is "basically alone in that" among explicitly paleo-sympathetic outlets.[4] (Having written favorably about Ron Paul and Rand Paul, the *American Conservative* also has a pronounced libertarian streak.) Other facets of the paleoconservative movement became gradually more accommodating of white supremacy, xenophobia, and even Holocaust denial. Commentary friendly to these ideas proliferated at fringe sites including *American Renaissance* and *VDARE,* which is named after Virginia Dare, the first white settler born in the British colonies in North America. (Dare vanished with the rest of the Roanoke colonists.)

"I started out as a paleoconservative," Kyle, a thirty-two-year-old attorney and alt-right member, told me in an interview via email. "I read Pat Buchanan's and Ann Coulter's books . . . I am how I am because I am well read."

But it would be wrong to suggest that the alt-right draws solely from the remnants of the paleocon movement. Some once called themselves libertarians and learned about the alt-right through the presidential campaigns of Ron Paul, whose noninterventionist foreign policy appealed to both groups. Others were libertarians who became active on college campuses, only to find their events continuously disrupted or shut down by leftists. Some of these libertarians radicalized in response, and their ideology morphed from "equal rights for all" into "destroy feminists and race activists as thoroughly as possible." Corrupted, you might say, by the dark side of the campus PC wars.

Before joining the alt-right, Cantwell—the "crying Nazi" mentioned earlier—had quite the intellectual journey. Two decades ago, his views were in line with Fox News, the only cable news network he watched. He dated black, Asian, and Latina women— he almost had a child with at least one of them, he told me—and harbored zero racial animosity. In 2009, he was arrested for driving under the influence, and started searching the internet for legal help. This search brought him into contact with the philosophy of libertarianism, which describes police officers (correctly, in my view) as an extension of the government that ought to be limited in their ability to disrupt people's lives, in keeping with the protections from unjust searches and seizures mandated by the Bill of Rights.

Eventually, this led him to get involved with the Ron Paul campaign, where he met anarcho-capitalists. Anarcho-capitalism, a more extreme version of libertarianism, holds that nearly every function of the government is illegitimate, and the state ought to be abolished so that all property can be privately owned. The rules for society would vary from fiefdom to fiefdom: on my property, my rules, on your property, yours. Cantwell came to find this position persuasive.

"I was trying to make a logical argument for the existence of the state and I felt that I was being bested," Cantwell told me. "So I revised my opinions."

Anarcho-capitalism might not seem like an obvious roadway to the alt-right, given that anarcho-capitalists are critical of the police and suspicious of authority, whereas the alt-right thinks of authoritarianism favorably, as long as it's the right-wing variety and not the left-wing kind. Sure enough, Cantwell harbored "violently anti-cop" and anti-authoritarian views during his anarcho-capitalist phase, he told me.

What happened next is a testament to the power of random encounters. Cantwell told me he saw a group of women and men on the street at night, involved in some kind of drunken domestic dispute. He tried to deescalate the situation, but one of the men came at him, and so he drew his gun.

"I was scared to death because I thought this guy was going to make me shoot him," said Cantwell. "Shockingly enough, I was rather glad to see the police pull up while I had a gun pointed at a man."

Cantwell told me he was surprised that the cops didn't immediately gun him down—he thought the cops were the bad guys. But these officers merely told Cantwell to lower his weapon, then asked what was going on. Cantwell had recorded the exchange with the drunk man on his cellphone, and after showing it to the cops, they gave him back his gun and sent him on his way.

"Boy, did I feel stupid about some of the shitty things I had said about police," said Cantwell.

The episode made Cantwell reconsider his strident anti-authoritarianism. He started listening to more people on the alt-right—at first in hopes of converting them to anarcho-capitalism, but later because he found their racial ideas alluring. The works of economist Hans-Hermann Hoppe, an anarcho-capitalist whose thinking provides a bridge to the alt-right, proved particularly influential. Hoppe's book *Democracy: The God That Failed* persuaded Cantwell that a truly anarcho-capitalist society would be authoritarian in character, rather than libertarian. (Hoppe, a fellow at the Ludwig von Mises Institute, does *not* describe himself as alt-right, and while he favors restrictive immigration policies, he has condemned restrictive trade policies as "inimical to human prosperity.")[5]

Cantwell gradually became persuaded that distinct ethnic groups have distinct interests, and that these interests do not align. Forcing these groups to occupy the same spaces in the same country was a recipe for disaster, and the cause of various social ills: violence, poverty, and so on. The world of cosmopolitan libertarianism, liberalism, and conservatism is a bad one, where ethnic tensions will rule.

"If my enemies get their way . . . we're all going to be some mongrel race of fucking savages, and the Jews are going to rule over all of us," he said.

While Cantwell came from anarcho-capitalism, the alt-right has drawn from all corners of the ideological spectrum, including the far left. Despite the movement's overall hatred of communists, it is not altogether uncommon to encounter former Marxists at alt-right rallies. Certain alt-right activists want something resembling economic equality for poor whites, and some alt-right leaders and friends of the movement have endorsed single-payer health care and abortion rights—both things that would give young men economic security, and thus more free time to advocate alt-right ideas.[6] Andrew Auernheimer, a neo-Nazi and alt-right hacker known online as "weev," was previously involved in the Occupy Wall Street movement.[7] Lane Davis, an alt-right blogger and conspiracy theorist now in prison for murdering his father during an argument, took an interest in Marxism, Occupy Wall Street, and even Islamic extremism before eventually finding a home on the far right.[8]

Even Richard Spencer, the former editor of the paleoconservative publication *Taki's Magazine* and the unofficial leader of the alt-right, sometimes sounds more positively disposed toward the left than the right. When I interviewed him, he criticized the "bumper-sticker Reaganism" of Turning Point USA, expressed skepticism of libertarianism and "free market economics," and spoke favorably of then-emerging Democratic Socialist candidate Alexandria Ocasio-Cortez. She resonates with people because she addresses the Zillennial generation's economic angst and has proposed solutions like greater health care coverage and basic income guarantees—things the alt-right should take seriously as possible means of alleviating the suffering of white Americans, according to Spencer.

"I want the alt-right to be something that you might associate with the left, in a way," he told me.

Spencer, who has moved from Montana to Arlington, Virginia, and back again, is credited with having coined the term "alt-right," and founded its online home, altright.com, in 2012. He talks like a philosopher, and dresses the part; the left-of-center magazine *Mother Jones* described him as "dapper," though many readers balked at this flattery.[9]

The two-word summary of Spencer's thinking is this: race matters. "Race is real," he told me. "Race is a highly predictive concept for thinking about society and economics, outcomes, and all that kind of stuff."

Unlike paleoconservatism, the alt-right is explicitly racial. Its motivating belief is identitarianism: the idea that people belong to racial groups, and that these groups possess very different characteristics. White people and black people have different cultures and traditions, and it would be better for everyone if they self-segregated into different countries. The same would be true for Latinos, Arabs, and so forth.

The left is often pilloried for embracing identity politics: separating people into categories based on race, gender, sexual orientation, or other attributes. But Spencer thinks this approach has merit—and should be extended to the kind of white European who descends from the culture of Rome.

"Conservatives love to hate identity politics," said Spencer. "I think actually the left is getting at something real when they say, 'I am not just an American citizen. I'm not just an individual consumer or producer in capitalism. I am an African,' and that emotional resonance, visceral resonance, is so real. The conservatives and libertarians as well just want to run away from that and pretend that it doesn't exist, or pretend that it is always bad."

Spencer, of course, is more adept than most at dressing up white nationalist ideas. Listen to virtually anyone else in the movement, and the cruelty of those ideas becomes more obvious. At the time this chapter was written, for instance, altright.com's lead article was a commendation of Attorney General Jeff Sessions for cracking down on marijuana users, because "pot makes you into an introspective, effeminate, 'open-minded,' bug man," according to alt-right writer Malcolm Jaggers. "Weed makes you a pussy who's stuck in your own mind with your precious thoughts. Needless to say, a preoccupation with others' feelings is not especially masculine."[10]

Masculinity is very important to the alt-right. Men should be tough, and violent when necessary. Alt-right activists associate femininity with liberalism and multiculturalism. One of the alt-right's favorite pejoratives is "cuckservative," a portmanteau of "conservative" and "cuckold," a term for a man whose wife sleeps with other men. Cuckservatives, according to the alt-right, have done nothing to prevent immigrants and minorities from figuratively coming into their houses and sleeping with their wives; to the extent the conservative movement has condoned and supported multiculturalism, conservatives are complicit in this cuckoldry, even appearing to derive sexual pleasure from their own humiliation. It's an ugly term with a racially charged history. The alt-right doesn't want people of color sleeping with white women, metaphorically *or* literally: the latter would dilute the purity of the white race.

In practice, these beliefs might not sound any less despicable than what the Ku Klux Klan or the Nazi Party believes, and alt-right activists frequently make statements about black and Jewish people that square with a KKK or Nazi worldview. Spencer and the more media-savvy members try to cloak the alt-right in a façade of respectability. They will say that *everyone* would be better served by a society separated into various racial collectives, but that the transition to this utopian future should ideally be peaceful and voluntary. At the rally in front of the Lincoln Memorial, Spencer was asked what he thought about interracial marriage, and replied, "Well, it's not ideal," but he didn't think it was an important concern for his movement. His hope was that white people would *want* to have white children, rather than mixed-race children, because they were proud of their race and their culture.

Despite the peaceful nature of the Lincoln Memorial event, alt-right events have occasionally played host to terrible things. Case in point: the infamous August 2017 rally in Charlottesville, Virginia, where supporters of the alt-right marched in opposition to the city's decision to tear down a statue of Confederate general Robert E. Lee, who is considered an icon of the movement. Removing images of white historical figures from public places is viewed by the movement as a form of *white* erasure, a complaint that calls to mind some of the left's grievances. Alt-right activists often chant "You will not replace us!" at their marches; they are specifically radicalized by the idea that multiculturalism is about erasing white identity.

The Charlottesville rally drew some of the most significant members of the alt-right, including Cantwell, Spencer, Baked Alaska, and Jason Kessler, the white nationalist who helped organize the event. It quickly descended into chaos. A counterdemonstrator, Heather Heyer, was run over and killed after an alt-right sympathizer drove his car into the crowd. On Twitter, Kessler responded to Heyer's death with a link to the *Daily Stormer*, an explicitly neo-Nazi website, and the following statement: "Heather Heyer was a fat, disgusting communist. Communists have killed 94 million. Looks like it was pay back time."[11]

Cantwell turned himself in to the authorities after learning there was a warrant out for his arrest; he was accused of pepperspraying counterdemonstrators in the face. Cantwell said it was self-defense, and that the media has been determined to misrepresent the situation so that he ends up in prison.

"The media has absolutely been saturated with fuckin' propaganda against me," he told me.

Since the alt-right—much like antifa—is prepared to meet aggression with violence, violence can and does ensue at their events. After Spencer spoke at the University of Florida in October 2017, three of his supporters drove to a bus stop and started yelling "Heil Hitler" at random commuters.[12] An argument followed; one of the white nationalists drew a gun and, at the behest of his compatriots, fired a single shot that hit no one. Police eventually caught the trio—brothers Colton Fears and William Fears, and Tyler Tenbrink—and arrested them. Tenbrink, the one who actually shot at the bus passengers, was a convicted felon in possession of an illegal gun. All three were charged with attempted homicide. Authorities dropped the charges against William Fears, though he was later arrested for domestic violence.

These incidents make several things clear. First, the alt-right is not fundamentally different from the KKK, the far-right white nationalist group that predates it in America.

Second, although alt-right activists like to complain that their free speech rights are being violated, they are even more confused about the First Amendment than their extremist counterparts on the left. The First Amendment does not guarantee anyone a platform on Twitter, nor does it establish a right to threaten to kill liberals, assault counterdemonstrators, or shoot at commuters.

Third, although Trump is not a member of the alt-right, it's possible to see why his victory gave the alt-right such hope. "Trump is overall a move in the right direction as far as recent presidents are concerned," Kyle told me. The alt-right attorney was disappointed that the president wasn't keeping some of his campaign promises—building the wall, pulling out of NAFTA, avoiding military intervention in Syria—but said that "Trump has added a nationalistic flair to American political discourse, which is invaluable."

Cantwell, for his part, denied that Trump was one of them. "All of Trump's children are married to, or dating, Jews," he said. "So the idea that he's like some kind of closet Nazi is foundationally ridiculous."

But it's not ridiculous for some alt-right-adjacent folks to occasionally think Trump is dog-whistling at them. Two weeks after the Charlottesville rally, the president gave a speech in Phoenix, asking, "Does anybody want George Washington's statue [taken down]? No. Is that sad, is that sad? To Lincoln, to Teddy Roosevelt. I see they want to take Teddy Roosevelt's down too. They're trying to figure out why, they don't know. They're trying to take away our culture, they're trying to take away our history." Whether Trump knows it or not (I'm betting not), this statement plays directly into alt-right fears about white culture being replaced.

Liberals could have scored a win here by retorting, *No one wants to tear down George Washington's statue. Washington isn't morally equivalent to Robert E. Lee.* Unfortunately, left-leaning political analyst Angela Rye had appeared on CNN just days before and declared, "I don't care if it's a George Washington statue, or a Thomas Jefferson statue, or a Robert E. Lee statue. They all need to come down."

The *Daily Beast*'s editor in chief at the time, John Avlon, who appeared in the same segment with Rye, immediately chimed in with, "You're feeding in to Steve Bannon and Trump."[13] And he was exactly right. As we will see throughout the rest of this chapter, there's a powerful symbiosis at work here. The right's extremism fuels the left, and the extreme left responds in a way that makes the extreme right feel vindicated. And vice versa.

A Tale of Two Tumblr Pages

In the previous section, I traced the intellectual roots of the alt-right and described the real-life activities of several of its best-known leaders and foot soldiers. But there's another story of where the alt-right came from, and you won't hear the names Buchanan or Spencer in this tale.

It's the story of Tumblr.

Tumblr, an online blogging platform and social networking community, debuted in 2007. "Tumblr is so easy to use that it's hard to explain," reads a note on Tumblr's website that captures its essence fairly well. The site is whatever its users want it to be: a blog, or a diary, or a place to post photos, videos, or whatever. (Prior to Yahoo's acquisition of the company in 2013, 11 percent of Tumblr's most popular blogs were pornographic.)

It was particularly popular with young, earnest, socially conscious, far-left folks who would come to be known to the right under the derisive monikers of "social justice warrior" and "cry-bully."

"If the generation of college-going millennials that followed the rise of this online culture could be described, as they are today by the conservative press in particular, as 'generation snowflake,' Tumblr was their vanguard," wrote Angela Nagle in her essential

2017 book, *Kill All Normies: Online Culture Wars from 4Chan and Tumblr to Trump and the Alt-Right.*

Tumblr users perfected the art of the callout—of publicly shaming someone else for saying something that was problematic on leftist grounds, such as sexism, racism, or ableism. But often their targets just didn't deserve anything approaching the level of ceaseless opprobrium the platform delivered. Consider a 2015 incident involving Paige Paz, a twenty-year-old self-described Tumblr artist who liked to draw pictures of characters from cartoon shows.[14] Paz had a habit of drawing different versions of the made-up characters: in one drawing, she chose to depict a pony character (from the show *My Little Pony: Friendship Is Magic*) as a Native American adult.[15] But this got her in trouble with the so-called crybullies—one Tumblr user commented about the not-a-pony picture, "This is stereotypical and therefore racist." It got worse: when Paz drew a dark-skinned character with slightly lighter skin, she was accused of racism. She was accused of transphobia for drawing characters as the wrong gender. She was accused of fatphobia for drawing characters who were thinner than they were supposed to be.

"If you support drawing canonically fat characters as skinny or worse, whitewashing PoC [person of color] representation, you can unfollow me right now because I don't need your shit," wrote one critic.

At one point there were as many as forty different Tumblr pages that existed for the sole purpose of calling out Paz.[16] Even if one thinks that what Paz did was somehow wrong, her critics were guilty of much worse sins. "I'll continue making fun of her lazy art and her bigotry until something changes," said one.[17] Others urged her to kill herself, which she eventually attempted, unsuccessfully.

Tumblr culture became toxic and militantly PC—but so did other corners of the internet, including Twitter, where some edgy young extremists goad each other to commit suicide by drinking bleach. In her book, Nagle highlights a few choice examples: Arthur Chu, a *Jeopardy* champion noted for his unusual winning strategy, once wrote on Twitter, "as a dude who cares [about] feminism sometimes I want to join all men arm-in-arm & then run off a cliff and drag the whole gender into the sea." And "Brienne of Snarth," a personality active on both Twitter and Tumblr, gave the following response to the death of a two-year-old who was killed by an alligator at a Walt Disney World resort in Florida: "I'm so finished with this white men's entitlement that I'm really not sad about a 2yo being eaten by a gator bc his daddy ignored signs."

There's a grating obnoxiousness to this brand of weird wokeness. It's purely performative, done for no other reason but to send a social signal: *I am the most progressive, because I am willing to say a truly horrible thing in service of my progressivism. I am better than you.*

"The hysterical liberal call-out produced a breeding ground for an online backlash of irreverent mockery and anti-PC," wrote Nagle. "After crying wolf throughout these years, calling everyone from saccharine pop stars to Justin Trudeau a 'white supremacist' and everyone who wasn't With Her a sexist, the real wolf eventually arrived, in the form of the openly white nationalist alt-right who hid among an online army of ironic in-jokey trolls."

At the same time some Tumblr and Twitter users were trying to crush the souls of people who wouldn't draw sufficiently over-weight anime characters, a corresponding culture of horror and abuse was rising on the right. Its homes were the forums Reddit and 4chan. Pepe the Frog originated on 4chan, as did the Republic of Kekistan—originally just *kek,* a variant of *lol,* or "laughing out loud," which itself was a holdover from earlier internet chatrooms.

The excesses of social justice Tumblr galvanized Reddit and 4chan, whose users associated callouts with thought control, censorship, and political correctness run amok. "One of the things that linked the often nihilistic and ironic chan culture to a wider culture of the alt-right orbit was their opposition to political correctness, feminism, multiculturalism, etc., and its encroachment into their freewheeling world of anonymity and tech," wrote Nagle.

Over time, online anti-PC culture drifted rightward, and

became as abusive and harassing as anything on the left. The GamerGate movement (for a brief overview of this, return to Chapter Two) mirrored the Tumblr activists' attacks on Paige Paz: legions of right-wing dudes sent death threats and rape threats to several prominent feminists who (gasp!) had dared to say that some videogames contained sexist tropes.

Many of the leaders of this movement—*Breitbart*'s Milo Yiannopoulos was one—declined to label themselves as alt-right, likely calculating that this would hurt their bids for mainstream attention. "Alt-lite" became their preferred description. But their audiences never fit so well into neat categorization, and many of their fans were either fellow travelers of the rising white nationalist tide, dabbling in it, or entrenched.

Is there a line between attacking feminists and minorities because you want to make some warped point about political correctness and doing it because you're a racist and sexist who actually hates them? If such a line even exists, many online cultural combatants have long since crossed it. And Spencer's movement was waiting to welcome them with open arms.

Living Hell

"The thing that is important to know about [the alt-right] is that they consider themselves victims of other races," Mary told me. "They believe this, that other races are coming to destroy them and they want to eliminate white people through interracial marriages and they want to destroy Western civilization. They want to take things from white people. It's very much like a victim mentality. Like they have to defend themselves from people of other races."

Mary speaks from a position of considerable knowledge. For three years—a time that she would later describe as a "living hell"—she was married to a member of the alt-right. ("Mary" is a pseudonym.) Her story is an illustrative glimpse into one young man's radicalization.

In the late 2000s, Mary was a conservative college student with an interest in writing. She met her future husband, Brad (not his real name), at a Republican political conference in Washington, D.C.

"This was during the Bush years," she told me. "I assumed that he, even if he was more conservative than me, that he must be somewhat mainstream if he'd be going at all."

There were warning signs. Mutual acquaintances warned Mary about Brad's college antics, which involved frequent clashes with the left over political correctness. Some said Brad was a racist. But to Mary, he seemed harmless—even dorky.

Months later, they connected on Facebook. Then they went on a first date. Mary thought Brad seemed friendly—not at all like his reputation. She asked him straight out whether he was some kind of white supremacist. He utterly denied it, she said.

Within two months, Mary was pregnant, and the couple decided to get married—something Mary now considers "probably a big mistake."

Mary received a clue that something was off about Brad on the day of their daughter's birth. Mary looks like the kind of woman a white supremacist would want to marry—she's light-skinned and blond-haired—but their infant daughter had brown hair, which Brad remarked upon almost immediately. He expressed optimism that she would grow out of it, according to Mary.

Over the next year, Brad was largely absent from the white nationalist movement, Mary told me. But he gradually became more and more involved with white supremacists. Sometimes he would invite such people to their apartment; more often, he communicated with them online or over the phone.

"You would rarely see these people in person," Mary told me. She was embarrassed when they hung out in public: Brad and his white nationalist friends would talk about things like "the Jewish problem" and "spiritual whiteness," she said.

Brad was also obsessed with guns, and routinely stockpiled ammunition. He became convinced that black people would riot if the jury decided to acquit George Zimmerman for Trayvon Martin's murder, and tried to persuade Mary as well.

"He's fascinated by guns, he owns an AR-15, he is always looking for reasons to buy ammunition," Mary told me. "He's very attached to the idea that there's eventually going to be a race war or something, where he's going to have to defend himself."

Zimmerman was indeed acquitted, but no such riots took place. Mary said she felt "foolish" for thinking Brad might have been right.

Mary slowly became both more aware of the depths of Brad's racism and less susceptible to him. They started fighting regularly. Mary developed a prescription drug addiction. Brad became more committed than ever to the alt-right cause, and more desperate to rope Mary into it. He brought her with him to a two-day alt-right conference in another city. This experience finally confirmed for Mary what had grown more and more apparent: she wanted no part of a movement whose adherents got together to chant "Sieg heil!" Two months later, they separated. They are now divorced, but share custody of their daughter.

It's difficult to say exactly how or why Brad became this way, and it would be foolish to think he wasn't always at least a little racist. But his desire to publicly associate with a movement dedicated to the cause of white identitarianism increased over time—in proportion to what he perceived as rising leftist identitarianism. Mary specifically cited leftist excesses on college campuses as one of the things that radicalized Brad.

"On campus, definitely," Mary told me. "[Campus leftists] have definitely fueled the radical right, I think, with their antics. I think that's how Brad got radicalized."

Mary told me that in college, Brad was involved in a conservative student group, and once invited a right-leaning congressman to speak on campus. In a turn of events that will be familiar to readers by now, student protesters crashed the event and disrupted the congressman's speech.

"They stormed the stage and attacked people, these demonstrators did," Mary told me. "I think that just pushed [Brad] further to the right. He just got more and more radical the more he was attacked on campus. It backfires, I think."

Red-Pilled

There is a critical early moment in the 1999 film *The Matrix* when the seemingly all-knowing Morpheus (played by Laurence Fishburne) offers protagonist Neo (played by Keanu Reeves) a choice: take the blue pill or the red pill. The blue pill would lead Neo back to the Matrix, a simulated reality where human beings go about their lives, blissfully unaware that they are actually slaves to a vast, totalitarian artificial intelligence system. The red pill would cause Neo to wake up—for the first time in his life—and join the human resistance in the actual world outside the Matrix, a place Morpheus refers to as "the desert of the real." This duality is also echoed in the climax of the second film, *The Matrix Reloaded*, when Neo must choose between two doors: one that will take him back to the beginning while ensuring humanity's survival, and one that will allow him to go forward but risks total extinction of humankind.

In the years since *The Matrix*'s release, the red pill has become an important metaphor for the men's rights movement, a mostly online community that believes men, rather than women, are the victims of discrimination in modern society. They cite custody battles, divorce proceedings, and sexual assault disputes as examples of situations where men are at a distinct disadvantage. Men's rights activists, or MRAs, refer to the act of discovering this truth as "red-pilling." There's no going back for them: their eyes have been opened to the way things really are.

Some of the MRAs' complaints contain tiny kernels of truth. For instance, while most people understand that men commit the overwhelming majority of violent crimes, less frequently discussed is the fact that most victims are also men, rather than women. Men, for whatever reason, commit suicide at a much higher rate than women. According to the American Foundation for Suicide Prevention, men are three and a half times more likely to kill themselves than women are.[18] In 2017, white men accounted for seven in every ten suicides. Among young people, female suicide rates have increased—but they're still significantly lower than the teen male suicide rate (5.1 per 100,000 girls vs. 14.2 per 100,000 boys).[19] Homelessness also affects more men than women.[20] MRAs claim that male victims don't get nearly as much attention as female victims—that modern society is relatively indifferent to male suffering.

The movement takes these grievances much too far, however, and the online forums and discussion sites of the men's rights movement are teeming with people who believe awful, misogynistic things about women and feminists—and hunger for revenge against them. An offshoot of the MRA community, Men Going Their Own Way (or MGTOW, pronounced like "mig toe"), believes men should disassociate themselves from women entirely.

It should come as no surprise that the radical element of the men's rights movement overlaps substantially with the alt-right. Young men who buy into their own victimhood and rail against a supposed women-centric modern culture and media establishment are vulnerable to being captured by charismatic extremists who give them an "other" to hate: globalism, social liberalism, immigrants, and more.

In the fall of 2017, I appeared on a panel at Harvard University that was cosponsored by the Open Campus Initiative student group, *Spiked* magazine, and the Institute for Humane Studies. My co-panelists were the feminist author Wendy Kaminer (mentioned in Chapter Four), *Spiked* editor Brendan O'Neill, and Harvard psychology professor Steven Pinker. We were asked to discuss the topic "Is Political Correctness Why Trump Won?"

Each of us thought the answer was at least a partial yes. For my part, I read a series of emails I had received in response to a *Reason* magazine article in which I made the case that the public voted for

Trump in order to fight back against political correctness run amok.[21] Voter after voter told me that this was *exactly* the reason they had voted for Trump.

"I too am sick of the antics of the PC crowd telling me what to think," wrote one. "Best regards for a Merry Christmas, happy holiday or whatever our betters tell us to call it."

"I support gay marriage and transsexual people's rights," wrote another. "However, I do not support them to the exclusion of other citizen rights . . . this blind adherence to political correctness was my main issue in the recent political arena."

Pinker's comments at the Harvard event have stuck with me as well.[22] He worried that the alt-right and other extremist ideologies were winning over vulnerable young people precisely because campus political correctness had rendered certain truths unsayable on campus.

"People who gravitate to the alt-right . . . swallow the red pill, as the saying goes, when they are exposed for the first time to true statements that have never been voiced in college campuses or in the *New York Times* or in respectable media," said Pinker. These statements "are almost like a bacillus to which they have no immunity, and they are immediately infected with a feeling of outrage that these truths are unsayable, and have no defense against taking them to what we might consider rather repellent conclusions."

Pinker gave the example of differences between the sexes. "This is not controversial to anyone who has even glanced at the data," said Pinker. "Men and women give different answers as to what they want to do for a living and how much time they want to allocate to family vs. career and so on. But you can't say it." Indeed, at Harvard University, President Larry Summers drew furious criticism from faculty in 2005 for discussing scientific research related to this issue, and later resigned.

As Pinker emphasized during his remarks, some evidence of certain sex-based differences would not mean that women should be treated differently, or that stereotypes about the sexes should be taken seriously, or that broad conclusions should be drawn. But a young person, having learned that this truth was withheld from him for so long, is unlikely to accept the qualifying arguments for why these facts ultimately don't mean very much. The person "will be vindicated when people who voice these truths are suppressed, shouted down, assaulted," according to Pinker. "All the more reason to believe the left, mainstream media, and universities can't handle the truth."

It would, of course, be wrong to blame the left for the alt-right's bad behavior and odious beliefs. The alt-right is a white nationalist movement, wholly undeserving of public sympathy. Its ascendance is a testament to the enduring power of racism in the twenty-first century.

But by turning away from bedrock principles of liberalism, free speech, and inclusion, the left has made it easier for people to swallow the red pill. Shutting down abhorrent far-right speakers backfires in that it distracts from the speakers' messages, casting them as martyrs and making their critics on the left seem like the intolerant ones. And of course, the tendency among some on the left to label everyone on the right a Nazi—not just Richard Spencer but Charles Murray and Ben Shapiro as well—creates a boy-who-cried-wolf problem and promotes ignorance. I disagree vehemently with many of Shapiro's opinions, but it's ludicrous to call him a Nazi or associate him with the alt-right. (Not least of all because Shapiro is in fact Jewish, and has been subjected to considerable anti-Semitic harassment from pro-Trump trolls.)[23] Or consider this: in the summer of 2017, a fact-checker for the *New Yorker* named Talia Lavin claimed that a wheelchair-bound ICE agent had a Nazi iron cross tattooed on his shoulder. She was mistaken; the cross was Maltese, the symbol of the agent's Marine platoon.[24] Lavin resigned from the *New Yorker,* but the left-wing watchdog group Media Matters hired her as a "researcher on far-right extremism" a few weeks later.[25]

The alt-right, thankfully, has earned less attention since the

2017 Charlottesville march. But it would be a mistake to think the movement—a living, breathing example of racial identity politics taken to a xenophobic extreme—has disappeared.

"The play is not over," Spencer told me. "There are going to be more acts to it."

WHEN EXTREMES MEET

I always made one prayer to God, a very short one. Here it is: "O Lord, make our enemies quite ridiculous!" God granted it.

—Voltaire

"America is a racist, sexist, classist, homophobic country," the speaker, Amanda, told an audience of perhaps sixty students. Later, she would challenge the students to "know their own intersectional story," since all struggles against oppression are part of the same global conflict. "If Mother Nature is your shit, then fuck with Mother Nature," she said. "Your issue is connected to every other fucking issue."

But one issue loomed larger than all the others and was always present.

"Capitalism is in the room with every social justice issue we talk about," said Amanda.

Amanda's specific issue that day was reclaiming the concept of the "nasty woman," the derogative label Trump had applied to Hillary Clinton during the third presidential debate. During her presentation, Amanda reverently played a clip of the speech given by Ashley Judd at the Women's March in Washington, D.C., in which the actress proudly declared, "I am a nasty woman."

The presentation was part academic lecture, part sermon, part poetry slam—delivered by a tall, rail-thin black woman wearing a black button-down shirt and a tie. Amanda is not her real name: I have chosen to redact her identity, since I never asked for permission to quote her, and was not formally invited to attend the conference at which she spoke. Indeed, I overheard the first half of her presentation while hiding in a stairwell adjacent to the conference room.

The event in question was a national convention for students interested in social justice, diversity, and leadership on their campuses. It was hosted by a nonprofit organization that sponsors training programs for schools. The young people who attend these kinds of events return to their colleges ready to preach the gospel of social justice to their peers. Curious about the sort of professional training the would-be leaders of the college activism movement were receiving, I decided to attend. (For reasons that will become clear in the very next paragraph, I have redacted the name of this convention and the organization responsible for it.)

A ticket to the convention cost an eye-popping $400–$500 per person, with the exact price depending on how early you registered. According to its schedule, the convention consisted of a series of presentations, workshops, and small-group discussions. For the discussions, participants were divided into twenty groups of ten people. It seemed likely to me I would have to either pretend to be a student or risk being thrown out. Instead, I opted to sneak in without registering, listen in on a few conversations, and sample one of the lectures. The first thing I saw was one student holding another, who was crying. After hurrying past a public restroom that had been relabeled "gender neutral" by decree of a flyer depicting the symbol for a man, a woman, and a triceratops along with the message "All are welcome," I found myself in the stairwell next to the room where Amanda was speaking, watching through the window of a door.

Amanda would frequently ask the audience to respond to questions. "Who put this motherfucker in office?" she asked, referring to You-Know-Who.

"White people!" a number of students, many of them white

themselves, shouted in response. Other answers were given as well. Eventually Amanda noted that many educated women voted for Trump. When Amanda said something the audience liked, they would respond not by clapping—clapping creates too much noise, which can be distressing to survivors of various traumas, or so the activists believe—but by snapping their fingers.

Occasionally Amanda would randomly call on a specific person to respond to what she had just said as a means of silencing the side conversations that some students were having. Shortly after the Ashley Judd clip wrapped up, this was exactly what happened to Michael (not his real name).

Michael, I would later learn, was a puffy white kid with extremely blond hair. The subject of Amanda's lecture had turned to the plight of women in America. Michael couldn't help himself: he pushed back. It seemed like Amanda just wanted to bash America. "Why don't we ever talk about women mistreated elsewhere?" Michael wanted to know. He pointed out that women in other parts of the world have it much worse. Women are still denied fundamental rights under the Islamic totalitarianism present in parts of the Middle East, and while sexual violence is rampant in the United States, American women have legal protections and recourse that other women do not.

"Now we're talking about sexual assault, something that might be triggering," said Amanda, warning the rest of the room. "And to be honest, he is triggering me."

Amanda, an administrator in a social justice and inclusivity office at a public university, then berated Michael and a friend seated next to him, another white student, for articulating this perspective. It was a tense moment that seemed to divide the room: many appeared to support Amanda, while others evidently thought she had gone too far. I followed Michael and his friend when they got up and left the room. The friend, a skinny guy dressed in a nice shirt and jacket (whose name I did not catch), was shaken. He felt like they had been called out and shamed for making a completely reasonable point. Amanda had treated them scornfully, even though they were just as committed to social justice as she was.

"If I didn't care about social justice, I wouldn't be here," he told me.

Another student, a woman of color, approached the young men to explain to them where they had gone wrong.

Not everyone was on Amanda's side, though.

"The whole point of this conference is inclusion, and that was *not* inclusive," I overheard a female student admit.

THIS BOOK HAS been the story of two extremes, woke intersectional safe-space progressivism and red-pilled identitarian right-wing populism—where they come from, what happens when they clash, and why they ultimately depend upon each other.

That said, I don't mean to draw a false moral equivalency between the far left and the far right. Even the most unreasonable fourth-wave feminist, for example, is not an extremist in the same sense as Richard Spencer. And while the left has a lot of power on college campuses and a great deal of currency on social media sites run by tech companies that are themselves staffed by left-friendly young people, the federal government is currently under the control of Donald Trump, a left-winger's nightmare. Despite losing the House of Representatives in the 2018 midterm elections, Republicans still control the Senate, the Supreme Court, and most state legislatures. Political power, at least for now, is firmly in the right's grasp.

And it's probably likely to stay that way as long as the hard right's foes—the left, but also liberals, centrists, and libertarians—remain hopelessly divided. Like it or not, the intersectionality-driven leftist war on moderation and cross-ideological coalitions makes alliance-building harder. This infighting is a gift to Trump and those who continue to support him.

As I hope I've made clear, I'm sympathetic to many of the goals of intersectional progressives (except for democratic socialists, though I will make common cause with them on abolishing ICE, if they will have me). So are other libertarians, many liberals, and even some conservatives on specific issues. Where we disagree is on tactics. I have deep reservations about the left's intersectionality and safe-space-fueled illiberal streak as it relates to free speech, due process, tolerance, and individuality. It's not just that I personally object to these tactics; I also think that they are counterproductive, turning away far more people than they convert. They force progressive activists to battle each other, since the most marginalized person is awarded the most power and influence in any dispute. I hope my exhaustive chronicle of intersectionality-induced infighting prompts some self-reflection. Consider this conclusion a friendly appeal to dial down the performative social signaling, insistence on ideological purity, and embrace of the worst aspects of identity politics. If the left does this—makes peace with liberals for the good of the #Resistance—it can win. My concern is that something akin to the nightmare scenario will unfold: Zillennial leftists will become more radical and the far right more emboldened while the rest of us shrug and give up.

Throughout this book, I have not shied away from pointing out inconsistencies in intersectional progressivism as I see them. But I hope readers don't get the impression that I dislike the young people I interviewed. On the contrary, I was often impressed by their passion.

Take Ziad, a high school senior who drew media attention in the spring of 2017 when he answered a question on a college application by writing the words "black lives matter" over and over again (he took a picture of the answer and tweeted it; it quickly went viral). Ziad considers himself an activist—his Twitter handle is @ziadtheactivist—but doesn't think his stunt deserved praise: he was just making sure the admissions officers "remembered me for me." Ziad was one of the first people I interviewed for this book— he was the first teenager I asked to define "safety."

"I think of safety as the right of every person to leave their house or to leave wherever they live, to walk this world and to feel safe and comfortable in their own skin, in their own ways that they identify, and to not fear violence, not fear prejudice, not fear discrimination, to not fear being bothered or to not fear living," he said. "That's safety to me, whether it's violence, whether it's verbal assault, whether it's not being served at a town, or whatever it might be." I don't think anyone would disagree that that's a hopeful vision for the future, at the very least.

Now an undergraduate at Yale University, Ziad has cofounded a Gen Z consulting firm to help businesses understand what teens want. I met him in a coffee shop in Manhattan in the summer of 2018, more than a year after we had first spoken on the phone. Ziad skillfully interrogated my deeply held beliefs, which was an uncomfortable experience for me—I'm supposed to be the one asking the questions. Our discussion grew heated enough that a woman sitting next to us actually asked if we could keep it down. This was a young activist who wasn't afraid of difficult conversations; he enjoyed them. And though he was certainly on the left—he was relieved that I hadn't voted for Trump, and insistent that I raise progressive children—Ziad told me that, unlike many of his friends on campus, he wasn't sold on socialism.

In conversations with other young people, I found that many of them agreed with me that activist hostility to free speech was counterproductive.

"I don't understand why there's anything productive to come from shutting people down," Kat, a college student from San Francisco, told me. "I think if you actually have white supremacists in this community, then you should put them out there and let them go speak their ideas so everybody knows who they are."

I met her on a street corner in Berkeley where she was a spectator at the alt-right and antifa marches that ensued after the failed Yiannopoulos event in August 2017. A short twenty-six-year-old with pink hair and a nose ring, Kat hadn't come to throw punches, or start fires, or shout anybody down. She just wanted to talk to people. But talking to people was often frustrating.

"I started out coming to these rallies as an anti-Trump person, and then figured out that there was zero dialogue happening on that side of things," she told me. As for the other side, she thought the wildly pro-Trump and pro-Yiannopoulos people probably didn't even believe the things they were saying, but "if you don't let them talk you'll never know that."

It's helpful to remember that the illiberal left and illiberal right are still minorities. There are a lot of young people who feel the same way Kat does about the growing hostility to free speech and about the rising tides of identitarianism—who believe in the principles of civil debate and the foundations of a free society.

At some campuses, these young people are pushing back. During his sophomore year at Williams College, Zach Wood, a student of color who came from a disadvantaged background in the Washington, D.C., area, was involved in a campus group called Uncomfortable Learning. Under his leadership, the group invited a range of speakers to come to campus and talk about issues from a perspective students were unlikely to hear in class. Many of the speakers were controversial.

"I disagree with these speakers, too, not just on the issues in which I bring them to speak, but from what I gather, from what I've read, on most issues, in fact," Wood told me. "For me, part of intellectual growth, part of college, part of the experience, it's sort of all about engaging with those views, strengthening your own position, understanding the opposition, and gaining a deeper understanding of humanity."

In 2015, one would-be speaker, the anti-feminist Suzanne Venker, provoked blind fury from the campus's far-left students.

"There were some people who questioned the judgment and the decision, and they did so in a way that was thoughtful and reflective, but the most vocal opponents were the most radical students on campus," Wood told me. "There were students who would politically call themselves democratic socialists or Marxists or even communists or something of the sort, students who probably didn't think Bernie was far enough to the left. These were the students who were most critical of me at the time."

Wood had no choice but to cancel the event. But something good came out of it, anyway: he was able to write about the experience for the *Washington Post,* and he became a nationally known pro-free-speech student. He's now the author of a book on the subject, and a writer for the *Atlantic.*

What's so refreshing about Wood is that he holds conventionally liberal values—and sees free speech as one of those values.

I asked Wood why he was unlike so many of the other young, politically interested people I had interviewed for this book—the ones who thought talking to their enemies was a waste of time. Wood told me he had grown up with a mother who suffered from schizophrenia, and the process of trying to comprehend her behavior taught him the importance of seeking understanding and practicing empathy, even when it seemed futile.

"When I couldn't rationalize why she was being cruel, or why she was enraged by something, something that seemed insignificant, I had to remind myself of the fact that her brain was working differently," Wood told me. "From a very young age, I was in a situation in which I had to try to understand, to stretch myself in order to understand, and to try to empathize as well."

At other colleges, there are young people who share Wood's values. Over the past few years, the mainstream student libertarian movement has sternly rebuked both the alt-right and the anti-free-speech left, and is an important force for civil discourse on many campuses. When Richard Spencer tried to crash the February 2017 Students for Liberty (SFL) conference in Washington, D.C., attendees denounced him to his face until hotel security asked him to leave. (It was a private space and Spencer had not been invited.) Today the young libertarians of Students for Liberty promote free expression and the values of the Enlightenment, and are an antidote to illiberal extremism at colleges. In recent years, SFL has been most successful at spreading classically liberal values internationally, in places such as Africa and South America: in 2015, its student activists were closely involved in the successful effort to oust the corrupt left-wing president of Brazil, Dilma Rousseff. (Disclaimer: I was involved in the group as an undergraduate.)

I've spent a lot of space in this book scrutinizing leftist intolerance and infighting. That's because leftist Zillennial activists greatly outnumber their rivals on the right. But I wouldn't want anyone to come away with the impression that the left is the main threat to free speech. Indeed, over the two years I spent writing this book, conservative hostility to free speech norms appeared to grow tremendously. Many people on the far right—and not just the alt-right—are increasingly interested in regulating private social media companies as public utilities and forcing them to extend a platform to conservative views. The right can complain all it wants about Facebook and Twitter treating it unfairly, but calls for government to level the playing field are a direct assault on the First Amendment. This is not a good look for conservatives who claim to be supporters of free speech.

What will it take to save activism from itself and reassert liberal norms? I won't pretend that I have easy solutions. It seems fairly likely that two big factors in young people's lives—social media and the education system—are partly responsible for the present situation, though it's not obvious what should be done about it.

Given college's pivotal role in elevating unreasonable demands and fostering illiberalism, as well as its decreasing ability to guarantee any kind of economic security for graduates, one tempting answer is to encourage young people to do something other than waste their time pursuing a degree. If the university is a breeding ground for cultlike behavior, PTSD, and mountains of debt, why bother?

Beyond the liberal arts, many young people in more technical fields are doing something other than college, too. Silicon Valley is teeming with dropouts—people who decided the classroom experience wasn't worth it and was actually limiting their growth potential. The college bubble hasn't burst yet, and it could still be a long time coming, given the powerful government forces at work, but alternatives are at least proliferating. Competition breeds improvement; if colleges had to offer their services at a more competitive price, it's possible they wouldn't spend so much time and money policing microaggressions.

As for social media, some people think kids' dependency on it is rotting their brains. "It's not an exaggeration to describe iGen as being on the brink of the worst mental-health crisis in decades," wrote the psychologist Jean Twenge in an article about teen smartphone usage. "Much of this deterioration can be traced to their phones."[1] She cites higher rates of depression, unhappiness, and suicidal thoughts among teens who are addicted to their iPhones. "The more time teens spend looking at screens, the more likely they are to report symptoms of depression. Eighth-graders who are heavy users of social media increase their risk of depression by 27 percent, while those who play sports, go to religious services, or even do homework more than the average teen cut their risk significantly."

I'm a little skeptical of dramatic claims about teen depression, since authority figures have wrongly blamed new technology—radio, television, cellphones—for various social ills in the past. But if smartphone addiction does make teens depressed, it helps explain why mental health has become such a foundational aspect of the intersectional victims hierarchy.

Illiberal activists have a lot of power on campus and on social media. Elsewhere, their rage doesn't matter as much. Still, they have some ability to enact long-term, broad-based social change. The activist young people I spoke with for this book didn't plan to stick around campus forever. Many will graduate and find jobs in law, policy, tech, and finance. At a march against climate change in Washington, D.C., in the spring of 2017, I spoke with two female activists—students at the University of Virginia—about what they planned to do after college.

"We're both business majors and we're both also really passionate about sustainability, so I think for us it's a lot about the intersection of economics and business and these social issues and environmental issues," one of them said. "Activism is great, but I think the most change is probably going to come from the business side."

In Chapter Four, we saw how a small cabal of left-wing activists was able to hijack existing, well-intentioned harassment law in order to make campuses more repressive places. It's not impossible to imagine the same kind of thing happening in the workplace: picture a boss who is afraid to reprimand negligent young employees out of concern that they will say their PTSD is triggered.

It's never too late to begin fostering different attitudes and beliefs among the next generation. Well, okay, it *is* too late for millennials, and Gen Z is already in school. But someone else will come along after that. Better civic education in K–12 schooling might help them learn something about the First Amendment. And a saner approach to safety might make them more independent and responsible—and get them out of the house from time to time.

As for social media, who knows what will happen. The journalist Taylor Lorenz thinks "social" and "media" will split in the near future: "Tweeting out your opinions only to be shouted down by Nazis has caused many users to abandon posting on open social networks and instead spend more time in closed networks and group chats."[2] This could ameliorate some of the toxicity of online public discourse, which would have positive effects. It's my opinion that intersectionality has primarily been spread by social media.

It's all too easy to groan about "kids these days," but—as I hope I have made clear—whatever faults the Zillennial generation may possess, much of the blame lies with other parties. For instance, the Australian millionaire Tim Gurner chided millennials for spending all their money on "avocado toast" instead of saving up to buy their first homes. As I am a millennial who did not yet own a home at the time this book was written, let me make it abundantly clear that fancy brunches are not the thing preventing us from buying homes. The truth has two parts: (1) the housing crash, an economic disaster inflicted upon us by older Americans, is still fresh in our memory, and (2) our most promising job opportunities are in cities, where renting often makes more short-term sense than buying. (Besides, avocado toast is delicious.)

If Zillennial activism's illiberal tendencies are to be reined in, liberals will have to step up to the plate. Intellectual leaders who are still in relatively good standing with the left—a shrinking number, to be sure—need to persuade them that anti-free-speech extremism is self-defeating and counterproductive. Point out that when governments are empowered to trample individual rights—even out of a desire to do well by the marginalized—disaster results. Given the realities of the Trump years, a governmental initiative to curb hate speech wouldn't be aimed at racial microaggressions—it would be used to punish NFL players who kneel during the anthem.

One of the most interesting arguments against free speech that I encountered in the wild while doing research for this book was the idea that free speech was impossible as long as power imbalances endured between any two people. Before society can enjoy free speech, it is first necessary to eliminate all inequities from society. After structural oppression has been defeated, then we can practice free speech.

My questions are these: How would we ever build a more equal society without free speech? How could we decide who needed a boost and who needed a penalty? What authority can be trusted with the adjudication of this transfer of power? The Trump administration? Tech giants? A university administration?

We need free speech because we still need to hash all of this out—because liberal norms of tolerance, civility, openness, individual rights, and freedom of expression are still the best tools we have for bettering our society. In these difficult conversations, everybody has a vested interest in participating—and that includes the left. Activists, you may not think it's your job to educate me, but I invite you to try.

ACKNOWLEDGMENTS

This little project took quite some time, and I am most grateful to my wife, Carrie, for helping me see it through. Caesar and Oliver, as well.

I would also like to thank my family—Ryan Soave, Kaitlin Soave, Stephanie Soave, Bob Soave, and all the Straszes—and a few close friends who served as sounding boards—Del Bodary, Pat Zabawa, Elizabeth Nolan Brown, Asawin Suebsang, and Prateik Dalmia.

My colleagues at *Reason* magazine are experts at separating good ideas from bad, and I'm grateful for their advice—particularly my editors, Katherine Mangu-Ward, Peter Suderman, Nick Gillespie, and Matt Welch.

This book wouldn't have been possible without the support of The Fund for American Studies. Thanks especially to Roger Ream and Daniel McCarthy. I should also recognize the Foundation for Individual Rights in Education, the Charles Koch Institute, the Institute for Humane Studies, the Student Free Press Association, and Students for Liberty; each of these groups has aided my professional endeavors tremendously.

Thanks as well to all those involved in the production of this book, specifically Wes Neff, Adam Bellow, Alan Bradshaw, and Ellis Levine.

A few others I need to mention: Lisa Kennedy, Lenore Skenazy, Emily Yoffe, Crystal Johns, and Linda LeFauve.

Last, I am eternally grateful to everyone who agreed to be interviewed for this project. I'm sure it wasn't easy for you to trust a stranger with your stories—particularly one you might view as an opponent. Be that as it may, I remain your most well-wishing adversary.

NOTES

PROLOGUE: ARRESTED DEVELOPMENT

1. Julie Rowe, "Elated Campus Erupts After Obama's Historic Win," *Michigan Daily*, November 5, 2008, https://www.michigandaily.com/content/2008-11-05/campus-erupts-after-obama-landslide.

2. Robby Soave, "Elite Campuses Offer Students Coloring Books, Puppies to Get over Trump," *Daily Beast*, November 16, 2016, http://www.thedailybeast.com/elite-campuses-offer-students-coloring-books-puppies-to-get-over-trump.

3. David Burt, Drew Henderson, and Everett Rosenfeld, "On the Morning of Sept. 11, 2001 . . . ," *Yale Daily News*, September 9, 2011, http://yaledailynews.com/blog/2011/09/09/on-the-morning-of-sept-11-2001.

4. Jennifer Kabbany, "Ivy League University Hosts Post-Election 'Breathing Space': Puppy Cuddling, Coloring, Chocolate," *College Fix*, November 10, 2016, http://www.thecollegefix.com/post/29898.

5. David Finkelhor, "Five Myths About Missing Children," *Washington Post*, May 10, 2013, https://www.washingtonpost.com/opinions/five-myths-about-missing-children/2013/05/10/efee398c-b8b4-11e2-aa9e-a02b765ff0ea_story.html.

6. D'Vera Cohn et al., "Gun Homicide Rate Down 49% Since Peak; Public Unaware," Pew Research Center, May 7, 2013, http://www.pewsocialtrends.org/2013/05/07/gun-homicide-rate-down-49-since-1993-peak-public-unaware.

ONE: INTERSECTIONAL A.F.

1. Women's March, "Our Mission," https://www.womensmarch.com /mission1.
2. Shikha Dalmia, "The Pointless Women's March Against Trump," *Reason*, January 12, 2017, http://reason.com/archives/2017/01/12/the-pointless -upcoming-womens-march-agai.
3. Elizabeth Nolan Brown, "Women's March Waffles on Sex-Worker Rights, Disinvites Women Who Oppose Abortion," *Reason*, January 17, 2017, https://reason.com/blog/2017/01/17/womens-march-strikes-sex-worker -rights.
4. Emma Green, "These Pro-Lifers Are Headed to the Women's March on Washington," *Atlantic*, January 16, 2017, https://www.theatlantic.com /politics/archive/2017/01/pro-lifers-womens-march/513104.
5. Kimberlé Crenshaw, "Demarginalizing the Intersection of Race and Sex: A Black Feminist Critique of Antidiscrimination Doctrine, Feminist Theory and Antiracist Politics," University of Chicago Legal Forum, 1989: Is. 1, Article 8. Available at: http://chicagounbound.uchicago.edu/uclf /vol1989/iss1/8.
6. *DeGraffenreid v. General Motors Assembly Div., Etc.,* 413 F. Supp. 142 (E.D. Mo. 1976), https://law.justia.com/cases/federal/district-courts/FSupp/413 /142/1660699.
7. Anna Julia Cooper, *A Voice from the South* (1892), https://docsouth.unc .edu/church/cooper/cooper.html.
8. "The Combahee River Collective Statement," April 1977, http://circuitous .org/scraps/combahee.html.
9. Patricia Hill Collins, *Black Sexual Politics: African Americans, Gender, and the New Racism* (New York: Routledge, 2004), 11.
10. Louis Peitzman, "Where 'The Handmaid's Tale' Went Wrong," *BuzzFeed*, July 11, 2018, https://www.buzzfeed.com/louispeitzman/the-handmaids -tale-season-2-what-went-wrong.
11. C. Osler, "'Fat Studies' Embrace Diversity and Take on the Biases of Being Overweight," *USA Today College*, February 22, 2016.
12. Course description for "Every Body Matters: Embracing Size Diversity," Lindsey Schuhmacher, instructor, Portland State University, https://cap stone.unst.pdx.edu/courses/every-body-matters-%E2%80%93-embracing -size-diversity.
13. Jade Pearl Frost, "Emerging Feminisms: When You're Not Physically Masculine: Colorado College's Body Privilege," *Feminist Wire*, September 15, 2016, http://www.thefeministwire.com/2016/09/body-privilege.

14. Jeffrey Aaron Snyder and Amna Khalid, "The Rise of 'Bias Response Teams' on Campus," *New Republic,* March 30, 2016, https://newrepublic .com/article/132195/rise-bias-response-teams-campus.

15. Derald Wing Sue et al., "Racial Microaggressions in Everyday Life: Implications for Clinical Practice," *American Psychologist* 62, no. 4 (2007): 271–86, https://world-trust.org/wp-content/uploads/2011/05/7-Racial -Microagressions-in-Everyday-Life.pdf.

16. Fernanda Zamudio-Suaréz, "What Happens When Your Research Is Featured on 'Fox and Friends,'" *Chronicle of Higher Education,* June 29, 2016, https://www.chronicle.com/article/What-Happens-When-Your /236949.

17. Robby Soave, "Oberlin College Is Hiring Students to Be Social Justice Activists, Host Microaggression Training," *Reason,* October 26, 2017, http://reason.com/blog/2017/10/26/oberlin-microaggressions-students.

18. Paul F. Campos, "The Real Reason College Tuition Costs So Much," *New York Times,* April 4, 2015, https://www.nytimes.com/2015/04/05/opinion /sunday/the-real-reason-college-tuition-costs-so-much.html.

19. Mark J. Perry, "More on My Efforts to Advance Diversity, Equity, and Inclusion and End Gender Discrimination in Michigan," *AE Ideas* (blog), American Enterprise Institute, May 17, 2018, http://www.aei.org /publication/more-on-my-efforts-to-advance-diversity-equity-and -inclusion.

20. "The Top 10 Colleges with the Hottest Student Bodies, Ranked," *Maxim,* January 27, 2017, https://www.maxim.com/women/college-hottest-girls -2017-1.

21. "Arizona State University," Urban Dictionary, https://www.urbandictionary .com/define.php?term=Arizona%20State%20University.

22. Katy Waldman, "The Trapdoor of Trigger Warnings," *Slate,* Sepember 5, 2016, http://www.slate.com/articles/double_x/cover_story/2016/09/what _science_can_tell_us_about _trigger_warnings.html.

23. Michael E. Miller, "Columbia Students Claim Greek Mythology Needs a Trigger Warning," *Washington Post,* May 14, 2015, https://www.washing tonpost.com/news/morning-mix/wp/2015/05/14/columbia-students -claim-greek-mythology-needs-a-trigger-warning.

24. Open letter by students of the Adalberto and Ana Guerrero Center, African American Student Affairs, Asian Pacific Student Affairs, LGBTQ Resource Center, Native American Student Affairs, the Women's Resource Center, and others to the University of Arizona, March 8, 2016, available at https://d1ai9qtk9p41kl.cloudfront.net/assets/db/14576311585113.pdf.

25. Samantha Harris, "Think Trigger Warnings Are Never Mandatory on

Campus? Think Again," Foundation for Individual Rights in Education, August 31, 2016, https://www.thefire.org/think-trigger-warnings-are -never-mandatory-on-campus-think-again.

26. Nathan Heller, "The Big Uneasy," *New Yorker,* May 30, 2016, https://www .newyorker.com/magazine/2016/05/30/the-new-activism-of-liberal-arts -colleges.

27. Elan Morgan, "21 Reasons Why It Is Not My Responsibility as a Marginal-ized Person to Educate You About My Experience," *Medium,* August 30, 2014, https://medium.com/@schmutzie/why-it-is-not-my-responsibility-as -a-marginalized-individual-to-educate-you-about-my-experience-915b4ec 08efd.

28. Hannah Wilder, "The Unicorn Ally," *Pyromaniac Harlot's Blog,* April 3, 2012, https://pyromaniacharlot.wordpress.com/2012/04/03/the-unicorn -ally.

29. https://twitter.com/kittypurrzog/status/1001922246460428288. No longer available online.

30. Kristin Lopez, "Marvel's 'Ant-Man and the Wasp' and Hollywood's Misunderstanding of Disability," *Daily Beast,* July 6, 2018, https://www .thedailybeast.com/marvels-ant-man-and-the-wasp-and-hollywoods -misunderstanding-of-disability-2.

31. Fredrik deBoer, "I'm Fed Up with Political Correctness, and the Idea That Everyone Should Already Be Perfect," *Quartz,* January 29, 2015, https://qz .com/335941/im-fed-up-with-political-correctness-and-the-idea-that -everyone-should-already-be-perfect.

32. Andrew Sullivan, "Here Comes the Groom: A (Conservative) Case for Gay Marriage," *New Republic,* August 28, 1989, https://newrepublic.com/article /79054/here-comes-the-groom.

33. Justin McCarthy, "Two in Three Americans Support Same-Sex Marriage," Gallup, May 23, 2016, https://news.gallup.com/poll/234866/two-three -americans-support-sex-marriage.aspx.

34. James Kirchick, "Dykes vs. Kikes: Chicago's Dyke March Targets LGBTQ Jews with Old-fashioned Anti-Semitism," *Tablet,* June 26, 2017, https://www .tabletmag.com/jewish-news-and-politics/238762/dykes-vs-kikes.

35. Jewish Voice for Peace, "Linda Sarsour, a contributor to JVP book 'On Antisemitism: Solidarity and the Struggle for Justice'" (video), Facebook, April 28, 2017, https://www.facebook.com/JewishVoiceforPeace/videos /10156056191824992.

36. "Petition for Accountability for DSA's Medicare for All Campaign," January 10, 2018, http://archive.is/iOj9Y#selection-155.0-155.185.

37. Bari Weiss, "When the Left Turns on Its Own," *New York Times*, June 1, 2017, https://www.nytimes.com/2017/06/01/opinion/when-the-left-turns -on-its-own.html.

38. Dominic Holden, "Poll Finds Gay Men and Older LGBT People Are Most Opposed to a Brown Stripe in the Pride Flag to Represent People of Color," *BuzzFeed*, June 28, 2018, https://www.buzzfeed.com/dominicholden/poll -finds-gay-men-and-older-lgbtq-people-are-most-opposed.

39. Elisa Chavez, "Revenge," *Seattle Review of Books*, January 3, 2017, http://www.seattlereviewofbooks.com/notes/2017/01/03/revenge.

TWO: NAZI PUNCHING

1. Sean Langille, "Limo Torched in DC Protest Belongs to Muslim Immigrant, May Cost $70,000 in Damages," *Washington Examiner*, January 23, 2017, http://www.washingtonexaminer.com/limo-torched-in-dc-protests -belongs-to-muslim-immigrant-may-cost-70000-in-damages/article /2612747.

2. Philip Wegmann, "What I Saw at the Anti-Trump Riot in DC," *Washington Examiner*, January 20, 2017, http://www.washingtonexaminer.com/what -i-saw-at-the-anti-trump-riot-in-dc/article/2612548.

3. Natasha Lennard, "Neo-Nazi Richard Spencer Got Punched—You Can Thank the Black Bloc," *The Nation*, January 22, 2017, https://www.thenation .com/article/if-you-appreciated-seeing-neo-nazi-richard-spencer-get -punched-thank-the-black-bloc.

4. Carlos Lozada, "The History, Theory and Contradictions of Antifa," *Washington Post*, September 1, 2017, https://www.washingtonpost.com /news/book-party/wp/2017/09/01/the-history-theory-and-contradictions -of-antifa.

5. Omar Wasow, "Do Protests Matter? Evidence from the 1960s Black Insurgency," Department of Politics, Princeton University, February 2, 2017, http://www.omarwasow.com/Protests_on_Voting.pdf.

6. Moises Velasquez-Manoff, "How to Make Fun of Nazis," *New York Times*, August 17, 2017, https://www.nytimes.com/2017/08/17/opinion/how-to -make-fun-of-nazis.html.

7. Velasquez-Manoff, "How to Make Fun of Nazis."

8. Graeme Wood, "His Kampf," *Atlantic*, June 2017, https://www.theatlantic .com/magazine/archive/2017/06/his-kampf/524505.

9. Jo Freeman, "A Short History of the University of California Speaker Ban," 2000, http://www.jofreeman.com/sixtiesprotest/speakerban.htm.

10. Robert Cohen, "What Might Mario Savio Have Said About the Milo Protest at Berkeley?," *The Nation,* February 7, 2017, https://www.thenation .com/article/what-might-mario-savio-have-said-about-the-milo-protest -at-berkeley.

11. Juniperangelica Xiomara Cordova-Goff, "Campus Must Prioritize Safety of Marginalized over Free Speech," *Daily Californian,* May 1, 2017, http:// www.dailycal.org/2017/05/01/399178.

12. "The GamerGate-Supporting Journalist Who Hates Gamers," Storify, October 21, 2014, https://storify.com/x_glitch/the-gamergate-supporting -journalist-who-hates-game. (Storify has shut down; see https://www .salon.com/2014/10/28/gamergates_fickle_hero_the_dark_opportunism _of_breitbarts_milo_yiannopoulos/.)

13. Elliot Kaufman, "Campus Conservatives Gave the Alt-Right a Platform," *National Review,* August 15, 2017, http://www.nationalreview.com/article /450469/campus-conservative-organizations-alt-right-platform-free -speech-milo-yiannopoulos-charlottesville-terrorist-attack.

14. Robby Soave, "UC-Berkeley Protesters Set Campus on Fire, Shut Down Milo Yiannopoulos Event," *Reason,* February 1, 2017, http://reason.com /blog/2017/02/01/uc-berkeley-protesters-set-campus-on-fir.

15. Vice News, "Campus Argument Goes Viral as Evergreen State Is Caught in Racial Turmoil (HBO)," YouTube, posted June 16, 2017, https://www .youtube.com/watch?v=2cMYfxOFBBM.

16. Herbert Marcuse, "Repressive Tolerance," in Robert Paul Wolff, Barrington Moore Jr., and Herbert Marcuse, *A Critique of Pure Tolerance* (Boston: Beacon Press, 1965), http://www.marcuse.org/herbert/pubs/60spubs/196 5MarcuseRepressiveToleranceEng1969ed Ocr.pdf.

17. Stephen R. C. Hicks, "Free Speech and Postmodernism," http://www .stephenhicks.org/wp-content/uploads/2012/01/hicks-freespeechpost modernism.pdf.

18. Matt McManus, "Post-Postmodernism on the Left," *Quillette,* June 13, 2018, https://quillette.com/2018/06/13/post-postmodernism-on-the-left.

19. Robby Soave, "*End of History* Author Francis Fukuyama Thinks Leftist Identity Politics Helped Create Trump," *Reason,* August 31, 2018, https:// reason.com/blog/2018/08/31/francis-fukuyama-identity-politics -trump.

20. *Matal v. Tam,* 582 U.S. ___ (2017), https://supreme.justia.com/cases /federal/us/582/15-1293/opinion3.html.

21. *Matal v. Tam,* 582 U.S. ___ (2017) (Kennedy, J., concurring), https:// supreme.justia.com/cases/federal/us/582/15-1293/opinion4.html.

22. Robby Soave, "Professor Injured by Crazed Mob at Middlebury Speaks Out: 'This Was the Saddest Day of My Life,'" *Reason,* March 6, 2017, http://reason.com/blog/2017/03/06/professor-injured-by-crazed-mob-at-middl.

23. Richard Delgado and David H. Yun, "'The Speech We Hate': First Amendment Totalism, the ACLU, and the Principle of Dialogic Politics," *Arizona State Law Journal* 27 (1995): 1281–96, https://papers.ssrn.com/sol3/papers.cfm?abstract_id=2094597.

24. "Academic Value" (letter to the editor), *Michigan Daily,* September 25, 2007, https://www.michigandaily.com/content/daily-academic-value.

25. Alex Morey, "Campus Disinvitations Set Record in 2016," Foundation for Individual Rights in Education, December 20, 2016, https://www.thefire.org/campus-disinvitations-set-record-in-2016; "Disinvitation Report 2014: A Disturbing 15-Year Trend," Foundation for Individual Rights in Education, May 28, 2014, https://www.thefire.org/disinvitation-season-report-2014.

26. Robby Soave, "Millennials More Likely to Support Censorship of Offensive Speech Than Older Americans," *Reason,* November 20, 2015, https://reason.com/blog/2015/11/20/millennials-more-likely-to-support-censo.

27. Zack Beauchamp, "The Myth of a Campus Free Speech Crisis," *Vox,* August 31, 2018, https://www.vox.com/policy-and-politics/2018/8/31/17718296/campus-free-speech-political-correctness-musa-al-gharbi.

28. Robby Soave, "Some Pundits Say There's No Campus Free Speech 'Crisis.' Here's Why They're Wrong," *Reason,* March 19, 2018, https://reason.com/blog/2018/03/19/some-pundits-say-theres-no-campus-free-s.

29. Lloyd Grove, "Why Did Fox News Welcome Date Rape Apologist Mike Cernovich?," *Daily Beast,* August 9, 2016, https://www.thedailybeast.com/why-did-fox-news-welcome-date-rape-apologist-mike-cernovich.

30. Matt Labash, "A Beating in Berkeley," *Weekly Standard,* September 1, 2017, http://www.weeklystandard.com/a-beating-in-berkeley/article/2009498.

31. "Behind Every Fascist, a Liberal: Report from Students at UC Berkeley," It's Going Down, September 28, 2017, https://itsgoingdown.org/behind-every-fascist-liberal-report-students-uc-berkeley.

32. "Resistance for Scout: Fighting in Their Memory," It's Going Down, September 19, 2017, https://itsgoingdown.org/resistance-scout-fighting-memory.

33. Daniel Tilles, "The Myth of Cable Street," *History Today* 61, no. 10 (2011), http://www.historytoday.com/daniel-tilles/myth-cable-street.

34. Robby Soave, "Former President Obama Criticizes Leftist Shutdown Culture," *Reason,* July 17, 2018, https://reason.com/blog/2018/07/17/obama -nelson-mandela-lecture.

THREE: OFF TO THE RACES

1. Emma Richter, "Racial Slurs Written on Dorm Door Name Tags," *Michigan Daily,* September 17, 2017, https://www.michigandaily.com/section/crime /racial-slurs-written-dorm-door-name-tags.
2. Frederick Douglass, "A Plea for Free Speech," http://www.speeches-usa .com/Transcripts/fredrick_douglas-boston.html.
3. Robert Shibley, "Martin Luther King's Last Speech Discussed Our First Amendment," Foundation for Individual Rights in Education, January 21, 2013, https://www.thefire.org/martin-luther-kings-last-speech-discussed -our-first-amendment.
4. Lee Rowland, "Donald Trump Has Free Speech Rights Too," ACLU, April 20, 2017, https://www.aclu.org/blog/free-speech/donald-trump-has -free-speech-rights-too.
5. Peter Salovey, "Free Speech, Personified," *New York Times,* November 26, 2017, https://www.nytimes.com/2017/11/26/opinion/free-speech-yale-civil -rights.html.
6. Michelle Ye Hee Lee, "'Hands Up, Don't Shoot' Did Not Happen in Ferguson," *Washington Post,* March 19, 2015, https://www.washingtonpost .com/news/fact-checker/wp/2015/03/19/hands-up-dont-shoot-did-not -happen-in-ferguson.
7. Robby Soave, "Cop Who Killed Tamir Rice Was Previously Kicked Off Force for 'Dismal' Gun Performance, Emotional Instability," *Reason,* December 3, 2014, http://reason.com/blog/2014/12/03/cop-who-killed -tamir-rice-was-previously.
8. Associated Press, "Latest on Police Custody Death," April 28, 2015, https:// web.archive.org/web/20150428170503/http://www.apnewsarchive.com /2015/The-latest-on-Baltimore-police-custody-death-More-than-150 -fires-in-Baltimore-city-says/id-0b32a37d8b0440b8a444403f5c7ad647.
9. "Herstory," Black Lives Matter, https://blacklivesmatter.com/about /herstory.
10. Jacob T. Levy, "The Defense of Liberty Can't Do Without Identity Politics," Niskanen Center, December 13, 2016, https://niskanencenter.org/blog /defense-liberty-cant-without-identity-politics.
11. John Malcolm and John-Michael Seibler, "Criminal Justice Reform Is Alive

and Well in Congress," *Daily Signal,* October 3, 2017, http://dailysignal
.com/2017/10/03/criminal-justice-reform-alive-well-congress.

12. Camryn Easley, "ACLU, Free Speech for Who?" Black Voice, October 2,
2017, https://blackvoicewm.weebly.com/campus-events/aclu-free-speech
-for-who.

13. "The Trump Effect: The Impact of the 2016 Presidential Election on Our
Nation's Schools," Southern Poverty Law Center, November 28, 2016,
https://www.splcenter.org/20161128/trump-effect-impact-2016
-presidential-election-our-nations-schools#executive-summary.

14. Maajid Nawaz, "I'm a Muslim Reformer. Why Am I Being Smeared as an
'Anti-Muslim Extremist'?" *Daily Beast,* October 29, 2016, http://www
.thedailybeast.com/im-a-muslim-reformer-why-am-i-being-smeared-as
-an-anti-muslim-extremist.

15. Elizabeth Nolan Brown, "Hate Crimes in 2016: New FBI Numbers Show
Little Change," *Reason,* November 13, 2017, http://reason.com/blog/2017
/11/13/hate-crimes-in-2016-report.

16. Madeline Masucci and Lynn Langton, "Hate Crime Victimization, 2004–
2015," Bureau of Justice Statistics, NJC 250653, June 2017, https://www.bjs
.gov/content/pub/pdf/hcv0415.pdf.

17. Robby Soave, "Cops Have No Idea if Hate Crime Laws Stop Hate Crimes,"
Reason, May 14, 2018, https://reason.com/blog/2018/05/14/hate-crime-us
-commission-on-civil-rights.

18. Mike Hayes, Albert Samaha, and Talal Ansari, "'Imagine Being Surrounded by People Who Hate You and Want to See You Dead,'" *BuzzFeed,*
September 27, 2017, https://www.buzzfeed.com/mikehayes/we-found-154
-incidents-of-college-hate-speech-and-violence.

19. Robby Soave, "Hate or Hoax? When It Comes to Campus Bias Incidents,
We Usually Have No Idea," *Reason,* September 29, 2017, http://reason.com
/blog/2017/09/29/hate-or-hoax-when-it-comes-to-campus-bia.

20. Luke O'Brien, "The Making of an American Nazi," *Atlantic,* December 2017,
https://www.theatlantic.com/magazine/archive/2017/12/the-making-of
-an-american-nazi/544119.

21. Haley Samsel and Maria Carrasco, "American University Student Protesters Block Traffic in Bender Tunnel to Demand Support for Students of
Color," *Eagle,* May 6, 2017, http://www.theeagleonline.com/article/2017/05
/american-university-student-protesters-block-traffic-in-bender-tunnel.

22. Robby Soave, "Duke Student Who Hung a Noose on a Tree Made a Bad
Pun. Expel Him Anyway?," *Reason,* May 4, 2015, http://reason.com/blog
/2015/05/04/duke-student-who-hung-a-noose-on-a-tree.

23. Henry L. Washington Jr., "'Did You Change Your Mind?': A Black Duke Student Responds to the 'Noose' Apology," *NewBlackMan (in Exile)* (blog), May 1, 2015, http://www.newblackmaninexile.net/2015/05/did -you-change-your-mind-black-duke.html.

24. Mara Rose Williams, "Racist Graffiti Painted on Car Near K-State Was a Fraud," *Kansas City Star,* November 6, 2017, http://www.kansascity.com /news/local/article183086416.html.

25. Samantha Schmidt, "A Black Student Wrote Those Racist Messages That Shook the Air Force Academy, School Says," *Washington Post,* November 8, 2017, https://www.washingtonpost.com/news/morning-mix/wp/2017/11 /08/a-black-student-wrote-those-racist-messages-that-shook-the-air -force-academy.

26. John Counts, "Ann Arbor Woman Pleads Guilty to Making Up Hate Crime," *MLive,* March 7, 2017, http://www.mlive.com/news/ann-arbor /index.ssf/2017/03/ann_arbor_woman_pleads_guilty_1.html.

27. Chris Schilling, *The Body and Social Theory* (Los Angeles: Sage, 2012), https://www.amazon.com/Social-Published-association-Culture-Society /dp/0857025333.

28. Robin DiAngelo, "White Fragility," *International Journal of Critical Pedagogy* 3, no. 3 (2011): 54–70, http://libjournal.uncg.edu/ijcp/article /view/249.

29. @serpysoup, https://twitter.com/serpysoup/status/909936389889781760 (no longer available online).

30. Celine Ryan, "Student Op-Ed Calls White People 'An Abomination,'" *Campus Reform,* November 29, 2017, https://www.campusreform.org/?ID =10206.

31. Haley Toy, "University Event Highlights 14 Ways 'Whiteness' Oppresses Society," *College Fix,* November 30, 2017, https://www.thecollegefix.com /post/39489.

32. Ekow N. Yankah, "Can My Children Be Friends with White People?" *New York Times,* November 11, 2017, https://www.nytimes.com/2017/11/11 /opinion/sunday/interracial-friendship-donald-trump.html.

33. Maggie DeHart, "It Is Not Okay to Be White" (letter to the editor), *State News,* November 13, 2017, http://statenews.com/article/2017/11/letter-its -not-okay-to-be-white.

34. Emma Victoria, "In Today's Society, Is It Reasonable for Women to Hate Men?" *Affinity,* November 27, 2017, http://affinitymagazine.us /2017/10/27/in-todays-society-is-it-reasonable-for-women-to-hate -men; Siraj Hashmi, "Teen Magazine Blames Otto Warmbier's 'Whiteness' for His Death," Red Alert Politics, June 20, 2017, http://redalertpolitics

.com/2017/06/20/teen-magazine-blames-otto-warmbiers-whiteness
-death.

35. "After Texas Massacre, Drexel Prof. Asks: 'What Makes White Men So
    Prone to This Kind of Behavior?,'" *Democracy Now!*, November 6, 2017,
    https://www.democracynow.org/2017/11/6/after_texas_massacre_drexel
    _prof_asks.

36. Cole Delby, "Read Cole Sprouse's Powerful Take on Whiteness and Mass
    Shootings," *Huffington Post*, October 2, 2017, https://www.huffingtonpost
    .com/entry/read-cole-sprouses-powerful-take-on-whiteness-and-mass
    -shootings_us_59d27a4be4b048a443242dbc; E. A. Crunden, "When We
    Talk About Mass Shootings, We Are Talking About White Men," *Think-
    Progress*, October 3, 2017, https://thinkprogress.org/shootings-white-men
    -las-vegas-e378cfad534b; John Haltiwanger, "White Men Have Com-
    mitted More Mass Shootings Than Any Other Group," *Newsweek*, Oc-
    tober 2, 2017, http://www.newsweek.com/white-men-have-committed
    -more-mass-shootings-any-other-group-675602.

37. David P. Thomas and Zoe Frances Luba, "White Fragility and the White
    Student Abroad: Using Critical Race Theory to Analyse International
    Experiential Learning," *Canadian Journal of Development Studies* 39, no. 2
    (2018): 182–98, http://www.tandfonline.com/doi/full/10.1080/02255189
    .2017.1366894.

38. Syllabus for American Whiteness (Soc 295), Professor Karla Erickson,
    Spring 2015, DePauw University, https://libguides.depauw.edu/ld.php
    ?content_id=16164654.

39. Toni Airaksinen, "Prof Pledges to 'Deconstruct Whiteness' in All Her
    Courses," *Campus Reform*, August 9, 2017, https://www.campusreform
    .org/?ID=9569.

40. David Brancaccio and Janet Nguyen, "Half of White Millennials Say
    Discrimination Against Whites Is as Big a Problem as Discrimination
    Against People of Color," *Marketplace*, November 8, 2017, https://www
    .marketplace.org/2017/11/07/economy/white-millennials-attitudes
    -discrimination-people-color.

41. Britton O'Daly, "ANAAY Blasts Dance Group," *Yale Daily News*,
    December 5, 2017, https://yaledailynews.com/blog/2017/12/05/anaay
    -blasts-dance-group.

42. Association of Native Americans at Yale, "The Association of Native Ameri-
    cans at Yale condemns Shaka at Yale's cultural appropriation," Facebook,
    December 2, 2017, https://www.facebook.com/associationofnativeamerican
    satyale/photos/a.821843194499639. 1073741829.154559944561304/1965722
    533445027/?type=3&theater.

43. Cathy Young, "To the New Culture Cops, Everything Is Appropriation," *Washington Post,* August 21, 2015, https://www.washingtonpost.com /posteverything/wp/2015/08/21/to-the-new-culture-cops-everything-is -appropriation.

44. Robby Soave, "Oberlin College Students: Cafeteria Food Is Racist," *Daily Beast,* December 20, 2015, https://www.thedailybeast.com/oberlin-college -students-cafeteria-food-is-racist.

45. Elliot Dordick, "Pitzer College RA: White People Can't Wear Hoop Ear-rings," *Claremont Independent,* March 7, 2017, http://claremontindependent .com/pitzer-college-ra-white-people-cant-wear-hoop-earrings.

46. "Maybe Don't Dress Your Kid Up as Moana This Halloween?" *Cosmopoli-tan,* October 23, 2017, http://www.cosmopolitan.com/lifestyle/a13069023 /moana-halloween-costume-racist.

47. Conor Friedersdorf, "A Police Killing Without a Hint of Racism," *Atlantic,* December 2017, https://www.theatlantic.com/politics/archive/2017/12/a -police-killing-without-a-hint-of-racism/546983.

48. Eldridge Cleaver, *On the Ideology of the Black Panther Party, Part 1* (San Francisco: Ministry of Information, Black Panther Party, n.d.), http:// freedomarchives.org/Documents/Finder/DOC513_scans/BPP_General /513.BPP.ideology.bpp.pt.1.pdf.

FOUR: BURN THE WITCH

1. Michelle Goldberg, "I Believe Juanita," *New York Times,* November 13, 2017, https://www.nytimes.com/2017/11/13/opinion/juanita-broaddrick -bill-clinton.html.

2. Molly Redden, "Gloria Steinem on Her Bill Clinton Essay: 'I Wouldn't Write the Same Thing Now,'" *Guardian,* November 30, 2017, https://www .theguardian.com/books/2017/nov/30/gloria-steinem-on-her-bill-clinton -essay-i-wouldnt-write-the-same-thing-now.

3. Doug P., "Awkward! MoveOn.org Establishes 'New Definition of Chutzpah' by Supporting This Hashtag," Twitchy, October 16, 2017, https://twitchy .com/dougp-3137/2017/10/16/awkward-moveon-org-establishes-new -definition-of-chutzpah-by-supporting-this-hashtag.

4. Emily Yoffe, "Why the #MeToo Movement Should Be Ready for a Backlash," *Politico,* December 10, 2017, https://www.politico.com/magazine/story /2017/12/10/yoffe-sexual-harassment-college-franken-216057.

5. Martha Weinman Lear, "The Second Feminist Wave," *New York Times Magazine,* March 10, 1968, https://timesmachine.nytimes.com/times machine/1968/03/10/90032407.pdf.

6. Lear, "The Second Feminist Wave."

7. Kay Hymowitz, "'We Believe the Children,' by Richard Beck" (book review), *New York Times,* August 21, 2015, https://www.nytimes.com/2015/08/23/books/review/we-believe-the-children-by-richard-beck.html.

8. Alexander Cockburn, "Katha's Silence," *Counterpunch,* October 26, 1999, https://www.counterpunch.org/1999/10/26/katha-s-silence.

9. Constance Grady, "The Waves of Feminism, and Why People Keep Fighting Over Them, Explained," *Vox,* last updated July 20, 2018, https://www.vox.com/2018/3/20/16955588/feminism-waves-explained-first-second-third-fourth.

10. Robby Soave, "Tennessee Student Accused of Sexual Harassment Because He Wrote Instructor's Name Wrong," *Reason,* October 4, 2016, https://reason.com/blog/2016/10/04/u-tennessee-student-accused-of-sexual-ha.

11. Mike Vilensky, "CUNY: Don't Address Students as 'Mr.' or 'Ms.,'" *Wall Street Journal,* January 26, 2015, https://www.wsj.com/articles/cuny-dont-address-students-as-mr-or-ms-1422323867.

12. Nathan Fenno, "Former USC Kicker Matt Boermeester Loses Bid to Return to School," *Los Angeles Times,* September 8, 2017, http://www.latimes.com/sports/sportsnow/la-sp-boermeester-court-hearing-20170908-story.html.

13. "U.S. Department of Education's Office for Civil Rights 'Dear Colleague' Letter, April 4, 2011," Foundation for Individual Rights in Education, April 4, 2011, https://www.thefire.org/us-department-of-educations-office-for-civil-rights-dear-colleague-letter-april-4-2011.

14. Jake New, "Burden of Proof in the Balance," *Inside Higher Ed,* December 16, 2016, https://www.insidehighered.com/news/2016/12/16/will-colleges-still-use-preponderance-evidence-standard-if-2011-guidance-reversed.

15. Robby Soave, "OCR to Frostburg State University: Common Sense, 'Reasonable Person' Standard Violate Title IX," *Reason,* September 12, 2016, http://reason.com/blog/2016/09/12/ocr-to-frostburg-state-university-common.

16. Max Kutner, "U.S. Students Filed Record 10,000 Civil Rights Complaints Last Year," *Newsweek,* May 4, 2016, http://www.newsweek.com/department-education-office-civil-rights-report-455752.

17. Robby Soave, "Prof Who Faced Down Title IX Inquisition Unmasks Money-Making Scheme for Lawyers, Bureaucrats," *Reason,* May 29, 2015, http://reason.com/blog/2015/05/29/prof-who-faced-down-title-ix-inquisition.

18. Robby Soave, "Female Student Said, 'I'm Fine and I Wasn't Raped,' University Investigated, Expelled Boyfriend Anyway," *Reason,* April 19,

2016, http://reason.com/blog/2016/04/19/female-student-said-im-fine-and-i-wasnt.

19. "FIRE Responds to White House Task Force's First Report on Campus Sexual Assault," Foundation for Individual Rights in Education, April 29, 2014, https://www.thefire.org/fire-responds-to-white-house-task-forces-first-report-on-campus-sexual-assault.

20. Robby Soave, "Betsy DeVos: The Era of Weaponized Title IX in Campus Rape Cases Is Over," *Reason,* September 7, 2017, http://reason.com/blog/2017/09/07/betsy-devos-rape-ocr-title-ix-campus.

21. Sarah Alexander, "25 Feminists Break Down Why We Must #StopBetsy and Stand with Campus Sexual Assault Survivors," *Ms.,* September 7, 2017, http://msmagazine.com/blog/2017/09/08/25-feminists-break-must-stopbetsy-stand-campus-sexual-assault-survivors.

22. "The Feminist Majority Foundation's Statement on Secretary DeVos's Statement on Title IX Rollback," Feminist Daily Newswire, September 7, 2017, https://feminist.org/blog/index.php/2017/09/07/the-feminist-majority-foundations-statement-on-secretary-devos-statement-on-title-ix-rollback.

23. Robby Soave, "We Need to Talk About Black Students Being Accused of Rape Under Title IX," *Reason,* September 14, 2017, http://reason.com/blog/2017/09/14/we-need-to-talk-about-black-students-bei.

24. Alyssa Milano (@Alyssa_Milano), "One in five women are sexually assaulted in college," Twitter, October 24, 2017, 6:46 a.m., https://twitter.com/Alyssa_Milano/status/922821699980075009; NARAL (@NARAL), "1 in 5 women will be sexually assaulted on a college campus. DeVos rescinding survivor protections is a slap in the face to them. #StopBetsy," Twitter, September 22, 2017, 9:18 a.m., https://twitter.com/naral/status/911263346938216450.

25. Robby Soave, "Junk Science and Campus Rape," *Reason,* November 2015, http://reason.com/archives/2015/10/20/junk-science-and-campus-rape.

26. Jake New, "One in Five?" *Inside Higher Ed,* December 15, 2014, https://www.insidehighered.com/news/2014/12/15/critics-advocates-doubt-oft-cited-campus-sexual-assault-statistic.

27. Nick Anderson and Scott Clement, "1 in 5 College Women Say They Were Violated," *Washington Post,* June 12, 2015, http://www.washingtonpost.com/sf/local/2015/06/12/1-in-5-women-say-they-were-violated.

28. "Washington Post–Kaiser Family Foundation Survey of College Students on Sexual Assault," *Washington Post,* n.d., http://apps.washingtonpost.com/g/page/national/washington-post-kaiser-family-foundation-survey-of-college-students-on-sexual-assault/1726.

29. Hillary Clinton (@HillaryClinton), "Every survivor of sexual assault

deserves to be heard, believed, and supported," Twitter, November 22, 2015, 5:09 p.m., https://twitter.com/hillaryclinton/status/6685971492911 84128?lang=en.

30. David Lisak et al., "False Allegations of Sexual Assault: An Analysis of Ten Years of Reported Cases," *Violence Against Women* 16, no. 12 (2010), https://journals.sagepub.com/doi/abs/10.1177/1077801210387747.

31. Cathy Young, "Weekly Standard: The Feminine Lie Mystique," Vermont Public Radio, July 29, 2011, https://www.npr.org/2011/07/29/138816111 /weekly-standard-the-feminine-lie-mystique.

32. Robby Soave, "Only 2–8% of Rape Reports Are False? Betsy DeVos Is Still Right to Fix Title IX," *Reason*, September 11, 2017, http://reason.com/blog /2017/09/11/devos-campus-rape-reports-false-title-ix.

33. Amanda Marcotte, "Rape Victims Are Common. Rapists Are Not," *Slate*, May 1, 2014, http://www.slate.com/blogs/xx_factor/2014/05/01/campus _sexual_assault_statistics_so_many_victims_but_not_as_many_pre dators.html.

34. David Lisak, "Repeat Rape and Multiple Offending Among Undetected Rapists," *Violence and Victims* 17, no. 1 (2002): 73–84, http://www.davidlisak .com/wp-content/uploads/pdf/RepeatRapeinUndetectedRapists.pdf.

35. Linda M. LeFauve, "Campus Rape Expert Can't Answer Basic Questions About His Sources," *Reason*, July 28, 2015, http://reason.com/archives /2015/07/28/campus-rape-statistics-lisak-problem.

36. Laura Starecheski, "The Power of the Peer Group in Preventing Rape," *Morning Edition*, NPR, August 18, 2014, https://www.npr.org/sections /health-shots/2014/08/18/339593542/the-power-of-the-peer-group-in -preventing-campus-rape.

37. Le Fauve, "Campus Rape Expert Can't Answer Basic Questions About His Sources."

38. Robby Soave, "How an Influential Campus Rape Study Skewed the Debate," *Reason*, July 28, 2015, http://reason.com/blog/2015/07/28/campus-rape -stats-lisak-study-wrong.

39. Kevin M. Swartout et al., "Trajectory Analysis of the Campus Serial Rapist Assumption," *JAMA Pediatrics* 169, no. 12 (2015): 1148–54, https://jamanet work.com/journals/jamapediatrics/fullarticle/2375127.

40. Robby Soave, "Campus Rape Expert Who Misrepresented His Work Faces Powerful New Criticism," *Reason*, August 11, 2015, http://reason.com/blog /2015/08/11/campus-rape-expert-who-misrepresented-hi.

41. Adam Marcus, "University Says No Misconduct in Campus Rape Paper," Retraction Watch, August 18, 2016, http://retractionwatch.com/2016/08/18 /university-says-no-misconduct-in-campus-rape-paper.

42. Isaac Chotiner, "A New Standard for Sexual Consent," *Slate,* September 5, 2017, http://www.slate.com/articles/news_and_politics/interrogation/2017/09/in_search_of_a_new_ standard_ for_sexual_consent_on_campus.html.

43. Anneta Konstantinides, "Horrifying Details of Vanderbilt Gang Rape Revealed," *Daily Mail,* last updated June 19, 2016, http://www.dailymail.co.uk/news/article-3648743/Jury-finds-Vanderbilt-football-player-Brandon-Vandenburg-GUILTY-raping-girl-dorm-room.html.

44. Lydia DePillis, "Rape on Campus: Not as Prevalent as It Is off Campus," *Washington Post,* December 19, 2014, https://www.washingtonpost.com/news/storyline/wp/2014/12/19/rape-on-campus-not-as-prevalent-as-it-is-off-campus.

45. Sarah Ellison, "After a Rape Story, a Murder, and Lawsuits: What's Next for the University of Virginia?" *Vanity Fair,* September 9, 2015, https://www.vanityfair.com/news/2015/09/university-of-virginia-most-horrible-year.

46. Robby Soave, "Is the UVA Rape Story a Gigantic Hoax?" *Reason,* December 1, 2014, http://reason.com/blog/2014/12/01/is-the-uva-rape-story-a-gigantic-hoax.

47. T. Rees Shapiro, "Jury Awards $3 Million in Damages to U-Va. Dean for Rolling Stone Defamation," *Washington Post,* November 7, 2016, https://www.washingtonpost.com/local/education/jury-to-deliberate-damages-to-u-va-dean-in-rolling-stone-defamation-lawsuit/2016/11/07/e2aa2eb0-a506-11e6-ba59-a7d93165c6d4_story.html.

48. T. Rees Shapiro, "Fraternity Chapter at U.-Va. to Settle Suit Against Rolling Stone for $1.65 Million," *Washington Post,* June 13, 2017, https://www.washingtonpost.com/local/education/fraternity-chapter-at-u-va-to-settle-suit-against-rolling-stone-for-165-million/2017/06/13/35012b46-503d-11e7-91eb-9611861a988f_story.html.

49. Robby Soave, "Appeals Court Sides with UVA Fraternity Brothers, Against *Rolling Stone* in 'Jackie' Rape Dispute," *Reason,* September 18, 2017, http://reason.com/blog/2017/09/19/appeals-court-sides-with-uva-fraternity.

50. Robby Soave, "Charlottesville PD Find Zero Evidence to Support UVA Rape Claims," *Reason,* March 23, 2015, http://reason.com/blog/2015/03/23/charlottesville-pd-find-zero-evidence-to.

51. Robby Soave, "Dear Prudence Meets Due Process," *Reason,* December 2017, http://reason.com/archives/2017/11/16/dear-prudence-meets-due-proces.

52. Sirius XM Progress (@SXMProgress), Twitter, https://twitter.com/SXMProgress.

53. Zerlina Maxwell, "No Matter What Jackie Said, We Should Generally

Believe Rape Claims," *Washington Post,* December 6, 2014, https://www
.washingtonpost.com/posteverything/wp/2014/12/06/no-matter-what
-jackie-said-we-should-automatically-believe-rape-claims.

54. Jessica Valenti, "Inconsistencies in Jackie's Story Do Not Mean That She
Wasn't Raped at UVA," *Guardian,* March 25, 2015, https://www.the
guardian.com/commentisfree/2015/mar/24/inconsistencies-jackie-story
-rolling-stone-rape.

55. Emily Yoffe, "The Bad Science Behind Campus Response to Sexual Assault," *Atlantic,* September 8, 2017, https://www.theatlantic.com/education
/archive/2017/09/the-bad-science-behind-campus-response-to-sexual
-assault/539211.

56. KC Johnson and Stuart Taylor Jr., *The Campus Rape Frenzy: The Attack on
Due Process at America's Universities* (New York: Encounter Books, 2017),
135, https://books.google.com/books?id=Prn2DQAAQBAJ&pg=PT81&lpg
=PT81&dq=kc+johnson+danielle+dirks&source=bl&ots=EaFa3BuJ_1&si
g=n8gGKq0BqvcuQPDTWjqzJZGqzHk&hl=en&sa=X&ved=0ahUKEwi
_sNu2n7HYAhUhm-AKHU5MAYQQ6AEISTAF#v=onepage&q=kc%
20johnson%20danielle%20di.

57. "Group of Students Protesting Suzanne Goldberg's Class Today," posted
by bwog, Vimeo, n.d., https://vimeo.com/236995142.

58. Lara Witt, "10 Things Every Intersectional Feminist Should Ask on a First
Date," *Everyday Feminism,* December 8, 2017, https://everydayfeminism
.com/2017/12/intersectional-feminist-first-date.

59. Elizabeth Bruenig, "Why Are Millennial Women Gravitating to Bernie
Sanders?," *New Republic,* February 9, 2016, https://newrepublic.com/article
/129483/millennial-women-gravitating-bernie-sanders.

60. No Friend of Kissinger Scott Wooledge (@Clarknt67), "Lena Dunham's
site: 'Hillary Clinton cannot be faulted, criticized, or analyzed for even one
more second,'" Twitter, November 15, 2016, 9:57 a.m., https://twitter.com
/Clarknt67/status/798585763923378176.

61. Elizabeth Bruenig, "Feminist Gloria Steinem Says Young Women Support
Bernie Sanders Because They Want Attention from Boys," *New Republic,*
n.d. (ca. March 2016), https://newrepublic.com/minutes/129335/feminist
-gloria-steinem-says-young-women-support-bernie-want-attention
-boys.

62. Amanda Marcotte, "Just Like a Bernie Bro, Sanders Bullies Clinton," *Salon,* April 15, 2016, https://www.salon.com/2016/04/15/just_like_a_bernie
_bro_sanders_bullies_clinton_brooklyn_debate_confirms_sanders_
campaign_is_sticking_by_sexist_ambition_witch_stereotype.

63. Brandy Zadrozny, "'Unsafe and Just Plain Dirty': Women Accuse Vice of

'Toxic' Sexual-Harassment Culture," *Daily Beast,* November 15, 2017, https://www.thedailybeast.com/unsafe-and-just-plain-dirty-women -accuse-vice-of-toxic-sexual-harassment-culture.

64. "On Our Radar—Feminist News Roundup: The Whiteness of #MeToo," BitchMedia, November 23, 2017, https://www.bitchmedia.org/article/on -our-radar/gloria-steinem-and-vice-chaos.

65. Scott Stump, "Pita Taufatofua, the Flag Bearer from Tonga, Shines on *Today* Show," *Today,* August 8, 2016, https://www.today.com/news/pita -taufatofua-flag-bearer-tonga-shines-today-show-t101587.

FIVE: LGB VS. T

1. "Reed College," *Princeton Review,* n.d., https://www.princetonreview.com /schools/1023568/college/reed-college.

2. Jack Halberstam, "Hiding the Tears in My Eyes: *Boys Don't Cry*—A Legacy," *Bully Bloggers,* December 7, 2016, https://bullybloggers.wordpress .com/2016/12/07/hiding-the-tears-in-my-eyes-boys-dont-cry-a-legacy -by-jack-halberstam.

3. Gabriel Arana, "White Gay Men Are Hindering Our Progress as a Queer Community," *Them,* November 9, 2017, https://www.them.us/story/white -gay-men-are-hindering-our-progress.

4. Garance Franke-Ruta, "An Amazing 1969 Account of the Stonewall Uprising," *Atlantic,* January 24, 2013, https://www.theatlantic.com/politics /archive/2013/01/an-amazing-1969-account-of-the-stonewall-uprising /272467.

5. Jamilah King, "Meet the Trans Women of Color Who Helped Put Stonewall on the Map," *Mic,* June 25, 2015, https://mic.com/articles/121256/meet -marsha-p-johnson-and-sylvia-rivera-transgender-stonewall-veterans# .D03bcv6gV.

6. "Jean O'Leary—Part 1," *Making Gay History: The Podcast,* https:// makinggayhistory.com/podcast/episode-14-jean-oleary-part-1.

7. Heather Saul, "Germaine Greer Defends 'Grossly Offensive' Comments About Transgender Women," *Independent,* October 26, 2015, https://www .independent.co.uk/news/people/germaine-greer-defends-grossly -offensive-comments-about-transgender-women-just-because-you-lop -off-a6709061.html.

8. Lizzie Crocker, "Rose McGowan's Trans Diss to Caitlyn Jenner," *Daily Beast,* November 18, 2015, https://www.thedailybeast.com/rose-mcgowans -trans-diss-to-caitlyn-jenner.

9. Martin Coulter, "Transgender Activist Tara Wolf Fined £150 for Assaulting 'Exclusionary' Radical Feminist in Hyde Park," *Evening Standard,* April 13, 2018, https://www.standard.co.uk/news/crime/transgender-activist-tara-wolf-fined-150-for-assaulting-exclusionary-radical-feminist-in-hyde-park-a3813856.html.

10. Sammy Caiola, "More Than a Quarter of California Teens Are Gender Nonconforming, New Study Shows," Capital Public Radio, December 14, 2017, http://www.capradio.org/articles/2017/12/14/more-than-a-quarter-of-california-teens-are-gender-nonconforming-new-study-shows.

11. Rachel Torgerson, "Gigi Hadid, Zayn Malik 'Vogue' Cover Story Slammed for Take on Gender Fluidity," *Cosmopolitan,* July 13, 2017, http://www.cosmopolitan.com/style-beauty/fashion/a10303113/gigi-hadid-zayn-malik-august-vogue-gender.

12. https://www.youtube.com/watch?v=YgQy70_LPS4.

13. Katie Herzog, "The Detransitioners: They Were Transgender, Until They Weren't," *The Stranger,* June 28, 2017, https://www.thestranger.com/features/2017/06/28/25252342/the-detransitioners-they-were-transgender-until-they-werent.

14. Jesse Singal, "What's Missing from the Conversation About Transgender Kids," *The Cut,* July 25, 2016, https://www.thecut.com/2016/07/whats-missing-from-the-conversation-about-transgender-kids.html.

15. Jesse Singal, "How the Fight over Transgender Kids Got a Leading Sex Researcher Fired," *The Cut,* February 7, 2016, https://www.thecut.com/2016/02/fight-over-trans-kids-got-a-researcher-fired.html.

16. Jesse Singal, "A Lot of People, Myself Included, Have Been Misreading the Single Biggest Published Study on Childhood Gender Dysphoria Desistance and Persistence," *Medium,* last updated March 28, 2018, https://medium.com/@jesse.singal/everyone-myself-included-has-been-misreading-the-single-biggest-study-on-childhood-gender-8b6b3d82dcf3.

17. Dawn Ennis, "We Warned the Atlantic About Jesse Singal, but They Ignored Us," *Medium,* last updated June 20, 2018, https://medium.com/@lifeafterdawn/we-warned-the-atlantic-about-jesse-singal-but-they-ignored-us-beaee469d3f8.

18. Harron Walker, "What's Jesse Singal's Fucking Deal?," *Jezebel,* June 19, 2018, https://jezebel.com/whats-jesse-singals-fucking-deal-1826930495.

19. Dana Beyer, "The Lambda Literary Foundation Trips but Rights Itself Quickly and with Dignity," *Huffington Post,* last updated March 23, 2017, https://www.huffingtonpost.com/dana-beyer/the-lambda-literary-found_b_9526090.html.

20. Alice Domurat Dreger, "Zero Tolerance: Censored by the Left," Alice Dreger.com, June 1, 2016, http://alicedreger.com/zero.

21. Ben Kamisar, "Trump Appeals to LGBTQ Community in Convention Speech," *The Hill,* July 21, 2016, http://thehill.com/blogs/ballot-box /presidential-races/288807-trump-to-appeal-to-lgbt-community-in -convention-speech; "Donald Trump's Entire Republican Convention Speech," posted by CNN, YouTube, July 21, 2016, https://www.youtube .com/watch?v=Fs0pZ_GrTy8.

22. Eugene Scott, "LGBT Americans Feel Trump Has Sacrificed Them to Shore Up His Evangelical Base," *Washington Post,* October 10, 2017, https://www.washingtonpost.com/news/the-fix/wp/2017/10/10/lgbt -americans-feel-trump-has-sacrificed-them-to-shore-up-his-evangelical -base.

23. Bari Weiss, "Why Hasn't Trump Lost the Evangelical Vote? Ralph Reed Explains," *New York Times,* June 20, 2018, https://www.nytimes.com/2018 /06/20/opinion/trump-evangelicals-ralph-reed.html.

24. Julie Moreau, "129 Anti-LGBTQ State Bills Were Introduced in 2017, New Report Says," NBC News, January 12, 2018, https://www.nbcnews.com /feature/nbc-out/129-anti-lgbtq-state-bills-were-introduced-2017-new -report-n837076.

25. Danielle Corcione, "We Need Gender Neutral Bathrooms Everywhere," *Teen Vogue,* May 14, 2018, https://www.teenvogue.com/story/we-need -gender-neutral-bathrooms-everywhere.

26. Robby Soave, "Title IX Is a Dangerous Tool for Extending Transgender Kids' Rights," *Reason,* May 16, 2016, https://reason.com/blog/2016/05/16 /title-ix-is-a-dangerous-tool-for-extendi.

27. "Shapiro: Why Do Transgender Pronouns Matter?" Daily Wire, January 25, 2018, https://www.dailywire.com/news/26363/watch-shapiro-why -do-transgender-pronouns-matter-daily-wire.

28. "Gender Pronouns," Lesbian, Gay, Bisexual, Transgender Resource Center, University of Wisconsin–Milwaukee, https://uwm.edu/lgbtrc/support /gender-pronouns.

29. Robby Soave, "So Brave: This University of Michigan Kid Selected 'His Majesty' as Personal Pronoun," *Reason,* September 29, 2016, https://reason .com/blog/2016/09/29/so-brave-this-university-of-michigan-kid.

30. "Genders, Rights and Freedom of Speech," YouTube, posted by The Agenda with Steve Paikin, October 26, 2016, https://www.youtube.com/watch?v =kasiov0ytEc.

31. Bradford Richardson, "University of Toronto Historian: Biological Sex a 'Very Popular Misconception,'" *Washington Times,* December 2, 2016,

https://www.washingtontimes.com/news/2016/dec/2/university
-historian-biological-sex-misconception.

32. Rebecca Joseph and Mike Drolet, "Laurier University Accused of Censorship After TA Reprimanded for Playing Gender Pronoun Debate Clip," Global News, last updated November 20, 2017, https://globalnews .ca/news/3868080/laurier-accused-of-censorship-after-ta-reprimanded -for-playing-gender-pronoun-debate-clip.

33. WLU Rainbow Centre, "Dear Laurier Community," Facebook, November 21, 2017, https://www.facebook.com/WLURainbowCentre/posts /1628430573891091.

34. Maggie Astor, "Violence Against Transgender People Is on the Rise, Advocates Say," New York Times, November 9, 2017, https://www.nytimes .com/2017/11/09/us/transgender-women-killed.html.

35. A. Williams, "Risk Factors for Suicide in the Transgender Community," European Psychiatry 41 supp. (April 2017): S894, https://www.sciencedirect .com/science/article/pii/S0924933817318357.

36. Megan Gannon, "Race Is a Social Construct, Scientists Argue," Scientific American, February 5, 2016, https://www.scientificamerican.com/article /race-is-a-social-construct-scientists-argue.

37. Jesse Singal, "This Is What a Modern-Day Witch Hunt Looks Like," New York Magazine, May 2, 2017, http://nymag.com/daily/intelligencer/2017/05 /transracialism-article-controversy.html.

38. Kelly Oliver, "If This Is Feminism . . . ," Philosophical Salon, May 8, 2017, http://thephilosophicalsalon.com/if-this-is-feminism-its-been-hijacked -by-the-thought-police.

39. Justin Weinberg, "Philosopher's Article on Transracialism Sparks Controversy," Daily Nous, May 1, 2017, http://dailynous.com/2017/05/01 /philosophers-article-transracialism-sparks-controversy.

40. Helen Griffiths, "Amid Controversy, 'Stonewall' Screening Postponed," Catalyst, October 25, 2015, http://catalystnewspaper.com/news/amid -controversy-stonewall-screening-postponed.

41. Arana, "White Gay Men Are Hindering Our Progress."

42. Decca Aitkenhead, "RuPaul: 'Drag Is a Big F—You to Male-Dominated Culture," Guardian, March 3, 2018, https://www.theguardian.com/tv-and -radio/2018/mar/03/rupaul-drag-race-big-f-you-to-male-dominated -culture; Caroline Framke, "How RuPaul's Comments on Trans Women Led to a Drag Race Revolt—and a Rare Apology," Vox, March 7, 2018, https://www.vox.com/culture/2018/3/6/17085244/rupaul-trans-women -drag-queens-interview-controversy.

43. "RuPaul Accepts an Award for RuPaul's Drag Race at the 21st Annual

GLAAD Media Awards in Los Angeles," YouTube, posted by GLAAD, April 21, 2010, https://www.youtube.com/watch?v=wlmiOH-B8Yw.

44. Lauren Herold, "How RuPaul Became a Leading Icon in the Gay Community," *Mic,* May 29, 2013, https://mic.com/articles/44947/how-rupaul -became-a-leading-icon-in-the-gay-community.

45. E. Alex Jung, "Real Talk with RuPaul," *Vulture,* March 2016, http://www .vulture.com/2016/03/rupaul-drag-race-interview.html.

SIX: BERNIE WOULDA WON

1. John Haltiwanger, "This Is the Platform That Launched Alexandria Ocasio-Cortez, a 29-Year-Old Democratic Socialist, to Become the Youngest Woman Ever Elected to Congress," *Business Insider,* November 6, 2018, https://www.businessinsider.com/alexandria-ocasio-cortez-platform -on-the-issues-2018-6.

2. "Watch: Alexandria Ocasio-Cortez and Ada Colau Interviewed by Amy Goodman," *Democracy Now!,* July 16, 2018, https://www.democracynow .org/live/watch_alexandria_ocasio_cortez_ada_colau.

3. Gary Zabel, "Safe Space Socialism," Dig Boston, November 16, 2017, https://digboston.com/safe-space-socialism.

4. Jacqueline Thomsen, "Ocasio-Cortez Defends Banning Press from Event: We Wanted 'Residents to Feel Safe,'" *The Hill,* August 18, 2018, http:// thehill.com/homenews/campaign/402451-ocasio-cortez-defends -banning-press-from-event-we-wanted-residents-to-feel.

5. Anna Heyward, "Since Trump's Victory, Democratic Socialists of America Has Become a Budding Political Force," *The Nation,* December 21, 2017, https://www.thenation.com/article/in-the-year-since-trumps-victory -democratic-socialists-of-america-has-become-a-budding-political -force.

6. "Uniting to Build a Socialist Feminist Movement," *Democratic Left,* May 2, 2017, https://democraticleft.dsausa.org/2017/05/02/uniting_to_build_a _socialist_feminist_movement_dl.

7. Nice! (@TheCathBoo), "Those 'extremely pro-abortion' women still don't think 'abortion is good' while they're getting one. Only Lena Dunham thinks that way," Twitter, December 10, 2017, 4:02 p.m., https://twitter.com /AntifaEzraPound/status/940008837813121024.

8. Scott Alexander, "Book Review: Singer on Marx," *Slate Star Codex,* September 13, 2014, http://slatestarcodex.com/2014/09/13/book-review -singer-on-marx.

9. "Critical Theory," *Berkeley Academic Guide 2018–19,* UC Berkeley, http://

guide.berkeley.edu/graduate/schools-departments-graduate-groups
/critical-theory.

10. "Graduate Program: Social, Cultural, and Critical Theory (Minor)," University of Arizona, last revised November 1, 2016, https://grad.arizona
.edu/catalog/programinfo/SCCTMING.

11. "Critical Theory in the Global South," Program in Critical Theory, Northwestern University, http://www.criticaltheory.northwestern.edu
/mellon-project/critical-theory-in-the-global-south.

12. "About UCI Critical Theory," School of Humanities, University of California, Irvine, http://www.humanities.uci.edu/critical/about/about.php; "Critical Theory," Department of Comparative Literature, University at Buffalo, http://www.complit.buffalo.edu/graduate/critical-theory.

13. Tom Bemis, "Karl Marx Is the Most Assigned Economist in U.S. College Classes," *Marketwatch,* January 31, 2016, https://www.marketwatch.com
/story/communist-manifesto-among-top-three-books-assigned-in
-college-2016-01-27.

14. Phillip W. Magness, "Commie Chic and Quantifying Marx on the Syllabus," PhilMagness.com, August 15, 2016, http://philmagness.com/?p
=1804.

15. Bryan Caplan, "The Prevalence of Marxism in Academia," Library of Economics and Liberty, March 31, 2015, http://econlog.econlib.org/archives
/2015/03/the_prevalence_1.html.

16. Neil Gross and Solon Simmons, "The Social and Political Views of American Professors," working paper, September 24, 2007, http://citeseerx
.ist.psu.edu/viewdoc/download?doi=10.1.1.147.6141&rep=rep1&type
=pdf.

17. Tom Hayden and Dick Flacks, "The Port Huron Statement at 40," *The Nation,* July 18, 2002, https://www.thenation.com/article/port-huron
-statement-40.

18. Herbert Mitgang, "Michael Harrington, Socialist and Author, Is Dead," *New York Times,* August 2, 1989, https://www.nytimes.com/1989/08/02
/obituaries/michael-harrington-socialist-and-author-is-dead.html.

19. Ezra Klein, "Bernie Sanders: The Vox Conversation," *Vox,* July 28, 2015, https://www.vox.com/2015/7/28/9014491/bernie-sanders-vox
-conversation.

20. Steven Perlberg, "How 'Abolish ICE' Went from Twitter Slogan to Winning Over Progressives and Dividing Politics," *BuzzFeed,* July 28, 2018, https://
www.buzzfeednews.com/article/stevenperlberg/abolish-ice-sean
-mcelwee.

21. Catherine Rampell, "Millennials Have a Higher Opinion of Socialism

Than of Capitalism," *Washington Post,* February 5, 2016, https://www
.washingtonpost.com/news/rampage/wp/2016/02/05/millennials-have-a
-higher-opinion-of-socialism-than-of-capitalism.

22. "Public Service Loan Forgiveness," Federal Student Aid, U.S. Department
of Education, https://studentaid.ed.gov/sa/repay-loans/forgiveness-can
cellation/public-service#qualifying-employment.

23. David O. Lucca, Taylor Nadauld, and Karen Shen, "Credit Supply and the
Rise in College Tuition: Evidence from the Expansion in Federal Student
Aid Programs," Staff Report No. 733, Federal Reserve Bank of New
York, July 2015, revised February 2017, https://www.newyorkfed.org
/medialibrary/media/research/staff_reports/sr733.pdf.

24. Grey Gordon and Aaron Hedlund, "Accounting for the Rise in College
Tuition," National Bureau of Economic Research, November 13, 2017,
http://www.nber.org/chapters/c13711.pdf.

25. Richard Vedder and Justin Strehle, "The Diminishing Returns of a College
Degree," *Wall Street Journal,* June 4, 2017, https://www.wsj.com/articles
/the-diminishing-returns-of-a-college-degree-1496605241.

26. Simone Pathe, "These College Majors Will Get You a Well-Paying Job,"
PBS NewsHour, February 25, 2015, https://www.pbs.org/newshour/nation
/college-majors-will-get-well-paying-job.

27. M [hammer/sickle] for the People (@AudaciousBeat), "I'm a trans woman.
I #ResistCapitalism because private property and capital are the basis of
my exploitation and my oppression," Twitter, February 25, 2017, 12:21 p.m.,
https://twitter.com/AudaciousBeat/status/835585655371612161.

28. Lamont Lilly (@LamontLilly), "'True revolutionaries are guided by great
feelings of love.'—Che Guevara," Twitter, January 3, 2018, 2:59 p.m., https://
twitter.com/LamontLilly/status/948690214662352896.

29. "Che Guevara," Wikiquote, https://en.wikiquote.org/wiki/Che_Guevara.

30. Lamont Lilly, "Lamont Lilly to Peace and Freedom Party: 'True Socialism
Must Connect to the Most Marginalized,'" Workers World, August 26,
2016, https://www.workers.org/2016/08/26/lamont-lilly-to-peace-and
-freedom-party-true-socialism-must-connect-to-the-most-marginalized.

31. Marwa Eltagouri, Professor Who Tweeted, 'All I Want for Christmas Is
White Genocide,' Resigns After Year of Threats," *Washington Post,* December 29, 2017, https://www.washingtonpost.com/news/grade-point
/wp/2017/12/29/professor-who-tweeted-all-i-want-for-christmas-is-white
-genocide-resigns-after-year-of-threats/?utm_term=.3401f677dc13.

32. wint (@dril), "'im not owned! im not owned!!', i continue to insist as i
slowly shrink and transform into a corn cob," Twitter, November 10, 2011,
4:20 p.m., https://twitter.com/dril/status/134787490526658561.

33. Christopher Muther, "The Airlines Call It Basic Economy. Misery Class Is More Accurate," *Boston Globe,* February 23, 2017, https://www.boston globe.com/lifestyle/travel/2017/02/23/the-airlines-call-basic-economy -misery-class-more-accurate/bS6Xt2wy9oDFk5Xw7IrUEM/story.html.

34. Annie Lowrey, "Why the Phrase 'Late Capitalism' Is Suddenly Everywhere," *Atlantic,* May 1, 2017, https://www.theatlantic.com/business/archive/2017 /05/late-capitalism/524943.

35. Oscar Rickett, "Stop Pretending These Leaders Are Woke Baes," *Vice,* August 9, 2017, https://www.vice.com/en_nz/article/a3e55j/stop-pretending -these-global-leaders-are-woke-baes.

36. Robert Pear, Rebecca R. Ruiz, and Laurie Goodstein, "Trump Administration Rolls Back Birth Control Mandate," *New York Times,* October 6, 2017, https://www.nytimes.com/2017/10/06/us/politics/trump-contra ception-birth-control.html.

37. Jimmy Vielkind, "Socialists Divided over Cynthia Nixon," *Politico,* July 12, 2018, https://www.politico.com/story/2018/07/12/cynthia-nixon-demo cratic-socialist-715382.

SEVEN: THE OTHERS

1. David Roberts, "The 5 Most Important Questions About Carbon Taxes, Answered," *Vox,* last updated October 18, 2018, https://www.vox.com /energy-and-environment/2018/7/20/17584376/carbon-tax-congress -republicans-cost-economy.

2. Bobby Magill, "Americans Used a Lot Les Coal in 2016," *Scientific American,* April 8, 2017, https://www.scientificamerican.com/article/americans -used-a-lot-less-coal-in-2016.

3. Ronald Bailey, "Global Tree Cover Has Expanded More Than 7 Percent Since 1982," *Reason,* September 4, 2018, https://reason.com/blog/2018/09 /04/global-tree-cover-has-expanded-more-than.

4. Joshua S. Goldstein and Steven Pinker, "Inconvenient Truths for the Environmental Movement," *Boston Globe,* November 23, 2015, https:// www.bostonglobe.com/opinion/2015/11/23/inconvenient-truths-for -environmental-movement/esDloe97894keW16Ywa9MP/story.html.

5. "Towards a Red and Green Future? Marxism, Critical Theory, and Environmental Philosophy," Undergraduate Education, Michigan State University, April 16, 2016, http://undergrad.msu.edu/events/view/id/122.

6. Jonathan Stein, "Ron Paul—It's Real, Get Over It," *Mother Jones,* November 1, 2007, http://www.motherjones.com/politics/2007/11/ron-paul-its -real-get-over-it/2.

7. Michael T. Heaney and Fabio Rojas, "The Partisan Dynamics of Contention: Demobilization of the Antiwar Movement in the United States, 2007–2009," *Mobilization: An International Journal* 16, no. 1 (2011): 45–64, http://www-personal.umich.edu/~mheaney/Partisan_Dynamics_of_Contention.pdf.

8. Phillip Valys, "Who Is Marjory Stoneman Douglas High School?" *Sun-Sentinel,* February 17, 2018, https://www.sun-sentinel.com/local/broward/parkland/florida-school-shooting/fl-fea-stoneman-douglas-shooting-profile-school-pride-20180217-story.html.

9. Ed Morales, "Emma González: La Nueva Cara of Florida Latinx," *Washington Post,* March 1, 2018, https://www.washingtonpost.com/news/post-nation/wp/2018/03/01/emma-gonzalez-la-nueva-cara-of-florida-latinx.

10. Allie Nicodemo and Lia Petronio, "Schools Are Safer Than They Were in the 90s, and School Shootings Are Not More Common Than They Used to Be, Researchers Say," News@Northeastern, Northeastern University, February 26, 2018, https://news.northeastern.edu/2018/02/26/schools-are-still-one-of-the-safest-places-for-children-researcher-says.

11. Eric Levitz, "There Is No 'Epidemic of Mass School Shootings,'" *New York Magazine,* March 1, 2018, http://nymag.com/daily/intelligencer/2018/03/there-is-no-epidemic-of-mass-school-shootings.html.

12. Mike Dunham, "Let's Not Underestimate Our Handgun Problem in the Assault Weapons Debate," *Medium,* March 14, 2018, https://medium.com/s/story/a-follow-up-on-parkland-why-focusing-on-assault-weapons-over-handguns-will-squander-the-chance-to-590ac6c75161.

13. Ian Johnston, "Suicide Rates Boosted by Easy Access to Guns, Researchers Say," *Independent,* August 18, 2017, https://www.independent.co.uk/news/health/suicide-rates-maryland-rural-urban-firearms-guns-johns-hopkins-united-states-a7898951.html.

14. Lorraine Adams and Dale Russakoff, "Dissecting Columbine's Cult of the Athlete," *Washington Post,* June 12, 1999, http://www.washingtonpost.com/wp-srv/national/daily/june99/columbine12.htm.

15. Dave Cullen, "The Depressive and the Psychopath," *Slate,* April 20, 2004, https://slate.com/news-and-politics/2004/04/at-last-we-know-why-the-columbine-killers-did-it.html.

16. David Brooks, "The Columbine Killers," *New York Times,* April 24, 2004, http://www.nytimes.com/2004/04/24/opinion/the-columbine-killers.html.

17. Jessica Chasmar, "Pop-Tart Gun Suspension Upheld by Maryland Judge,"

Washington Times, June 17, 2016, http://www.washingtontimes.com/news /2016/jun/17/pop-tart-gun-suspension-upheld-by-maryland-judge.

18. Robby Soave, "School Suspends 5-Year-Old Girl for Holding Stick That Looked Like Gun," *Reason,* March 30, 2017, http://reason.com/blog/2017 /03/30/school-suspends-5-year-old-girl-for-hold.

19. Tom Koch, "Fourth Grader Suspended for Bringing His 'One Ring' to School," *Eyewitness News,* Los Angeles, February 3, 2015, http://abc7.com /news/boy-suspended-for-bringing-his-one-ring-to-school/502381.

20. Glenn Greenwald (@ggreenwald), "This is a bizarre and incredibly disingenuous statement from @Twitter," Twitter, July 27, 2018, 5:42 a.m., https://twitter.com/ggreenwald/status/1022824465623859200.

21. Donald J. Trump (@realDonaldTrump), "Twitter 'SHADOW BANNING' prominent Republicans," Twitter, July 26, 2018, 4:46 a.m., https://twitter .com/realDonaldTrump/status/1022447980408983552.

22. "Cara Daggett," Professor Watchlist, July 10, 2018, https://www .professorwatchlist.org/2018/07/10/cara-daggett.

23. James Hohmann, "The Daily 202: Koch Network Warns of 'McCarthyism 2.0' in Conservative Efforts to Harass Professors," *Washington Post,* August 1, 2018, https://www.washingtonpost.com/news/powerpost/paloma /daily-202/2018/08/01/daily-202-koch-network-warns-of-mccarthyism-2-0 -in-conservative-efforts-to-harass-professors/5b611a871b326b0207955e90.

24. Michael Vasquez, "Leaked Memo from Conservative Group Cautions Students to Stay Away from Turning Point USA," *Chronicle of Higher Education,* June 15, 2018, https://www.chronicle.com/article/Leaked-Memo-From -Conservative/243688.

25. Tom McKay, "Tweets About Diapers Broke the Entire Conservative Youth Movement," *Gizmodo,* February 26, 2018, https://gizmodo.com/tweets -about-diapers-broke-the-entire-conservative-yout-1823345007.

EIGHT: BLEACHED

1. Oliver Darcy, "The Untold Story of Baked Alaska," *Business Insider,* April 30, 2017, http://www.businessinsider.com/who-is-baked-alaska-milo -mike-cernovich-alt-right-trump-2017-4.

2. Image of T-shirt with Donald Trump atop a tank, FullRedneck.com, http:// www.fullredneck.com/wp-content/uploads/2016/11/Best-Donald -Trump-Shirt-8.png.

3. Olivia Nuzzi, "Five Myths About the Alt-Right," *Washington Post,* November 23, 2016, https://www.washingtonpost.com/opinions/five-myths

-about-the-alt-right/2016/11/23/66e58604-b0c2-11e6-be1c-8cec35b1ad25
_story.html.

4. Dylan Matthews, "Paleoconservatism, the Movement That Explains Donald Trump, Explained," *Vox,* May 6, 2016, https://www.vox.com/2016 /5/6/11592604/donald-trump-paleoconservative-buchanan.

5. Hans-Hermann Hoppe, "Libertarianism and the Alt-Right," speech delivered at the twelfth annual meeting of the Property and Freedom Society in Bodrum, Turkey, on September 17, 2017, https://misesuk.org /2017/10/20/libertarianism-and-the-alt-right-hoppe-speech-2017.

6. Dylan Matthews, "Why the Alt-Right Loves Single-Payer Health Care," *Vox,* April 4, 2017, https://www.vox.com/policy-and-politics/2017/4/4 /15164598/alt-right-single-payer-health-care-trump.

7. Xeni Jardin, "Andrew 'Weev' Auernheimer, Hacker in AT&T iPad Case, on Occupy Wall Street," Boing Boing, October 20, 2011, https://boingboing .net/2011/10/20/andrew-weev-auernheimer-hacker-in-att-ipad-case-on -occupy-wall-street.html.

8. Joseph Bernstein, "Lane Davis's Civil War," *BuzzFeed,* last updated July 18, 2018, https://www.buzzfeednews.com/article/josephbernstein/lane-davis -ralph-retort-seattle4truth-alt-right.

9. Ethan Gach, "Wolfenstein 2 Collectible Mocks Progressive Magazine over Its Coverage of White Nationalists," Kotaku, October 29, 2017, https:// kotaku.com/wolfenstein-2-collectible-mocks-progressive-magazine-ov -1819952709.

10. Malcolm Jaggers, "Marijuana Makes You a Leftist," AltRight.com, January 6, 2018, https://altright.com/2018/01/06/marijuana-makes-you-a-leftist.

11. Matt Pearce, "Tweet from the Account of Charlottesville Rally Organizer Insults Slain Protester Heather Heyer," *Los Angeles Times,* August 19, 2017, http://www.latimes.com/nation/la-na-charlottesville-organizer -20170818-story.html.

12. Matt Pearce, "White Nationalist Shot at Protesters After Richard Spencer Speech in Florida, Police Say," *Los Angeles Times,* October 20, 2017, http:// www.latimes.com/nation/la-na-richard-spencer-speech-20171020-story .html.

13. Katelyn Caralle, "CNN Commentator: Washington, Jefferson Statues 'Need to Come Down,'" *Washington Free Beacon,* August 17, 2017, http:// freebeacon.com/issues/cnn-commentator-washington-jefferson-statues -should-come-down.

14. Clinton Nguyen, "An Attempted Suicide Forced a Tumblr Community to Open Its Eyes About Bullying," *Vice,* November 6, 2015, https://

motherboard.vice.com/en_us/article/3da838/an-attempted-suicide
-forced-a-tumblr-community-to-open-its-eyes-about-bullying.

15. Drawing by Zamiio7o and comments, Tumblr, July 31, 2015, http://
zamiio7o.tumblr.com/post/125515519690/satouusagi-zamii070-i-was
-drawing-and-then-i.

16. https://archive.is/VJe0h.

17. https://archive.is/MhRe9.

18. "Suicide Statistics," American Foundation for Suicide Prevention, https://
afsp.org/about-suicide/suicide-statistics.

19. Susan Scutti, "Suicide Rate Hit 40-Year Peak Among Older Teen Girls in
2015," CNN, August 3, 2017, http://www.cnn.com/2017/08/03/health/teen
-suicide-cdc-study-bn/index.html.

20. Glen Poole, "Homelessness Is a Gendered Issue, and It Mostly Impacts
Men," *Telegraph*, August 6, 2015, http://www.telegraph.co.uk/men/thinking
-man/11787304/Homelessness-is-a-gendered-issue-and-it-mostly-impacts
-men.html.

21. Robby Soave, "Trump Won Because Leftist Political Correctness Inspired
a Terrifying Backlash," *Reason*, November 9, 2016, http://reason.com/blog
/2016/11/09/trump-won-because-leftist-political-corr.

22. "Steven Pinker: Political Correctness Might Be Redpilling America,"
YouTube, posted by Learn Liberty, January 2, 2018, https://www.youtube
.com/watch?v=kTiRnbNT5uE.

23. "ADL Report: Anti-Semitic Targeting of Journalists During the 2016
Presidential Campaign," Task Force on Harassment and Journalism, Anti-
Defamation League, October 19, 2016, https://www.adl.org/sites/default
/files/documents/assets/pdf/press-center/CR_4862_Journalism-Task
-Force_v2.pdf.

24. ICE (@ICEgov), "Read the full ICE statement regarding erroneous attacks on ICE employee for #military tattoo," Twitter, June 18, 2018, 9:03
a.m., https://twitter.com/ICEgov/status/1008741913355276288/photo/1
?ref_src=twsrc%5Etfw%7Ctwcamp%5Etweetembed%7Ctwterm%5E10
08741913355276288&ref_url=https%3A%2F%2Fwww.thewrap.com%2
Fmedia-matters-ex-new-yorker-fact-checker-talia-lavin-ice-agent-false
-naz.

25. Jon Levine, "Media Matters Hires Ex–New Yorker Fact Checker Who
Falsely Said ICE Agent Had Nazi Tattoo," The Wrap, July 20, 2018, https://
www.thewrap.com/media-matters-ex-new-yorker-fact-checker-talia
-lavin-ice-agent-false-nazi-tattoo.

EPILOGUE: WHEN EXTREMES MEET

1. Jean M. Twenge, "Have Smartphones Destroyed a Generation?," *Atlantic*, September 2017, https://www.theatlantic.com/magazine/archive/2017/09 /has-the-smartphone-destroyed-a-generation/534198.
2. Taylor Lorenz, "Social and Media Will Split," NiemanLab, December 2017, http://www.niemanlab.org/2017/12/social-and-media-will-split.

INDEX